Notes of a Moscow Pianist

Notes of a Moscow Pianist

by

Dmitry Paperno

AMADEUS PRESS
Portland, Oregon

ISBN 1-57467-034-4

Printed in Singapore

Published in 1998 by
Amadeus Press (an imprint of Timber Press, Inc.)
The Haseltine Building
133 S.W. Second Avenue, Suite 450
Portland, Oregon 97204, U.S.A.

Library of Congress Cataloging-in-Publication Data

Paperno, Dmitriĭ, 1929–
[Zapiski moskovskogo pianistra. English]
Notes of a Moscow pianist / by Dmitry Paperno.
p.   cm.
Translation of: Zapiski moskovskogo pianistra.
Includes discography (p.   ) and index.
ISBN 1-57467-034-4
1. Paperno, Dmitriĭ, 1929–   . 2. Pianists—Soviet Union—Biography.
I. Title.
ML417.P25A3   1998
786.2′092—dc21
[B]   97-21882
CIP
MN

To the memory of Ida, my mother . . .
and to three generations of my beloved

Lucya

Anya

Sasha

Sam

Contents

Photographs follow page 96

Foreword

These memoirs captured me so powerfully that I literally read them in one breath, with great interest and empathy. I remember personally much that the author is writing about, yet he has shown me many things in an absolutely new light. I have even made some discoveries for myself.

For some readers this book might seem too nostalgic, but I think that this touch of nostalgia bears witness to the spontaneity and sincerity of the author.

Above all, Dmitry Paperno is a highly talented pianist and a man of intelligence. He found himself in the center of Moscow's musical life during and after World War II, while at the same time he experiences all the zig-zags of a career that depended on the musical bureaucracy and the authorities. In the midst of all this, he describes the events and people absolutely honestly and impartially.

Not many memoirs of Soviet musicians are published in the West. This book is a remarkable contribution to the chronicle of contemporary Russia's musical life.

Vladimir Ashkenazy

Preface to the American Edition

Many years after this book was written and published in Russian, I began to realize fully what an agonizing period my family and I had just gone through. The painful adaptation to a completely different new life in the United States had lasted at least eight years and, to my regret, affected my relations with quite a few people, some of them dear to me. The damned "Soviet mentality" long implanted into all of us there; the inadequate language skills that prompt some people to take immediate advantage of you; the overall discomfort, stress, and many more personal aspects of the breaking up of our lives—let me assure my friendly fellow Americans that they are fortunate never to have gone through this kind of experience. But blaming our difficult emigration from the Soviet Union in the middle of the 1970s, with all the devastation it brought, serves as only a poor excuse. Mea culpa . . . those who can hear me, please take it into account.

On the other hand, looking back, I can hardly complain of our destiny in this country. I have taught at DePaul University for about twenty years and have given a start to many good professionals who will always remember our studio; I have concertized in many American and European cities, made six recordings (four on compact disc), and had two books published, the one you hold in your hands, in its original Russian (Hermitage, Ann Arbor, Michigan, 1983), and *Postscriptum* (AMGA Editions, Paris, 1987). With no false modesty, the list doesn't look too bad, does it?

Now I feel deeply satisfied to see my *Notes of a Moscow Pianist* published in English, better late than never, and hope that it will make interesting and rewarding reading for my Western colleagues and music

11

lovers alike. In it, I attempt to present the decades of my musical life in the U.S.S.R., particularly in Moscow, through my own experience and point of view, which although not always objective and faultless, is always to the best of my knowledge and sense of fairness.

Perhaps my strongest motivation to write and subsequently to translate this book was to familiarize the Western public with my great teacher, Alexander Borisovich Goldenweiser—a person and musician of great scope. As Andrei Lishke, reviewing the Russian-language edition for the Paris journal *Continent* put it, "As the noble figure of Glazunov towers above the darkness of human baseness in Shostakovich's *Testimony*, the remarkable image of Paperno's teacher Goldenweiser dominates *Notes*. A friend of Leo Tolstoy, a man of rare spiritual power, Goldenweiser left forever on his students the noble imprint of his personality, both musical and moral." The transference of this image justifies, at least for me, the whole idea of the book, and the long and scrupulous work on it.

Unless context or I indicate otherwise, when I write *now* or *today* in the pages to come, I am referring to the early 1980s. Believing it would be worthwhile to fill the gap between 1983 (when the Russian-language edition of *Notes* was first published) and the present, I have added new material, both in the occasional endnote to the original text and in the newly written Epilogue that concludes this book, in which I give more scope to the positive aspects of our American experience— my growing satisfaction with my teaching at DePaul University and the awaited activation of my concert life. Naturally, in a few cases my musical reminiscences of 1985–86 coincide with those offered in *Postscriptum*. My sincere thanks to Hermitage and AMGA for publishing my original *Notes* and *Postscriptum*, respectively.

My special thanks to James Ginsburg, my young friend and recording producer, without whose enterprise and persuasiveness this English-language edition (as well as my career as a compact disc recording artist) might not have come about.

And one more thing. One reason for the success of *Notes* is its candid, speechlike language, which conveys my thoughts and reminiscences in the most immediate fashion. To preserve this style, I decided to make an initial raw translation myself, so to some extent you are going to encounter uncommon spellings of Russian names, as well as some angular syntax and a shortage of *thes*, *as*, and *have beens*. I want to express my sincere thanks to Dr. Helen Marlborough for her painstaking editing of my manuscript, retaining the Russian flavor with the least sacrifice of literary English. My intent is to have the book relay to you a more genuine and personal Russian touch.

Dmitry Paperno
Chicago, 1996

Preface to the
Russian Edition

An aging Russian musician sits at a typewriter at his home in the north side of Chicago. If someone had said ten years ago that this was a description of the author of this book, I would have perceived it as an absurd fantasy.

In 1972, my name was well known in both the performing and music teaching fields in Moscow. I was considered the leading pianist in Mosconcert (the bureau in charge of all concerts in the city); I played at least two concerts every year in Moscow and performed regularly in Leningrad, Kiev, Baku, Tbilisi, Riga, Tallinn, and other cities that were by no means open to all performers. The Moscow Recording House and Melodiya released my recordings approximately every four years. I also performed abroad, even in capitalist countries. From 1967 to 1973, I taught successfully as a part-time instructor at the Gnessin Institute, which had become quite a prestigious school of music in the last decades. What more could a musician want?

Our profession, perhaps more than any other, holds us continually in the grip of its power, occupying our thoughts and feelings. The point here is not only the amount of time spent composing or practicing. Music becomes a part of our life and reminds us of this in the most unexpected moments. As a profession it involves a complex mixture of talent, ability to work, intellect, temperament, and ambition—something similar to voluntary hard labor. Having once experienced its sweetness, one will never abandon it.

The painful disappointment and unprecedented satisfaction that only music can give are the motivating forces in a musician's fate. Only through constant connection with his life's work can he remain worthy of his own respect. Without this bond—the incessant effort to achieve and maintain perfection—a person cannot truly be considered a musician.

> Until the poet is called
> For hallowed sacrifice by Apollo
> In the cares of the bustling world
> He is small-mindedly absorbed;
> His sacred lyre is silent;
> His soul is steeped in chilly sleep,
> And among the worthless children of the earth
> He is perhaps the most worthless of all.
> —Pushkin, *The Poet*, 1827

As long as a musician's work is needed by others and brings self-satisfaction, his life does not pass in vain. It gives stimulation for continued work and fills his life with meaning. It is unneccessary to prove how important this was under Soviet conditions. Furthermore, with a little bit of egoism, one could say that the recognition of and satisfaction with the main work of his life helped to remove the musician temporarily from the surrounding cruelty, hypocrisy, and incivility.

From this book the reader will learn how disillusionment gradually penetrated my basic field of activity: concert performing. As regards my pedagogy, that was unexpectedly dealt a blow in 1973, in such a cruel and senseless way that I simply could not reconcile myself to it. This manifestation of our callous bureaucratic system was greater than an injustice against me personally—anyone could be its next victim.

Five years earlier, in August 1968, something happened that dispelled the desperate hopes for a softening of this system. Many Soviets perceived the tragic invasion of Czechoslovakia as proof that we were fated to endure such a regime. That millions of our compatriots malevolently commented, "Serves them right! Imagine, trying to live differently from us" (and that even more didn't know what to think) proves that our people cannot be measured by one standard. For years, many of us attempted to close our eyes to the surrounding injustice and lies (call it "socialist idealism").

Besides family, school, books, and all the other common companions of childhood, my generation was influenced by the ominous terror of the 1930s; "friendship" with Hitler; the destruction of postwar hopes; the savage reaction in literature, music, and science; and the medieval darkness of Stalin's last years. And it is impossible to erase from our childhood the strongest impressions of another sort: the skillful propaganda romanticizing the revolution and the Civil War, the bright images of our role models of that time, and the general outburst of patriotism in World War II. We—with all the good and the bad in us—are the product of this epoch.

Furthermore, for young musicians in the 1930s, '40s, and '50s who were connected with Moscow (first at the Central School of Music—later, at the Moscow Conservatory), modern Russian music, its successes and growing authority, its outstanding composers, performers, and teachers were all ours, the Soviets', and were a source of patriotic pride. The bond between generations in Russian and Soviet music was obvious, and we prepared to succeed the people with whom fate had so fortunately placed us.

No wonder then that it had taken a long time for the dogmatism, incompetence, indifference, and cruelty generated from above to complete their destructive work on our minds and hearts. The complete havoc wrought upon Soviet music in 1948; the campaigns against "formalism" and "cosmopolitism"; the stifling conditions for the distribution of jobs after graduating from the Conservatory; Khrushchev's speech at the Twentieth Party Congress on the nightmarish crimes of Stalin; countless meetings and conversations with people in trains, planes, and hotels during endless concert tours around the country—all this cannot be forgotten and has left its mark. Sooner or later, according to dialectics, this conglomeration of contradictory events and impressions changes one's perception of reality. Thus, toward the beginning of the 1970s, two lines of my life, the civic and the professional—which until this time had developed more or less in parallel—gradually joined together, soldered by bitter disillusionment.

I would not have written about this in such detail if my fate were not typical of a whole generation of Moscow musicians, my friends and colleagues. This generation definitively contributed to the development of Soviet music. We were the first students admitted to the Moscow Conservatory after the war (the second half of the 1940s) in perhaps the most dramatic period of its history. And here we approach the main point—how and when the idea arose to write this book.

For those who have left the Soviet Union, scattered now throughout the West, the names Goldenweiser, Igumnov, Goedike, Neuhaus, Oborin, Oistrakh, and many others mentioned in the book are not just names. We saw them on the streets of Moscow and heard them in concert halls—they were a part of our life. The unique images of these remarkable people must not disappear from our memory.

Soviet music historiography, with its official limitations, cannot convey to the reader the many varied human features even of those it sincerely wants to preserve. With their departure the ties of the following generations to that unforgettable period in the life of the Conservatory are gradually breaking apart. Consequently, a truthful and interesting book, written from a freer perspective, was needed—even though it would inevitably be subjective.

Furthermore, Western musicians and inquisitive music lovers have always been interested in the phenomenon of the Soviet performing school—that brilliant gold mine of talents who conquered the world as early as 1927, at the first Chopin Competition in Warsaw. A book about the actual creators of this phenomenon, therefore, and the Conservatory that gathered them under its wing, is not intended solely for a Russian audience. The Western reader has a right to know these people, whom we will always recall with admiration and gratitude.

In spite of some literary experience (critical articles for the magazine *Soviet Music* and a short memoir on Goldenweiser, *Memories of a Teacher*), the idea of myself as a possible author of the book which you now hold in your hands arose much later, after my emigration. In 1980, I was asked to write two essays on Russian programs to be performed by the Chicago Symphony Orchestra. In the second, I included some personal impressions from my acquaintance with Shostakovich, which evoked a special interest from the audience. It was then, urged on by a few American friends, that I thought, "After all, why not?" I believe, without false modesty, that I am, perhaps, one of the few Russian émigrés who not only has something to recall of musical Moscow in the last several decades but who could also give an account of this on paper. Others are either too busy with their concert duties, do not have even my small literary experience, or simply are not inclined to disrupt their everyday routine. For me, the importance of such a book became ever more apparent, and I was ready to devote a significant amount of time to working on it.

This book is not an autobiography. The reader is presented with events as they develop chronologically through the eyes of a participant and witness. Under these conditions, it is hard for the author to remain entirely objective or to avoid frequent mention of himself. I have tried to do this without vanity, however, following the advice of experienced writers of memoirs, so as not to distort the book's message. Not being a sociologist by profession or a fighter by nature, I wrote simply as a musician, touching politics only so that situations did not seem smoothed over or ambiguous. After all, the whole agony of Russia—her fate—will remain with us, never completely understood by the West.

Of course, I wanted the book to be read with interest by all, not only by musicians. I tried not to overload it with personal or particularly professional descriptions. It would surely have been possible to bring in still more examples of the brilliant wit of Sollertinsky, Kondrashin, Rostropovich, or Rozhdestvensky, but I restrained myself from turning it from an interesting and sometimes diverting account into something that was merely entertaining. This period in the history of Soviet music is already too fraught with drama and tragedy.

I should note one intentional deviation from objectivity in the book: I tried, wherever possible, not to name people who, from my point of view, are dishonorable and heartless, and whose contribution to the history of Soviet music is more negative than positive.

A few inaccuracies can be found in the text in some dates and quotations given. Frequently, in citing individuals' remarks, I retained the nature of their thoughts while expressing them in my own words (it surprises me that I did remember several of them word for word).

Readers' comments are invited and will be deeply appreciated.

Dmitry Paperno
Chicago, 1982

CHAPTER 1

School Years

I was born on 18 February 1929, in Kiev. There were no professional musicians in our family, but my mother, whom I lost when I was one year old, took piano lessons in her youth. In one surviving photograph she is sitting at the upright piano with an open score of Chopin's Étude in C minor, op. 10, no. 12 (the "Revolutionary") on the music stand. Apparently she had the technical ability to play this comparatively challenging piece. Much later I learned from my father that the tunes he hummed from the popular piano pieces of Beethoven, Chopin, and Tchaikovsky, were remembered from the 1920s, the time of his acquaintance with my mother and their brief marriage.

Soon after my mother died, my father started another family and did not take part in my upbringing. A talented engineer, an expert in the new field of chemical dyes, he was sent in 1931 on a scientific research mission to Berlin. This foreign contact, along with his caustic disposition, soon destroyed not only his promising career but virtually his whole life. In 1933, a large number of chemical specialists, including my father, were arrested after a slanderous denunciation. By that time, a series of trials in the industrial sphere (such as the Promparty trial and the Shahty case in the coal region) had already victimized many representatives of the country's scientific-technological elite. My father endured the first five years of prison camp with comparative ease, if that word has any place here. But his second arrest in 1941, right after the war started—the so-called second wave, when hundreds of thousands who had already served their camp terms became victims of a second repression, this time without any trial—and all that followed, turned the last ten years of his life into a nightmare.

21

I remember nothing from the two or three years I spent with my mother's family in a small Ukrainian town, Belaya Tserkov (White Church). My more definite recollections are associated with Kiev, when my unforgettable Grandpa and Nanny—my father's parents—undertook my upbringing. From that point on, my Aunt Ida, my father's sister, replaced my mother for me, and as the only child in the family, I grew up surrounded by love and care, and was even rather spoiled.

My impressions of Kiev are so sharply divided by the war that it seems I recall two different cities. The first, before the war, was a noisy, kind, southern City (with a capital letter, after Bulgakov)[1], with its many old houses gladdening the eye, its prerevolutionary movie theaters and pharmacies, many small shops, chestnut trees, and thundering streetcars. Beautiful Kreshchatik, the main street, began at the famous Bessarabian covered market, with streets sloping toward it from both sides, their very names scented with the aroma of the past—Funduckley, Proreznaya, Nikolai (with the circus and children's theater), Luteran. Along the shores of the Dnieper River was the marvelous monument to Prince Vladimir-Red-Sun, who brought Christianity to the Kiev Rus. I often strolled with my Nanny through the Merchant and Czar gardens; on one such afternoon I ran (to her horror) into a group of Ukrainian Communist Party leaders.

The war, which ruined central Kiev, destroyed for me all the visual and spiritual aspects of the city. My dear grandparents vanished with the thousands of others of defenseless victims in the infernal horror of Babi Yar. Kiev lost forever its fascination and its place as my native town. In the 1950s and '60s I performed several times in the Philharmonic Hall. Many people came backstage to see me—those who had known our family and simply music lovers. All the encounters were marked by some nostalgia, a preoccupation, an isolation from the present city's life. Now the brisk go-getters, the hypocrisy, the unmistakable touch of Black Hundred antisemitism[2]—the more repulsive because it was taken for granted—were shaping Kiev. It was not easy to get accustomed to a completely different city, now pompous and cold, even to the lack of cultured faces on the streets. I was leaving Kiev without any regret, not the way I had in my childhood. Now the city, as well as all my once-beloved Ukraine, remained for me just a formal place of birth.

We lived in a big building on the corner of Proreznaya and Musical Lane (or rather, blind alley) with the Conservatory House at the end of it and the black-marble Glinka monument in front. In the evenings, peasant girls who had come to Kiev to make some money as domestic servants and nannies gathered in the alley under the windows and sang at length many beautiful Ukrainian songs a capella. Many musicians since Glinka have considered peasant singing, with its expressiveness, melodic richness, and amazing, ancient polyphonic art, their first strong musical influence, and my childhood was no exception. My grandpa liked to croon many Russian and Ukrainian songs, such as "Unharness, Boys, the Horses" and "Along the Kazanka River." Very early, I think about the age of three, I came up to our upright piano and picked out, with one finger, the melodies I'd heard. I had perfect pitch, so it was easy for me. Within a short time, quite a few marches and popular songs, such as "The Red Cavalry," which came through the wall from the neighbors' radio, were added to my repertoire. All this became gradually "covered" with harmony, without which music no longer existed for me.

When I was four, my elders decided to introduce me to a musician they knew. A piano teacher started to come over to our place, but within a few months I hated these lessons and awaited them with dread, trying to explain my feelings by referring to my young female teacher's unsuitable name—Bespalets (in Russian, "fingerless"!). Now I realize that to accustom a child to music is a very delicate and many-sided process. Countless careers of gifted children have been, and unfortunately will be, ruined in the very beginning. An insufficient gift on the teacher's part, a lack of professional methods, a psychology incompatible with the pupil's, excessive initial demands, or, on the contrary, the unwarranted indulgence of a little slyboots—any of these things can do it. Besides, I was apparently too little then.

They left me alone, and after only two years I realized that another female friend of ours was leisurely, as if playing at music, drawing me back to the piano. Soon I was even able to write down a few small pieces of my own. It seemed to be getting serious. My Aunt Ida, whom I'll call "mother" from now on, decided to introduce me to the leading professor of the Kiev Conservatory—Konstantin Nikolaevich Mikhailov. He was a big elderly gentleman, a typical Russian lord in appearance, stalking along Musical Lane with his stick. Not without a little ruse (I was told he had "a piano with a tail"—a grand piano), I was brought to his apartment.

By that time the Central School of Music had opened in Kiev, the third of its kind after Moscow and Leningrad. The standard four-story secondary-school building was erected on a hill to the left of the Conservatory: Ukraine wanted to trump Moscow, where the famous school before and during the war had taken shelter in an old two-story building. Mikhailov said that I should enter school that same year. He did not teach children, so I was taken into the studio of another well-known professor, Arnold Anatolyevich Yankelevich. I am sure that this day must have been very important and joyful in my family. I myself cannot even remember the first day of school—1 September 1936. I was accepted at the age of seven, one year earlier than usual, and from then till my postgraduate degree from the Moscow Conservatory in 1955 I was one of the youngest in my class.

In Kiev, studies in general education were held in Ukrainian, and even though we moved to Moscow the next year, I can still understand and read the language. I believe that some pupils from those early times took up worthy positions in Soviet music, but I remember only the outstanding violinist Julian Sitkovetsky, because our roads met soon after in Moscow, where we became good friends until his untimely death in 1958.

Yankelevich found the right way to approach me—he was kind, and managed at the same time to warm up my ambition. Judging by my repertoire, I made good progress: Beethoven's Sonatina in F, the Waltz and "Dance of the Elves" from Grieg's *Lyric Pieces*, Glière's Rondo. My first-ever public performance was the students' concert in the Conservatory Hall—Grieg's Waltz and Maikapar's brisk "In the Smithy." After bowing to the audience, for some reason I jumped off the stage into the hall.

During the New Year's concert for the students in January 1937, the Christmas tree onstage suddenly caught fire. Several teachers, led by Abram Mikhailovich Loufer, the director of the Conservatory, rushed to drag the burning toys and cotton down from the tree. Fortunately, they managed to put out the dangerous fire—there were several hundred children, and only two exits. Loufer, one of the winners of the second Chopin Competition in Warsaw (fourth prize, 1932), was a first-rate pianist and administrator. This did not prevent him from finding himself virtually out of business in postwar Kiev, however. He was only forty-three when he died in 1948, and now not many remember him.

That spring, I first saw the man with whom my life would be forever connected. Surrounded by several professors, a lean and handsome, though not tall, old man was going toward the Conservatory. An aura of deep respect surrounded him. "Goldenweiser," somebody whispered. For us young schoolchildren, the words *Moscow, Conservatory, Goldenweiser,* seemed to be somehow inaccessible, almost unreal. Nevertheless, a few months later, in August 1937, my mother brought me to the Moscow apartment of Alexander Borisovich Goldenweiser, on Skatertny Lane, to play for him before the entrance examination to the Central School of Music. Her dream was to move me to Moscow where she and her husband had one room in a communal apartment in little Krapivensky Lane, which runs like the crosspiece in the letter *A* between Petrovka Street and Petrovsky Boulevard. My grandparents, on the contrary, did not want me to leave Kiev. ("God, if only he wouldn't pass the exam . . . .")

I was nervous, realizing the significance of the event. When I stumbled in the finale of the Beethoven Sonatina, an inimitable, ironic "No-o-o" was heard from the second piano, an intonation familiar to all Goldenweiser's students—one cannot convey its reproachful, and at the same time, encouraging meaning, something like "Come on!" Following an intense, competitive selection—two rounds, with several candidates for every opening—I was admitted. There was no turning back. Entering the Central School of Music made you a musician until your dying day; the rare exceptions only prove this statement.

Let me say a few words about the origin and history of the school that has raised several generations of talented and at times outstanding musicians. Just to name several of its alumni is enough to give an idea of the Soviet performing school that conquered the music world for decades. Ashkenazy, Berman, Davidovich, Kogan, Nikolayeva, Rostropovich, Rozhdestvensky, and Spivakov are only a few of those with world renown. Their number would increase to several dozen if we included musicians known chiefly in Europe. Hundreds of graduates of the legendary school, having won at least one major international competition, are touring in the Soviet Union and around the world, playing in the best orchestras and teaching in conservatories and colleges.

Everything started in 1932, on Goldenweiser's initiative, when about fifteen gifted children were united in the special children's group attached to the Moscow Conservatory. Shortly afterward, the first spe-

cial ten-year secondary school was organized. Apart from music studies, its pupils were given an all-around education. Besides Goldenweiser's leadership as the first artistic director, the school got active
help at the very beginning from the leading professors of the Conservatory, including pianists Konstantin Nikolaevich Igumnov and Heinrich Gustavovich Neuhaus, violinists Abram Ilyich Yampolsky, Lev
Moiseevich Tseitlin, Konstantin Georgievich Mostras, and the cellist
Semyon Matveevich Kozoloupov. Pupils came for lessons to the professors' studios in the Conservatory. Thus from early childhood on,
many of us spent time in the Conservatory at least once a week, walked
up its stairs, used its second-floor library, could see the outstanding
musicians and knew the numbers of their classrooms.

Before the war, our annual report concerts took place not only in
the Little (Maly) but also in the Grand (Bolshoi) Hall of the Conservatory—the most prestigious hall in the country. I still have the programs
of several such concerts and sometimes look through them with mixed
feelings. A very few participants still lead active concert lives; others
placed more emphasis on teaching; the rest were not successful in their
careers at all (with plenty of reason, unfortunately). The destiny of
many is not known to me. Quite a few are no longer alive—the war,
incurable diseases, several suicides. I will speak at greater length about
some of them later in this book.

Today the surviving participants of the group are over seventy. It
is strange and sad to recognize in the elderly, gray-haired people the
features of the boys and girls of the 1930s. As teenagers, the five most
gifted of them won crucial competitions. For instance, Rosa Tamarkina, an outstanding student of Goldenweiser (and later Emil Gilels'
first wife), at the age of sixteen won second prize in the third Chopin
Competition (Warsaw, 1937).

A spirit of high professionalism was implanted in us from early
childhood. A strong team of teachers managed to make the theory and
music history lessons, and later on elementary harmony and analysis,
lively and interesting for children. We were never bored with singing
and *solfeggio*, writing dictations, and making simple musical analyses.
But of course the cornerstone in our education was always our instrument—the specialty, as it was called in official documents. It is hard to
understand how some of my American students play their pieces without having a clear knowledge of their formal and especially harmonic
and polyphonic structure. What was an integral part of music for

youngsters from our school often appears a revelation for nineteen- or twenty-year-old American musicians. It is a pity to realize how much these gaps in music education have delayed, sometimes irreversibly, their professional growth.[3]

Many memories remain with those who studied in Alexander Borisovich's class during the prewar years. His way of talking with children, serious, without a trace of lisping or falseness, often with a faint note of humor, attracted us to him. At the same time he was very demanding, strict, sometimes irritable. In October 1953 Goldenweiser addressed the music teachers thus: "Pupils will forgive a teacher a hot temper, sharpness, sometimes even roughness if it comes from a wish that a pupil should play well. But pupils hate indifferent teachers." The following is an abridged fragment from the excellent memoirs of the well-known teacher and organist Leonid Isaakovich Roizman:

> They often said of Goldenweiser that he "loved his students too much" and always tried to promote them. To me it sounds like the best praise a teacher can deserve. . . . Yes, Alexander Boriso-vich loved his students. There was not a shadow of sentimental-ity in this feeling. In outward appearance his attentive attitude toward us showed itself in traits hardly noticeable to a stranger: coming across you in the Conservatory corridor, he would just pat your shoulder, give you an ironic glance, and instantly you would feel happy! Or he would speak quite sharply and ironi-cally of a student's features, or his playing.

His indisputable authority, erudition, and warmth, concealed under outward strictness, together with his strong will and dedication, exerted a great influence on us, both in human and in professional ways. It is worth at least mentioning his attitude toward his students' performances. To say nothing of public concerts and exams, I do not remember Alexander Borisovich ever missing our rehearsals for the soirees that took place in the small school building in Kislovsky Lane. A wintry Moscow morning, barely dawn at seven or eight o'clock, but our Old Man (as we used to call him behind his back) is already in the hall on the second floor, listening to us rehearse for the evening performance. And this is in spite of the several assistants who looked after us between his lessons.

In the last two years before the war (1939–41), Ilya Romanovich Kliachko was such an assistant for me, the kindest of men and a subtle musician. During our lessons he always involuntarily sang along "a falsetto," sometimes reaching a funny "peep" as the melody climbed up; there he would mutter some vivid words, his eyes closed, and rumple his soft, thin hair. He was totally impractical and absent-minded, a typical otherworldly character, but in music he missed nothing and was very demanding. Another pupil Goldenweiser entrusted to him was the exceptionally talented and motivated Tatiana Nikolayeva.

A little bit more about us—the prewar pupils of this school, the first of its kind. Despite the novelty of its principles and methods, its rigorous curriculum and heavy workload, we remained children, though perhaps more "difficult" than ordinary schoolboys and girls. We were friendly, played together, fell in love, quarreled, gossiped, sometimes behaved defiantly or simply were idlers. But even then we began to realize what a jealous person Music is, and how unforgiving she is of even the slightest neglect. At first it would be a parent's grumble, then an unfortunate lesson and an intent look from the teacher. Later the real punishment came—an inner discontent and a small scar left upon your soul when you spent a worthless day.

There was also the towering feeling of conquering a difficult piece—a teacher's praise, a successful performance. Starting from a complex, often boring, sight reading of a new piece, I did not spend so many hours, days, weeks at the piano in vain. Once mastered, the piece becomes part of my repertoire and I feel happy, noticing how obedient the once-awkward texture has become under my fingers, how natural and flexible this music sounds now.

In the last year before the war, a petite young girl from Baku joined our fifth grade to study with another famous old man, Konstantin Nikolaevich Igumnov. At twelve, Bella Davidovich played the Schumann Concerto with amazing precision and balance: it was obvious she had a bright future. Yet stepping away from the piano, she again became joyful, communicative, and funny. Almost sixty years have passed, and I can still picture the animated girl, dancing with zest at some party at my place in Krapivensky Lane. The war separated us, and we met again five years later as fellow students in the Conservatory.

The number of students was growing, and the small building could not provide enough space for the studies of all the groups and classes. If I am not mistaken, beginning in 1939 the administration had to rent two stories in neighboring public schools. Later, during the war, the school moved forever into the latest of them, on Sobinov Lane in the interior yards between the Nikitskaya Street and Arbat Square.

It was a standard four-story brick building with spacious classrooms and corridors where the noise and running about during recesses didn't differ at all from that in the regular secondary schools. The lessons in so-called military training were held in the same corridors—the students of the fifth and sixth grades, including the girls, marched, reported, and carried out the orders of a cultured instructor with a typical military carriage. (I suspect that he had survived the terror of 1937, when the elite of the Red Army was exterminated, thanks to being only a captain and not, say, a colonel.) I cannot resist sharing my recollection of one such lesson, when the sixth-grader Slava Rostropovich displeased our instructor somehow—apparently with his posture. The subsequent short dialogue was especially funny because both of them had trouble pronouncing the letters *r* and *l*, which they sounded almost like *w*:

> Captain Andreev: As you wewe! What's you-w name?
> Slava: Swawa Wostwopovich.
> Captain Andreev: Wostwopovich, attention!
> Slava (reprovingly): Not Wostwopovich—*Wost-wo-po-vich!*

Still in formation, we were literally choking with laughter by the end of this scene.

From the several grown-up concerts I heard before the war, I remember the high perfection of the duo-recital by Lev Oborin and David Oistrakh in the Little Hall. They were both in their early thirties but even then seemed to be Olympians who had reached the musical heights. For Oborin, indeed, the 1930s were the peak of his performing career. It's a pity that nowadays so few remember his prewar performances of Chopin's études or Rachmaninov's Third Concerto. With his brilliant victory as a nineteen-year-old in the first Chopin Competition in Warsaw (1927), Oborin's reputation as the first Soviet laureate stayed firm, whatever shining stars appeared on the pianistic horizon.

Speaking of Oistrakh, in that distant past he had only one serious rival—Miron Poliakin, an inspired representative of the same famous violin school (Leopold Auer's, in St. Petersburg) that gave the world Jascha Heifetz, Efrem Zimbalist, and Mischa Elman. Poliakin's inimitably bright playing delighted Neuhaus, Glazunov, and the outstanding violin professor Abram Ilyich Yampolsky, as well as thousands of music lovers. Unfortunately, the real scourge of this remarkable artist and very sensitive human being was intense stage fright. It explains the uneven level of his concerts, which prevented him from displaying his talent fully in the West, where he spent nine postrevolutionary years before returning to his native land. I heard one of numerous "Poliakin stories" from the well-known pianist Yakov Zak. After a concert, Poliakin is nervously pacing the floor of his dressing room, waving away the congratulations of friends and fans. "No, no, don't calm me down. I've ruined the concert—nothing worked." "But Miron, please, you cannot judge yourself so severely for just a few wrong notes." Poliakin, with sudden resentment: *"Wha-a-a-t?!"* (My fellow musicians will appreciate this humorous and typical situation: "An artist is his own best critic.")

Tragically, this permanent nervous burden contributed to his untimely death at the age of forty-six. In the spring of 1941, Miron Borisovich Poliakin died suddenly on a train, coming home from a concert tour in southern Russia.[4] I remember the shock of this death, and the widespread rumors among musicians about the autopsy results, which determined that his heart was like that of a very old man.

Besides the Poliakin-Oistrakh rivalry, there were other duels in the Soviet performing arts. In the 1930s, the exceptional popularity of Yakov Vladimirovich Flier triggered his competition with the rapidly rising young Emil Gilels. They first confronted each other at an international competition in Vienna in 1936, where the brilliant and temperamental Flier conquered the jury with his warhorse, Liszt's B minor Sonata (a remarkable teaching achievement by Igumnov). Gilels, who came in second, took his revenge two years later as the winner of the highly prestigious Eugène Ysaÿe Competition in Brussels, where the oldest jury member, Emil Sauer—one of the last living disciples of Liszt and Nikolai Rubinstein—predicted a brilliant future for Gilels. Flier took third prize, and the very young Arturo Benedetti Michelangeli, seventh.

A few surviving prewar concertgoers still remember Flier's Liszt Sonata, as well as his "Mazeppa," "Snowstorm," and Transcendental Étude in F minor, and Rachmaninov's Third Concerto; and from Gilels, Brahms' Paganini Variations, Stravinsky's *Petroushka*, and Tchaikovsky's First Concerto. Later, in the 1940s, Flier suffered deeply when hand problems forced him to abandon his great concert career for many years. Yet he found himself in teaching, raising an impressive pleiad of bright, assertive pianists who enjoyed great success with the audience. Gilels went on to grow steadily for many long years, competing with the brightly talented Sviatoslav Richter. The other pairs of rivals, who are distinguished either by their real superiority to others or by the public's appetite for piquant situations, will be mentioned in their proper chronological place in the story. Many got their start in Moscow in the 1930s, however—names like Sergei Prokofiev and Dmitri Shostakovich, the excellent coloratura sopranos Valeria Barsova and Debora Pantoffel-Netchetskaya, and the two enormously popular tenors of the Bolshoi, Ivan Kozlovsky and Sergei Lemeshev.

Without sharing all my early impressions of movies and theater, I would mention a particularly vivid memory of the emotional play *The Third Floor* (I don't remember the author, and the heartbreaking play quickly disappeared from the repertoire), with the remarkable actress Valentina Sperantova playing a boy in the leading role. More important was the striking and forceful music Prokofiev composed for Sergei Eisenstein's movie *Alexander Nevsky*. Even much later, and in spite of its naïve political bias (it was commissioned by Stalin), one would call the film powerful not least thanks to Prokofiev's music—expressive and brilliant in depicting both the enemy and the Russian olden times so dear to the author. Perhaps for the first time the dissonances and shrill sounds of the brass instruments did not grate on our classically trained ears—a cruel and ruthless struggle for life could not be represented otherwise. Ten years later, however, they tried to convince us Conservatory students of the harshness of Prokofiev's harmonies in the scene of the bloody battle on Tchudskoy Lake! I remember Khachaturian's irritated remark as chairman on our music history graduation exam: "I never heard anything harsh there." (He was known for his diplomatic caution in public statements, especially after the 1948 Central Committee decree on music.)

One other film worth mentioning was American, *The Great Waltz*, a sentimental and cleverly designed story of Johann Strauss Junior's life, with the beautiful actress Milica Koryus and scenes of Old Vienna, balls, revolutions, unusually emancipated people, and of course, the music itself—like champagne. All this was a dazzling contrast to our strictly regulated lives, not to mention the terrible things that were going on in the background, and that the grown-ups tried to keep from us. Stories went around about people who went to see *The Great Waltz* ten or even twenty times.

Near the end of third grade, in the spring of 1941, I had completed with Alexander Borisovich two Haydn sonatas, two or three cycles of not-too-complicated Beethoven variations, a lot of Bach (including many three-part inventions and the F minor Concerto), numerous études (mostly Czerny), some short pieces by Grieg, Schumann, Tchaikovsky, and so on. A. B. assigned us, the younger pupils, to play most études in keys a half-tone lower and higher also, with the same fingering—which was not easy but greatly developed our auditory and motor skills.

I played Haydn's C major Sonata in the 1939 school report concert in the Little Hall. In the finale I had a short memory slip. I almost stopped, but quick reflexes and the harmonic context sent an immediate order to my fingers, and those who did not know the music would hardly have noticed that anything had happened. Just then, somebody in the audience shouted, "That's a boy!" I learned later that it was seventy-year-old professor Anna Pavlovna Ostrovskaya, who recognized my resourcefulness with the spontaneity of an old musician.

I experienced real stage fright only once, when as a second-grader I played on the radio (live, of course) the "Red Army March" I had composed one evening as an assignment from our music education instructor. Another boy, my friend the violinist Emmanuel Boder, and I spent several hours in the uncomfortable studio then located in the Central Telegraph Building on Gorky Street (now Tverskaya). When at last the time came to play my unpretentious little piece, I was already feeling a kind of estrangement and hostility toward it and the whole surrounding bustle. My hands turned cold and wet. Having fairly bungled the middle section, I got up from the piano ashamed and disgusted with myself. Boder played very well, and I liked his piece. Neither of us made a composer, though.

In the spring of 1941, playing soccer during recess, I caught pneumonia. There was no penicillin then, and I spent two weeks languishing in bed, postponing my exams until the last possible date. Kliachko asked Alexander Borisovich if I could play only the first movement of Mozart's Sonata in B-flat, K. 570, to which he replied, "Nonsense—he'll learn all three movements" (which turned out to be right). I was not among the best in school, simply a good and reliable student. Having received from A. B. an interesting and challenging program for the summer, including Mendelssohn's G minor Concerto, I was ready to leave for young pioneer camp. It was the middle of June.

On 22 June 1941, a day that will never be forgotten, Nazi Germany, without a declaration of war, invaded the Soviet Union. For a number of reasons, which it would be irrelevant to mention here, the U.S.S.R. was unprepared for this war for survival, which took hundreds of thousands of lives in the first months. The enemy, instead of being "annihilated on its own territory," as we had been promised for years, was advancing deep into our country, sowing hate, cruelty, and death. Moscow changed drastically, becoming uncharacteristically strict and grim. In the evenings, the streets were deserted. Barrage air balloons were stationed on the boulevards, paper strips were glued to windows in case of bombing.

Soon the government decided to evacuate the Central School of Music to the old provincial town of Penza in central Russia. In the middle of July, most of the students and a few parents left Moscow by the single *echelon*, as they called the evacuation trains. It was a trip several days long, and to us it was an adventure—of course, we could not even imagine the seriousness of the overall situation, and where and how our own destiny might end.

In Penza, the school was assigned to the sturdy old building of the art college. About 150 beds and a dozen grand pianos were arranged in classrooms on its two floors. Two leading violin professors, Yampolsky and Mostras—remarkable persons and teachers—as well as the young piano professor and disciple of Neuhaus, Theodor Davidovich Gutman (d. 1994), were settled with their families in small, individual classrooms in the city's school of music, a few blocks from our dorm. Life, and then lessons, resumed in the new place.

From time to time the mothers, and in a few cases the fathers who for various reasons were not drafted, would join their adored children—they simply could not live apart. Family life as a whole and the parents' psychology in particular were rooted in an indestructible faith in the child's exceptional gift and brilliant career (though one was not encouraged to use this word in the Soviet Union). Their ambitions sometimes took a ridiculous, and occasionally a sad or even tragic form. It might turn out that the child did not live up to these great expectations, or lacked the psychological stability for this highly demanding occupation. The disappointment, in the intensely professional and anxious spirit of our school, was heartbreaking; it dashed all the family's dreams and hopes.

All the parents (about twenty-five people) were accommodated in a *single*-room dormitory (albeit a large one) with the grand piano for the students' daily practice in the middle. Even now, almost sixty years later, it's painful to recall the unbearable mix of sounds, odors, illnesses, passions—from great hope and pride in your child to the inevitable quarrels and outbursts of despair.

Our board of directors tried hard to maintain discipline among us, but it became increasingly difficult. The evening escapades of the teenagers—sometimes funny and impudent pranks, at other times approaching hooliganism—became more frequent. Once, we put fourteen-year-old Slava Rostropovich on the table in the middle of our room, covered him with a sheet, powdered his distinctive face with something white, and stuck a lit candle in his hands. The others crept under their beds, singing a kind of somber dirge. Soon, the mother-on-duty for that evening showed up and approached the "deceased" cautiously, trying to view his face. At the last moment, Slava blew the candle out, which triggered such a wild scene that the frightened guard felt lucky to run away. Slava stayed in Penza only a few months, but already we were struck by his unbelievably virtuosic cello playing. I recall the pieces of David Popper and his own "Dance of a Green Devil."

Quite a few students among us later became famous performers: violinists Leonid Kogan, Julian Sitkovetsky, Nina Beilina, Igor Bezrodny, and Rostislav Dubinsky, and pianists Lazar Berman, Leonid Brumberg, Evgeny Malinin, and others. Speaking of those who were not inferior to them, but who were simply not fated to enjoy success in their lives and careers, and were cut off prematurely, I must mention violinist Yosif Meister and pianist Alexey Yakovlev.

Yosif Meister was a brown-haired, rather undersized but sturdily built teen. He didn't appear Jewish, but his speech instantly revealed his descent from a typical small-town Ukrainian Jewish family. The boy was undoubtedly born to be a brilliant virtuoso, and he would have been, if only they had managed to implant in him the basics of real culture and to curb his aggressive, hot temper, with its intermittent bouts of anguish and melancholy. He had a natural sense of fairness and decency, though his deeds sometimes contradicted it. His stories of the machinations he arranged on the war-time Penza black market, annotated with juicy comments, lingered in the school's oral chronicles.

Meister's violin sound was not big but warm, his virtuosity outstanding, and I can hardly remember such another natural, God-given bow staccato. I have kept the program of the spring 1940 performance of four of our students with the orchestra, Meister among them. With the exception of Lazar Berman (Mozart's Concerto in A), the fate of the three others vividly illustrates the bitter disappointment that often awaits child prodigies. Nadezhda Retsker (Beethoven's Fourth Concerto) died in obscurity in Chicago in 1981; violinist Naum Latinsky (Paganini's Concerto in D) became a moderately successful soloist in the Moscow Concert Bureau. Meister, our hero, played the Mendelssohn—in short, he showed great promise. Somebody even favored him from behind the walls of the Kremlin: as another story from the Central School of Music's oral chronicles has it, once when little Yosia was late for a rehearsal of the school orchestra and was reprimanded by the conductor, he blurted out in a fit of rage, "My father will call Lazar Moiseevich [the infamous Kaganovich] and you're gonna find yourself in deep trouble!" Even in Penza, the local musicians knew his name, although they had never heard of our other star, Leonid Kogan. Several months later Meister's father, also short and aggressive but without any divine spark, took his son away to Tashkent for some reason. The boy fell madly in love there, suffered a lot, and came back grown-up and even sadder. He cared less about practicing and performing; his ambition faded. The wartime marked the beginning of his professional decline—and he was only seventeen!

I met Meister much later, at the end of the 1950s, as an assistant concertmaster with the Vilnius Symphony Orchestra. Not a trace of his bravado remained; the glint in his blue eyes had grown dim. Others who deserved it less than he performed as soloists with the orchestra where he sat in the second chair. Besides, he had married unhappily. His wife, with her everyday problems, did not want to understand him and did not care to hide it. In 1966, after two suicide attempts from which he was resuscitated with difficulty, he succeeded by taking dozens of sleeping pills.

The pianist Alexey Yakovlev, introverted, vulnerable, and clever, seemed to embody the Russian type of "unruly fellow." He had a genuine talent for music and chess, and unfortunately, a hereditary predisposition to alcoholism. In Penza he became a star pupil, playing Liszt's E-flat Concerto splendidly. The next year his teacher, Theodor Gutman, gave him the Tchaikovsky First. Today, gifted pianists of eighteen cope more or less successfully with this work, but in the 1940s it was an exceptional event. Alyosha, having fallen in love with this music, practiced as if obsessed, and played the Concerto in the spring of 1943 so impetuously that even some roughness in his technique was overwhelmed by his exceptional enthusiasm. Everyone felt that a great talent had been born, and soon we would listen to his playing in Moscow and take pride in our friendship.

In reality, he made little progress in the Moscow Conservatory after our return—the "green snake" of alcoholism had started its destructive work. Neuhaus, upon Gutman's recommendation, had accepted Alyosha in his studio, but soon turned him over to Emil Gilels. Not only did Alyosha fail to take part in the All-Union Competition at the end of 1945, but I can hardly recall any significant student performance of his. He was often seen in the foyer on the second floor, idling away his time playing one chess game after another, making funny and sarcastic remarks. His creativity at chess and elegant style made him unbeatable, especially in timed "blitz" games. I am positive that if he had taken chess seriously he would have become a really distinguished master.

In 1947 it was not easy for me to escape his influence, when after hours of chess bouts our visits to cheap Moscow restaurants became dangerously more frequent. After graduating from the Conservatory in 1949, Alexey went on destroying himself. He moved from one city to another, never able to stay; rumors of his adventures aroused pity. He obviously tried to dodge meetings with old friends. In the beginning of the 1970s, performing in Dushanbe (in Middle Asia) where Alexey had worked not long before, I called up the director of the music college to learn at least something about him. The man's voice filled with spite as soon as I mentioned Yakovlev.

Before our emigration I heard that Alexey had died in the early 1970s, and I am ashamed to say that we do not even know when and under what circumstances.[5] With these words, I want to pay final honors to the memory of two exceptionally gifted friends of my musical youth—Yosif Meister and Alexey Yakovlev.

To return to the first year of our evacuation—the war was becoming ominous. Kiev had fallen; in the middle of October the Germans approached the northern vicinity of Moscow; Leningrad was encircled by a cruel blockade. Gradually, even the youngest of us realized the terrible menace of the situation. Radios—the famous "black plates" of those days—were in only a couple of rooms (all receivers had been confiscated for the war). Information was inadequate, and in the evenings many of us went to the nearest town square to listen to the news through loudspeakers. For a while both our own conflicts and the inhabitants' hostility toward us as newcomers were forgotten. People held their breath as they listened to the names of surrendered cities, tried to catch gleams of hope even in the intonations of Moscow announcers, and dispersed in silence.

The idea of this war as a glorious hour in the history of the Soviet state has been expressed more than once. Yet for the Western person it is hard to understand how a tragedy for millions, which brought losses and hardship literally into every family, united all people for those four unforgettable years as never again in our history. Fascism, revealed as a ruthless animal, proved to be a deadly enemy not only of the regime but of every single person as well, for whom a hatred of the occupiers absorbed all the horror and the suffering of the 1930s. The war joined the people and gave them strength to go through an unheard-of ordeal, to withstand and win after all. One cannot say it better than Pushkin: "Who has helped us? The people's frenzy."

Even the continued, though less frequent, arrests could not affect this outburst of universal patriotism. One late evening they arrested before my eyes the quiet and intelligent Ghita Abramovna Balter, who taught music history. Her husband had been taken away in 1937, and now, five years later, they remembered his wife. She had the strength to knock on the nearest door and to tell my mother, who worked as a nurse in the isolation ward, "Ida, I've been arrested." Her ten-year-old boy, the bashful Alexander Krasinsky, was then withdrawn from the school boardinghouse and placed in one of the houses for "children of enemies of the people." Many years later, in the mid 1950s, after Stalin's death and the discharge and "rehabilitation" of his mother, Shura graduated with honors in physics from the old Tomsk University. A few years later, he died suddenly of a heart attack.

In spite of everything, in Penza we practiced with unprecedented intensity and persistence. Not one piano stood idle for even five minutes—one student took over from another. Some practiced fanatically, sparing neither themselves nor others. The lives of the two dozen men and women in the parents' room became a hell. In the evenings, the more obstinate of us walked about three blocks to the school of music to finish practicing, holding our sheet music in one hand and a vial of kerosene with a small wick on the top in the other. Power failures were quite common, and given the shortage of matches, we usually lit this primitive wick lamp at Gutman's room and walked upstairs slowly, shielding the flame from the draft. On winter evenings, the classrooms were so cold that one needed to wear gloves to practice. Besides, the sense of solitude in the deserted, dark building did not help to create comfortable working conditions.

Yet, we practiced. The sweetness of our "voluntary hard labor," once tasted in childhood, held us firmly. We were even making great progress. The older of us reached the level of concertos by Liszt, Chopin, Tchaikovsky, and Rachmaninov's Second. I, in particular, received serious attention after playing the Mendelssohn G minor (1942) and Grieg (1943) concertos.

How could one explain this collective phenomenon, displayed by mere children in those difficult times? The question is not simple; neither is the answer.

I hope that the next pages might help some young musician to see himself from the outside, with the eyes of an adult. We have to realize that only two or three years of being negligent and insufficiently demanding mark the end of a professional performer's career. After you are eighteen, there is no chance to make up for lost time. If your goal is just to "play a waltz for Aunt Harriet's birthday party" (in Neuhaus' words), you can skip these pages with confidence.

So first of all, we really were one collective—not only our performances, but our everyday practices as well, took place in sight of others, and a spirit of ambition or professional competition ran through the whole of our life. How could you skip one day of practicing when next to you Alexey Yakovlev, Leonid Brumberg, or Lazar Berman methodically turned out their six and more hours?

There were jokes and near-legends about the young Lazar Berman's practicing. His mother, the restrained, fragile, and very soft-spoken Anna Lazarevna, possessed rare strength of will. She had studied in the distant past with one of the famous female teachers of St. Petersburg, Isabella Vengerova, and she monitored the professional development of her extremely gifted only son, the meaning of her life, very strictly. Once, on the train to the city of Kuibyshev (formerly and currently Samara), where a group of our students was to perform in a couple of show concerts, Lyalik was "practicing" on the small table in their compartment when this dialogue allegedly took place: "Lyalik, now play the arpeggio in inversions." "Mother, I've played it already!" "Once more, then—I didn't hear it!" As the Italians say, "Se non é vero, é ben trovato," (if it's not true, it's well invented). In any event, it too became part of the school's oral chronicles.

Secondly, we all, and everyone around us at that time, considered it our duty to be responsible and conscientious. It was our way of struggling and surviving. We all wanted to believe that some time we would return to Moscow, to our homes, to our familiar classes, to our regular teachers; and we simply couldn't let our current instructors down when they were sharing all the hardships of evacuation with us.

And one more circumstance contributed enormously to our musical development: we constantly learned new music. Because the piano and string students lived and practiced in the same rooms, we all knew the concert repertoire for other instruments. Some of the pianists also played, for pleasure, the classical symphonies in four hands. I am sure we all remember the Pugnani-Kreisler Prelude and Allegro, which was played on rare holidays in our small hall by all violinists aged eight to eighteen, from tiny Sima Rakhlina to Leonid Kogan. The rapt children's faces, the severe, powerful music, the flickering candles—all this was impressive, and stayed in our memory.

More and more often we gathered around the large library table and listened to recordings (the noisy old 78s, of course), literally absorbing music that was new to us: symphonies, concertos, an enormous number of instrumental pieces and operatic arias. Rachmaninov, Chaliapin, Kreisler, Heifetz, Menuhin, Galli-Curci, Oistrakh, Gilels were among the performers. We entered a totally different world, forgetting everything around us. Who of the more talented and ambitious of us would *not* dream about this distant world of great music, which might one day open its door for us, too? But, above all, everyone was overwhelmed by the pleasure of music. We always drifted apart late, and for a long time could not fall asleep.

Our longing for live performers and concert halls combined pain-

fully with our dreams of Moscow. Shortly after reading, and then seeing, Chekhov's play in which the three sisters constantly repeat "to
Moscow!" I could appreciate how similar our feelings were—with one
difference: for the sisters it was simple to go to the city of their dreams
for a few days, while for us it was closed.[6]

At the end of 1941, late in the evening, somebody screamed over
and over in the corridors, "Victory near Moscow!" The Nazi advance
had been halted for the first time. It is hard for me to describe what
happened then: all of us, young and old, ran out of our rooms, scream-
ing and hugging each other. It was the first real sign that the war could
be won. (I may add, we were to stay in Penza for almost two long
years more.)

From time to time we attended the town officers' club, where lectures and reports on the war and the international situation were delivered by an intelligent speaker, an educated Muscovite, helping to keep
our spirits up at that difficult period. Some readers of my generation
might be pleased to learn that an American film from the 1930s, *In
Old Chicago*, made quite a strong impression on us then. Who could
have thought that almost forty years later I would live in that city?

In the spring of 1942 I wrote a letter to A. B. in the city of Nalchik
(in the North Caucasus), where he had been evacuated with a group of
leading Moscow cultural workers, including Miaskovsky and Prokofiev. My teacher's answer came with unexpected speed. Its tone was
calm, despite the extremely tense situation at the front, ending with the
advice to "play more Bach." I was so proud of this card that I carried
it with me everywhere, until it wore away to shreds. Somehow, I managed to preserve it all those long years.

Two popular pianists brought us real joy with their recitals in Penza:
Yakov Zak, who had won first prize at the third Chopin Competition
in Warsaw in 1937 (I still remember the great Toccata in C by Bach-
Busoni), and Isaac Mikhnovsky, the 1938 winner of the All-Union
Competition (Liszt's Eighth Rhapsody and the Mephisto Waltz).

Even though the time dragged, we were growing up noticeably,
reaching and crossing over a dangerous barrier. A wild large-scale scuf-
fle took place among the older boys, in which our future world-class
violinist revealed his dangerous and vindictive nature. On the whole,
though, we lived without serious conflicts. Some friendships born then
continued for many years. A few youthful love affairs that began in
Penza turned into long-lasting marriages. There was no room in our

school for antisemitism, which was flourishing loathsomely around us. In the one case I can recall, our younger boys, led by the Russian Evgeny Malinin, chased the half-Jewish Igor Bezrodny, who shouted at somebody in the heat of argument, "*Zhid!*" (the sadly popular Russian for "kike").

When in the summer of 1943 it was finally decided to move the school back to Moscow, we were more than happy. Our homecoming was set for October; even when we were still hours from Moscow, we all were glued to the windows, looking intently at the names of the rail stations and platforms, hardly believing our eyes. Later, I experienced a similar feeling, though to a lesser degree, each time I returned to Moscow from my concert tours. But it began in the fall of 1943. A brief but important and unforgettable period of our life was over.

After almost two and a half years' absence we are in Moscow again—the same room in our communal apartment, the familiar route from the Piotr to Nikita Arches to the Central School and Conservatory, the unforgettable long walks through Moscow with a few fellow students after our evening school hours. In the first winter after the war blackout lifted (1943–44), the evening Moscow streets were illumined; snow crunched under our feet, frequent and loud artillery salutes with fireworks celebrated each liberation of another city, after which Russian music poured from loudspeakers—fragments from symphonies and operas as well as orchestral miniatures by Tchaikovsky, Borodin, Rimsky-Korsakov, Rubinstein, Liadov, Glazunov. The terrible war still went on, tens of millions of people suffered and perished. For us, however, the thoughtless selfishness of youth made it possible to feel the joy of life; bright hopes prevailed.

One more circumstance that is very important in the context of this book—music had become a primary goal of my life. Two years of intensive studying had not passed in vain, and I had joined the group of the school's most promising students. Needless to say, this pleased my teacher a lot—A. B. loved to have strong, reliable pupils in his class, maybe more than anybody else. I remember clearly the outburst that revealed what might be called a jealousy of the past. You see, for two years I had studied in Penza with another teacher, Tamara Alexandrovna Bobovich, who incidentally was a healthy influence, and I'd made significant progress there. When I asked him once about some ballade or scherzo instead of the other Chopin piece he had assigned me, there was an unexpected but apparently long-accumulated explosion: "Here it is! We learned our impudence well in Penza! We are playing difficult pieces now! So you'll learn "Rondo à la Mazur" without wasting time on talking!" (I know it sounds almost funny now, translated, but not then. Need I add that I did play the Rondo?)

Sudden and often spontaneous anger, also a characteristic of Tolstoy, his lifelong idol, became more noticeable in Goldenweiser's later years. (Indulge yourself and reread the chapter on old Prince Bolkonsky from *War and Peace*, not neglecting his last days, please.) Almost nobody knew what kind of petty stings and inner struggles he had lived through for the past twenty years. Thank God they never dared to hurt him openly, even though the well-staged campaigns to persecute the best and noblest could have turned against anybody in any field—and did, too many times. (More about this later, when we'll talk of the 1940s and '50s.)

We are in the same classroom, studio 42, on the fourth floor of the Conservatory, which Alexander Borisovich took over in 1906 after Scriabin, who taught here briefly. Several portraits of his teachers and friends were hung on the walls—Prokunin, Pabst, Taneyev, Arensky, Siloti, Rachmaninov, Scriabin. There were two Bechstein pianos, one of which A. B. always locked upon leaving the studio, and an armchair for him in a remote corner by the window. Sofas and chairs lined the walls—several students were always waiting their turn to play.

The lessons were always different. Sometimes we were given several short remarks concerning phrasing, articulation (two elements of piano playing he was highly sensitive about), and dynamics, such as "Here use more legato in the upper voice, and there make the imitations in the subordinate voices clearer." Another time he would grow inspired, and suddenly the piece would reveal itself in all its facets—the form, inner development, the polyphony of its texture. He believed that a scrupulous execution of all a composer's indications and remarks could never suppress a student's creative individuality—only a lack of such individuality produces "dried-up elders in music."

Among his pupils were the great Samuel Feinberg, Grigory Ginsburg (a pity that these two are still little known in the West!), the splendid Rosa Tamarkina, Tatiana Nikolayeva, Dmitry Bashkirov, and Lazar Berman, to name just a few inimitable musical personalities. One could never tell that they all came from the same teacher's class, and this

is possibly the highest compliment to him. Perhaps only one thing uni-
fied us—an intolerance for irresponsible and careless playing. To tell
the truth, if only these professional qualities had been inculcated in
some of my American students from their childhood, would we sit
together for weeks, picking out from the music a three-part Bach fugue
or an exposition of the classical sonata?

One more feature of A. B., characteristic only of highly gifted
musicians, and something he preserved until his last days: an amazingly
spontaneous perception of music, apparent in two excerpts from his
diary. The first, from 1929, after the death of his first wife, is his reaction to Beethoven's Symphony no. 7, with Otto Klemperer conducting: "One of the most powerful musical impressions of my life. Words
fail me. A will to live and a belief in the meaning and profound significance of our existence are restored to me." And from 1956, following
a recital by Isaac Stern: "For a long time I have not had such artistic
joy." In our studio as well, our teacher often inspired us with his sincere expressions of admiration and astonishment at the eternal beauty
of music.

I usually chose the evening hours for our lessons. By seven or eight
o'clock, the other students often drifted away. Alexander Borisovich
stood up from his chair at the piano, and, having crossed his hands
behind him, would pace the floor slowly, sometimes stopping near
me. Once, playing Chopin's Fourth Ballade, I approached the second
theme in recapitulation, where something gloomy and tragic bursts
into the rapturous melody, and not a trace remains of the preceding
light coloring—despair prevails. Here A. B. clapped his hands several
times, as he used to do to stop a student who was getting carried away,
and said with excitement, "The man here can hardly catch his breath,
words fail him, and—[seeking an appropriate expression, then sud-
denly]—he starts to play an arpeggio!" Such an unexpected image gave
me more than a merely logical analysis of the tragic intensification of
this passage.

Another time, playing Chopin's B major Nocturne, op. 62, no. 1,
which has an amazing, almost oriental, melody in the coda, I heard his
rapturous "Aah!" He, who had probably heard this piece several hundred times, could not help being struck by the astonishing beauty of the
music. By the way, this Nocturne is associated, for me, with another
recollection: one conversation in the classroom turned to Yuli Krem-
lev's serious, and generally good, monograph on Chopin. Alexander

Borisovich said, "I read there that opus 62 [two nocturnes] is a fruit of the mind rather than of inspiration. How do you like that?" And then, in a sudden outburst, "I could not restrain myself and marked in the margin 'Idiot!'" As a matter of fact, he always regarded Mozart, Schubert, and Chopin with special admiration and reverence. When he was listening to the music of these three young geniuses, who did not live into their forties and who could have been his grandsons, the face of our wise old teacher often showed an expression of tenderness.

His passionate temperament was under the command of constant self-control and discipline. We should not forget that his fifteen-year association with Tolstoy had exerted enormous influence on Goldenweiser. His candid self-description, offered long ago, seemed paradoxical: "I am a very lazy person. Most of all in life I love to be alone, to stay at home and read books. And all my life I have to function, appear onstage, and speak at meetings. And all this I do, constantly fighting my own nature." Later we realized that this might be the key to understanding his personality.

To hear him talk was always interesting, no matter where he spoke—at his studio, meetings, or home. His animated and, I would say, old-fashioned Moscow speech abounded with analogies from the past and unexpected comparisons. He could not stand linguistic untidiness such as wrong accents or negligent syntax ("This is a translation from the German; it's not Russian!") His moods could be very different—calm and concentrated, captivated by music, laughing with all his heart, but you always felt the significance of his personality. In the next chapter we will talk about Alexander Borisovich's courage, so uncommon at the end of the 1940s. In the meantime, we will just confine ourselves to a few examples of his particular humor—biting and always pedagogically effective. (All occurred in the studio—impromptu, and in the students' presence.)

In his memoirs, Leonid Roizman tells of Goldenweiser's response, as an accompanist, to a student who was playing Mozart's Concerto in E-flat, no. 22, hastily and unevenly: "You know, when I play this piece with you, I experience the same sensation I have when walking my husky. I am dragged along uncontrollably, and it's beyond my power to resist." Lazar Berman plays Ravel's most delicate "Jeux d'Eau" with superfluous pressure. Goldenweiser reacts with an unexpected question: "Tell me: did you watch the film *The Soviet Whalers?*" Lyalik suspects some trick, but has nowhere to go. "Yes, Alexander Borisovich

—why?" The Old Man, noticeably contented: "Your playing could be a good musical illustration for it." And it seems none of us escaped the classic answer to our attempt to excuse an unfortunate lesson by saying that at home everything was working: "So play at home!"

We had enough love for him, and enough sense of humor, not to take offense at such bantering. Moreover, the very same Berman once brought A. B. his old recording of Mozart's Fantasy in D minor, which he made around the age of four! After listening, A. B. said, "I will tell you; you played better then than now." And Lyalik could not resist the temptation. "I had not studied with you then, you know, Alexander Borisovich!" It is hard to tell whether our Old Man would have forgiven anyone else such impudence. But then they both laughed— Berman, nervously, frightened by his own boldness, and A. B., wholeheartedly.

The last example comes from my own experience. In the fall of 1944, I reported to the studio a couple of weeks later than the other students. Alexander Borisovich, who incidentally was usually well informed about significant sports events, remarked sharply, but fairly, "Aha! So the soccer season is really over!"

I mentioned earlier that there were several assistants in A. B.'s class who took care of us between his lessons. The first year after returning to Moscow I studied with a pretty, sweet, very feminine woman who was then in her midforties—Leah Levinson, who'd been a student of Goldenweiser in the 1920s and '30s. Later, during my student and postgraduate years, our friendship would become permanent. In the meantime, I will only note that she was (and, thank God, still is—in April 1997 Ms. Levinson turned ninety-two) a superlative musician with refined taste. Her lessons were perhaps not exemplary in methodology—she interrupted students often, and repeated herself; but the main thing is that her suggestions and discoveries were simply invaluable! Toward me she felt a special affection—in 1944, I studied with her Chopin's Second Concerto, the same piece that she had coached Rosa Tamarkina in, several years earlier, for the third Chopin Competition in Warsaw (1937). This semi-legendary student of Goldenweiser won second prize there at the age of sixteen. Afterward, Tamarkina switched from Goldenweiser's studio to Igumnov's, which hurt our Old Man bitterly. She passed away in 1950 at the age of twenty-nine, after long suffering from a then-incurable disease. I think that in the sensitive heart of Leah I replaced her favorite in a way, which prompted her boundless tolerance toward me and our decades-long friendship.

In 1944 Goldenweiser transferred me to his other assistant at that time, Kliachko, with whom I had already studied for two prewar years. He had not changed at all—uncommonly kind in life and very strict in music. I still remember from his infrequent recitals his beautiful singing tone and flights of brilliant virtuosity. His hands were ideally suited to the piano—large, always warm and dry, very sensitive; the tips of the strong fingers even shivered slightly. The article "Reminiscences of V. V. Sofronitsky" (*Soviet Composer*, 1970) included an interesting story: Sofronitsky arrived at the Little Hall late in the evening, after Kliachko's recital, for a recording session. After a few Chopin mazurkas, he went into the dressing room to rest, and said that playing came easily to him that night. "The piano feels warm. There is a sense that a good man has just played it. . . ."

At last we could satisfy our craving for live concerts. For the first several months, it was like drinking bouts—we kept going to the Grand Hall of the Conservatory, missing almost nothing. If I remember correctly, we could get in then with our school ID, or, for the harder-to-get concerts, just by dodging the ushers, or as the Russians say, *bilkering*, running like a hare. This wasn't usually necessary, because many of the permanent concertgoers had not yet returned to Moscow from the front or evacuation, and sold-out houses were quite uncommon at that time. The repertoire of the symphony concerts was then rather narrow, primarily Russian and Soviet music; among the Western composers Beethoven prevailed, then Mozart, Liszt, Berlioz, and, less often, Brahms. But even this was enough to make us happy—the playing of the U.S.S.R. State Orchestra was always of a high standard. I remember several conductors from the older generation (Alexander Gauk, Nikolai Golovanov, Alexander Orlov); from the middle-aged (Nikolai Anosov, Konstantin Ivanov, Natan Rakhlin); and the quite young and handsome Kirill Kondrashin.

At the end of 1943, I was lucky enough to hear an introductory lecture by Ivan Ivanovich Sollertinsky before a performance of Brahms' Symphony no. 1. First of all, the very timbre of his voice—harsh, almost croaking—was striking. In the next minute I was captured by the fireworks of his images and comparisons, and the vivacity of his ideas. Many years later Kondrashin, who happened to have conducted this long-ago concert, was pleasantly surprised that I still recalled one of Sollertinsky's splendid images: "The Brahms First Symphony begins on such a level of emotional tension that it seems like you've just plugged your radio in at the very top of the wave." It would be hard to find a more precise image for the unique opening of this powerful music.

A brilliant, multitalented man, Ivan Ivanovich was able to lecture without preparation on old Russian painting, the Italian Renaissance, the history of drama, or the works of Mahler, whom he idolized. As one of the very few people close to the genius Shostakovich, Sollertinsky contributed to the influence of Mahler's epic, tragic, and at times grotesque music on the creative works of his friend.

All recollections concerning him note Sollertinsky's almost unbelievable linguistic abilities: he spoke more than two dozen foreign languages and dialects. Many examples of his peculiar and biting humor are still alive in the vocabulary of the Leningrad intelligentsia. From this source, I heard a funny story about an important representative from Nepal, a highly exotic place in the 1930s, who was visiting the Philharmonic. Naturally, Ivan Ivanovich was appointed to take care of him, and when this unusual couple returned to the concert hall after intermission, noticeably "warmed up" from the refreshment bar, the foreign guest was still giggling, having appreciated Sollertinsky's crisp anecdotes—in Nepalese.

Whatever this brilliant man's destiny might have been during the rage of the postwar reaction, it was hard to accept his sudden death at the age of forty-one, in February 1944, at Novosibirsk. The next day, the pianist Maria Yudina, one of Sollertinsky's longtime Leningrad colleagues, obviously shaken, honored his memory by crossing the audience in the Little Hall before her recital. Sure enough, the authorities did not forget the daring gesture.

The circle of concert instrumentalists was narrow—no comparison to the boom of the 1950s that followed—but each name is engraved in the history of the performing arts. (I am not speaking here of violinists, among whom Oistrakh reigned supreme.) The mainly classical programs presented by old Igumnov and Goldenweiser attracted a wide audience from the old-timers, who remembered them from prerevolutionary days.

When Igumnov managed to overcome the nervousness that plagued him all his life, audiences listened breathlessly to Beethoven's seventh and thirty-second sonatas, the Schumann "Kreisleriana," or sonatas by Chopin, Liszt, and Tchaikovsky. A long, singing tone, lyricism, wise and natural phrasing, all turned into masterpieces the miniatures of Russian composers, including Anton Rubinstein, who was almost forgotten by then. But when Igumnov could not cope with his nerves, most of the concert went "under the piano," and it was difficult to listen. A story went around about a concert he played in Tbilisi when the war was in full swing. In the middle of Chopin's C minor Nocturne, op. 48, the lights went out. For several minutes the audience sat in complete silence (they loved Igumnov very much in the Caucasus). When the lights came on again, instead of continuing to play, he addressed the hall. "You think I stopped because the lights went out? No, I just forgot." This tall, lean old man, with his long, dry face and stiff legs, possessed some special charisma. His pupils (Lev Oborin, Yakov Flier, Bella Davidovich, and many others) simply adored him.

The performance qualities of my teacher were nearly opposite: a display of logic, clarity of pianistic texture, a special speechlike manner of phrasing, with active beginnings of the musical intonations and contrasting recessions in the endings. Even now, when listening to Beethoven's Thirty-two Variations, Schubert's "Musical Moments," Chopin's Third Ballade, or Tchaikovsky's Variations in F, the image of the snowy-haired old man seated at the piano, "uttering" the music in his angularly declamatory manner, returns to me. Goldenweiser's diary entry from 2 February 1932, when he played the solo piano part in Scriabin's *Prometheus* in the Bolshoi Theater with Nikolai Golovanov conducting, shows how far his stage fright could reach on bad days:

> During the intermission it had not even entered my head to get nervous. I walked onstage—nothing unusual. I sat down, and all of a sudden felt a horrible emptiness to my right. It felt like I was flying somewhere, dizzy as if on the edge of a cliff. For a moment I was sure that I would either fall down or be forced to stop. . . . By a superhuman effort I managed to pull myself together. It is not 'stage fright,' it is some torturing nightmare. And so strange: yesterday, it was not there at all.

The concert in question was a repeat of the previous day's program, on the same stage and with the same group of performers. Now tell me how to find a logic in stage fright—or how to fight it.

Both Igumnov and Goldenweiser were especially impressive in their encores. Relaxed by then, they would play with calm wisdom, calling up in one's imagination the legendary figures of their predecessors (Tchaikovsky, Anton Rubinstein), and friends (Rachmaninov, Scriabin, Medtner).

The concerts of Vladimir Sofronitsky and Emil Gilels were also special occasions. It is a pity that Sofronitsky's name is so little known in the West. His somewhat enigmatic, reserved nature, a noble aristocratic appearance, and of course his unique, deeply individual manner of playing created a distinctive aura around him. With his lofty spiritual and emotional strength, he seemed descended from the astounding period of artistic blossoming in prerevolutionary Russia, a time bound up with the names of the poet Blok, the artist Vrubel, and the musicians Scriabin and Rachmaninov. The range of his repertoire was vast, and it is impossible to say what he could not manage successfully. He never performed with an orchestra or chamber ensemble—it is hard to imagine even the most adaptable partners making music with him. Some friends of his Leningrad years remembered only the Glazunov F minor and the Scriabin F-sharp minor concertos.

Sofronitsky's playing was a brilliant display of dialectics in performing art: indestructible logic, an almost architectural modeling of musical images, but at the same time a free and almost improvised manner of expression, in which unexpected subordinate voices and timbres were brought out. The creative labor of this powerful, flexible force was constantly evident. No wonder he was considered the best interpreter of Scriabin—never again will one hear such performances of Scriabin's sonatas nos. 3, 4, 7, and 10, nor of his études, preludes, and poems. Sofronitsky's rendition of the Waltz op. 38—a fragile dream with an ecstatic culmination and soaring coda—remains unforgettable.

It is difficult to express in words the musical beauty of Sofronitsky's performances. The grandeur and wisdom of Beethoven's late works, the kindness of Schubert, the romantic impetuosity of Schumann, the noble theatricality of Liszt, the suffering and epic might of Chopin, the energy and lyricism of Prokofiev, the Russian boundlessness of Tchaikovsky, Rachmaninov, and Medtner—all were within his grasp.

People waited for his concerts as for a grand occasion, and when he was at his best, they left shaken.

Sofronitsky never smiled while onstage. Statuesque and slender, he walked on for calls unhurriedly, often holding a snow-white handkerchief in his hand. Sometimes his last encore would be Scriabin's Twelfth Étude, op. 8, after which people in the large marble lobby of the Grand Hall seemed to behave differently, overwhelmed by the elemental, tragic power of his performance.

He did not enjoy playing in front of microphones and called his recordings "my corpses." Indeed, the spontaneity of his art could not be captured. During recording sessions, a performer is inevitably encumbered with concerns about technical precision. When certain spots did not work out after several takes, Sofronitsky would get nervous, jump up, and leave the studio, overstrained. "To the devil—I'll never be able to play it."

There were unfortunate concerts when it was hard to recognize him—the result of his low spirits and depression, a heavy heart, alcohol. Several times he would even interrupt them without finishing. The circumstances of his personal life, especially in his last years, were not happy, and teaching did not satisfy him. Sofronitsky allowed very few people to be close to him, and only those few were aware of how simple and complicated he was at the same time, vulnerable and naïve as a child with his love of funny jokes and playful tricks. Not everyone, even in Moscow, knew that he was the author of several clever palindromes (which are, unfortunately, untranslatable). Lazar Berman in his recollections of Sofronitsky brings up another example, when Sofronitsky called him up to report a clumsy error in a radio program, which cited "Works of Haydn performed by Mozart," and then added, "Now you call up your acquaintances, and I'll call my people." It's evident that the combination of naïveté and a sense of humor, as well as an ability to abstract oneself from external matters, even momentarily, often helped those marked with talent and spirituality to survive in those terrible postwar years. The surrounding cruelty and violence of the Stalinist era terrified and oppressed Sofronitsky immensely.

During his last years (1958–60), he often preferred to play in the Scriabin museum-apartment in Moscow, not far from Arbat Street, where up to a hundred people crowded into several small rooms to hear, most often, Schubert, Schumann, Chopin, Liszt, Rachmaninov, and of course, Scriabin. As it happened, these concerts were the highest revelations of this great artist. By 1961, he was seized with a terminal illness, and in August, after cruel suffering, Vladimir Vladimirovich Sofronitsky passed away.

The funeral service was held in the Little Hall of the Moscow Conservatory (the Grand Hall was closed for summer repairs). Thousands of people came to bid farewell and thank, for the last time, the great musician who had generously shared his unique artistic gifts. Even in his coffin, at sixty years of age, he did not look like an old man—only like one who had been through much and had suffered a great deal.

Another pianist who made an enormous impression on us during those last years of the war was Emil Gilels. In many respects the opposite of Sofronitsky, his art seemed to radiate health and reliability, one might say an Olympian spirit. His pianistic tone itself startled one with its unusually powerful, meaty *forte* and a velvety *piano* that penetrated everywhere.

Gilels' virtuosity has always been notable. As far back as 1933, as a sixteen-year-old, the brightly red-headed youth from Odessa astonished the audience and jury of the first All-Union Competition with a brilliant performance of Liszt's difficult transcription of Mozart's *The Marriage of Figaro*. His playing was not distinguished then by any special depth, and the tempos were sometimes too fast, but it was impossible to withstand his pianistic spontaneity. It was obvious that not only was a phenomenal virtuoso entering a major art but a personality as well, endowed with iron will, clarity of thought, and a healthy mental balance.

The great demands he made on himself, along with his purposeful studying under such an artist as Heinrich Neuhaus, resulted in Gilels' brilliant victory at the Ysaÿe Competition in Brussels in 1938. A quarter of a century later, Neuhaus remembered that the young Gilels, who had earlier been reluctant to learn the Schumann Concerto, said to him, "You know, Heinrich Gustavovich, it seems to me now that this is one of the most brilliant piano concertos!" Neuhaus added, "I was very proud then to see him grown up."

The 1940s became the middle period, as it were, in the development of this pianistic giant. Thoughtfulness, and the large scale of his conceptions, became part of his performing nature. Gilels continued to move along this path, developing into a mature, and later a wise, master. The late sonatas of Beethoven, Liszt's B minor Sonata, and the sonatas nos. 7 and 8 of Prokofiev (Gilels gave the latter's premiere in 1944) occupy a large place in his repertoire. One might argue over Gilels' Chopin, but even in the 1930s the shrewdest critics could detect the great passion of his artistic nature in his playing of the B-flat minor Sonata.

Gilels does not play often. His impetuous growth seems to demand time to realize and evaluate itself, in order to rise to the next higher stage. Though the composer did not seem close to his artistic personality, it was Gilels who in 1954 brought back to the concert stage the music of Nikolai Medtner, which had been banned during the witches' sabbath at the end of the 1940s. Having achieved this, he became the first pianist to perform once again Medtner's G minor Sonata, op. 22.

As with Oistrakh, a halo seems to surround the name of Gilels. Complete loyalty, at least superficially, in his relations with the authorities, had made him into a kind of banner of the Soviet performing arts. (In 1945, Stalin proudly called for Gilels to display his skill before the participants at the Potsdam Conference.) But as a man, Gilels is very hard to deal with. He is reserved and rarely smiles, chooses friends very carefully, and if he once dislikes someone, the feeling lasts forever. The story of his long, unexpressed rivalry with the other pianistic giant, Sviatoslav Richter, could be a bitter illustration to Balzac's *The Human Comedy*. The unbearable thought that someone is challenging the lion's autocracy makes him as overanxious and jealous as any *Homo sapiens*. Nevertheless, no one can accuse Gilels of having destroyed another's career or of chasing away less fortunate rivals, and in these days that means something. On the contrary, during the cruel years of 1949 and '50, when help was needed to ward off the dangers facing three almost doomed colleagues at the Conservatory, Gilels supported the daring initiative of my teacher.

In 1944, the war was moving toward a victorious end, and during concerts the Conservatory often shuddered from artillery salutes celebrating the liberation of another large city. One strong impression from that time was the autumn comeback concert of Heinrich Neuhaus, recently returned from an "evacuation" rather different from the others. Three years earlier, as the German army approached Moscow, Neuhaus had not moved with the Conservatory to the old city of Saratov in central Russia because his eldest son was dying of tuberculosis, and Neuhaus could not leave him. Shortly after, Neuhaus, whose father was German, was arrested, spent some time in jail, and was then expelled to the Urals. All his honorary titles and honors were taken away. It is hard to say what the end result of this wild arbitrariness would have been if this brilliant musician's influential friends had not eventually achieved his return to Moscow.

Incidentally, the young pianist and organist Leonid Roizman also stayed behind in Moscow at that time, as his father was dying. Meeting him after an interval of three years on the Conservatory's staircase, Neuhaus asked with charming amazement, "Haven't you been arrested?"

The demonstrative welcome for Neuhaus in the overcrowded Grand Hall was unusual for a Soviet audience. The crowd rose to its feet. The ovation, which simultaneously expressed both a protest and the joy of meeting a beloved artist again, lasted not less than five minutes. I recall nothing of the kind before any other concert. Neuhaus stood up several times, touched and confused, answering the stormy manifestation of love felt for him. The "voices from heaven" in the slow movements of Beethoven's Sonata in C minor, op. 111, his last, and the B minor Sonata by Chopin have stayed in everyone's memory. The spontaneous performance of the finale of Chopin's Sonata excited a new wave of ovation.

Thirty-five years later, I hung Neuhaus' photograph with his warm inscription, dated 1963, on the wall of my classroom at DePaul University. He looks out at you from a background made from a page of the first movement of this Sonata—an echo of that unforgettable, bygone recital.

January 1945, the premiere of Prokofiev's Symphony no. 5 in the Grand Hall. It was the only time I ever saw Prokofiev, who was conducting, and what I recall is not so much the music itself as an impression of something very significant and masterful. His unusual and angular motions must have sprung from insufficient conducting experience (in contrast to his pianistic skills). His indestructible confidence and the logic of each musical thought, however, coupled with the orchestra's enormous respect and attention, produced marvelous results. This was Prokofiev's last public appearance. Within a few days he suffered the first attack of the illness he fought for the last eight years of his life.

The great Yehudi Menuhin came to Moscow that same year, and the legendary idol simply proved we are all human. A. B., who attended Menuhin's concert at Tchaikovsky Hall, declared he would remember the slow movement of the Beethoven Concerto until his last days, but for those who expected technical perfection from this top-ranked violinist, his recital in the Grand Hall was a slight disappointment. Some of us, with the cruelty of youth, even demanded as encores the virtuoso miniatures we had recently heard on his recordings. After this our violinists began to play a popular Saint-Saëns Rondo Capriccioso at a much more reserved pace, in contrast to which the swift coda increased in virtuosic luster.

The intensity of Menuhin's concert career, which started when he was thirteen and included more than a hundred performances a year, exhausted the gifted adolescent's nervous system. His 1958 recital in Bucharest was marked by bow gnashing and a somewhat inexact intonation. A few days later, though, the packed Atheneum Hall enjoyed his and Oistrakh's performance of Bach's Double Concerto. Both played calmly and wisely—one of the greatest duos I've heard. Even now, divine sparks often break out in his playing.

At the end of 1945, the first postwar All-Union Competition was held in Moscow. Pianists Sviatoslav Richter and Victor Merzhanov shared first prize; the young Slava Rostropovich won the cello competition. Among violinists, the second and third prizes went to Boris Moribel and the brilliant Julian Sitkovetsky (both died in their thirties). Leonid Kogan did not make it to the final round, an obvious injustice that we soon witnessed more and more often. I must say that Merzhanov played magnificently then. His Scriabin Fifth Sonata, Brahms' Paganini Variations, and especially Rachmaninov's Third Concerto brought him the highest achievement of his life, sharing the prize with the brilliant Richter. Unfortunately his moment of fame was brief— quite soon, he began to lose his nerve onstage. Of course he did not possess Richter's scale and divine gift, and the tenth prize in the 1949 Chopin Competition was in fact the end of his career. Several of his recordings are known in the West, however, including the very good Twelve Études, op. 8, of Scriabin.

It is strange, but except for a general impression of the enormity of Richter's playing, I cannot remember his contest repertoire beyond Liszt's "Wilde Jagd" Étude and Tchaikovsky's First Concerto. Perhaps he was set on fire by the unexpected rivalry of Merzhanov (which is not in his nature at all). In any case, the spontaneity of his performance simply astounded the audience. All who had the luck to hear Richter in the second round in the Little Hall surely remember that he finished playing by candlelight (another power failure in the Conservatory). During the stormy Liszt Étude, one of the candles rocked and fell from the piano, and a chill of rapture swept the audience. As I was making my way out between the rows after his Tchaikovsky Concerto, I overheard one quite hearty and well-to-do listener comment to his neighbor, "Sounds funny, but my knees are still shaking."

The competition of 1945 proclaimed, as if officially, the emergence of a great new pianist.[7] One of the most dedicated laborers in the performing arts, Richter could spend half the night after a triumphal concert at the piano, scrupulously "cleaning up" the program that he had just played and preparing the next. And if something in his performance did not satisfy him, no delighted audience nor even his teacher, Neuhaus, could reassure him until he achieved, with the huge, powerful hands of a Master, what he himself intended.

The concerts of the great Romanian George Enescu were memorable events in 1946 Moscow. Besides being a notable composer, he was distinguished in three performance fields, as a conductor, a pianist, and a violinist—a unique example of versatility in twentieth-century music, which is otherwise marked by narrow specialization. In his recital in the Tchaikovsky Hall[8] at age sixty-five, Enescu played as a pianist with Oistrakh (I still remember a wonderful evenness of figurations in the development section of the first movement of Grieg's C minor Sonata), and then with Oborin as a violinist in the Franck Sonata. Among his students are two great performers, Yehudi Menuhin and the pianist Dinu Lipatti, whose tragically early death in 1950, at the age of thirty-three, could be compared only to the loss of Karl Thausig, the brilliant young pupil of Liszt, eighty years earlier.

The fascination of his name, and his nobility and kindness, inevitably attracted young people to Enescu, which brings to mind a funny story. A young Romanian violinist came to Enescu and asked him to accompany his debut in Paris, where Enescu had lived for many years. The old man, with his customary generosity to his young countrymen, could not deny his assistance. Shortly before the concert, Enescu came across his famous fellow pianist Alfred Cortot, and in order to remain with him longer, half jokingly asked him to be his page turner. In the good old days great artists must have been more easygoing in such situations—in any case, Cortot agreed, and the next day's *Figaro* ran this one-of-a-kind review: "A rather unusual concert took place last night in Gavo Hall. The person who should have played the violin played the piano; the one who should have played the piano turned the pages; and the one who ought to have turned pages played the violin instead."[9]

Meanwhile the spring of 1946—with its final exams in general education, music theory, and above all in our "specialty"—was approaching.[10] Among the other pianists, two students of Goldenweiser (one of them myself) and one of Neuhaus were graduating from the Central School. It was decided that our degree recitals would combine both the final exam and the audition for the Conservatory, and thus, the jury panel included all the Central School's piano teachers and two outstanding professors of the Conservatory. In a rare coincidence, all three of us played concertos by Saint-Saëns—I, the popular Second (G minor), and the other two, the less well-known Fourth (C minor). It was a successful day for us all, and I still remember the unusual words of praise I received, like "in Gilels' manner." On a sunny day in June 1946 we finished the Central School, which had been a primary reality of our lives, and became students of the Moscow Conservatory, in the most dramatic and turbulent period of its history.

CHAPTER 2

Moscow Conservatory

About our dear companions,
Who enlivened our world
With their presence,
Do not say with sorrow:
They are gone
But say with gratitude:
They were.

V. Zhukovsky

The student contingent of Soviet universities during the postwar years was heterogeneous in the extreme. In lecture halls, young girls with braided hair sat next to grown-up youths who had been to the front, sometimes even through the hell of German captivity, with all its long-term consequences. Our first-year group was no exception. Besides myself, the younger pianists included Bella Davidovich (the studio of Igumnov), returned from her native Baku, and Margarita Feodorova (the studio of Neuhaus), and among the older, Victor Nossov (the studio of Feinberg), grown wise from his war experience, to mention a few who later emerged on the concert stage.

We have chiefly happy memories of the time before February 1948. We were friendly, full of hopes, and proud of being students of the Moscow Conservatory. On marble slabs by the door to the Little Hall are the names of its best alumni: the first graduate ever to win the Gold Medal for both composition and piano, Sergei Taneyev (1875); a few years later, Alexander Siloti (1882) and Sergei Lyapunov (1883); a fabulous 1893, with Yosif Levin, Sergei Rachmaninov, and Alexander Scriabin; and here are our teachers, Konstantin Igumnov (1894); Alexander Goldenweiser (1897), and Rozina Bessi (later Levina; 1898). We were proud of our other professors as well. The kind Maria Solomonovna Nemenova-Luntz, one of the few pupils (and a favorite) of Scriabin, taught a concertmaster class. Pavel Alexeevich Lamm, who had restored the original score of *Boris Godunov* and was a loyal friend of Miaskovsky and Prokofiev, led the chamber ensemble.

Soviet musicology was characterized by tendentiousness and a chronic juggling of facts, in service to the time, but fortunately we attended the classes of two outstanding experts. The first was Igor Vladimirovich Spossobin, a powerfully built intellectual whose peasant, or *muzhik*, appearance contrasted with his brilliant mind, biting wit, and rare musical erudition. His ability to give instant illustrations of the most complicated and rare harmonic successions from the music literature still seems a small miracle to me. A famous specialist in the field of theory and harmony, he was severely criticized during the ideological purges of the Soviet musical science elite. At an ill-fated meeting in 1948, after one of his hypocritical fellow colleagues had urged him, "Igor Vladimirovich, come back to us, before it's too late" (in other words, disassociate from the gang of wicked, harmful "formalists"), a groan escaped Spossobin's mighty chest: "Oh, my God." He was only fifty-four when he died, disappointed, and as sure as fate, drowning his sorrows in drink.

The second was one of my favorite and most revered teachers, a giant in the field of music analysis: Victor Abramovich Tsuckerman. His amazing Russian was absolutely free of borrowed words, the sentences complete, the references exact and concise. In 1950, when the ominous campaign against cosmopolitism (our "cultural revolution" aimed primarily against Jewish intellectuals) was in full swing, his remarks became aphoristic: "In our day, if your antisemitism does not reach a zoological scale, you can be considered a most noble person."

To trick Tsuckerman with empty twaddle, as we managed to do with other instructors, was impossible. His quick smile and ironic, "True, but it does not answer the question," put you in your place then and there. The brilliance and artistry of his lectures were stunning. His piano playing, though dry, was very "honest," unlike other musicologists', with no skipped notes, even in the most difficult passages. A whole hour was given to the formal analysis of Chopin's First Prelude in C, which lasts no more than half a minute. Two double lessons were assigned for Liszt's B minor Sonata, and the brilliant craftsmanship of his analysis opened the hidden places of the great composers' work for us. Tsuckerman's simpler books, more easily understood by a broad circle of musicians, such as *Glinka's Kamarinskaya* (1957), or *Musical Genres and Bases of Musical Forms* (1964), read like poems on music. In this respect, though, he had a no-less-brilliant friend and rival, Lev Abramovich Mazel, whose small book, *Chopin's Fantasy in F Minor* (1937), is a delightful combination of genuine artistry and brilliant scientific analysis.[1]

This rare and lucky synthesis of music and science was the distinctive feature of both Spossobin and Tsuckerman.

Against this background the instructors of the military and Marxism-Leninism departments appeared in striking contrast. From the military department's recent frontline officers, it was hard to expect verbal elegance. We simply enjoyed their grammatical pearls, like "When I'm speaking a moth should fly," instead of the old saying, "When I'm speaking, you should hear a moth fly." (By the way, during our drill lessons a fragile old man with delicate features played different marches for us, decorating them with such dashing passages in double thirds that we got into conversation. It turned out that he had studied in the Moscow Conservatory at almost the same time as his older brother— Yosif Levin.) As for the teachers of Marxist philosophy and political economics (a complete waste of time), despite their rank as lecturers (the equivalent of American associate professors), they often shocked us with their uncouth, primitive vocabulary. My friend Lazar Berman even collected their gems in a special notebook, which was risky, but sometimes we couldn't resist.

At the same time, I do consider a brief study of dialectical laws to be a must for the cultural musician. A genuine dialectic runs through our developing art of music. Such concepts as "a unity of opposites" or "a transition of quantity to quality" can be very helpful for a composer and performer if applied creatively. For instance, Neuhaus, in my opinion, was right on the mark when he used dialectical notions in his lessons and lectures. But what a dead thing, and almost illiterate besides, they kept presenting us in the philosophy department! From time to time, Goldenweiser and Neuhaus had to invite our "Marxists" to report on international events at special meetings. It was uncomfortable to see our professors listening to this infantile narration of newspaper information, hiding their eyes and cringing at every literary lapse. Nevertheless, that is the way it was, and these politically infallibles poked their noses into all Conservatory affairs and music; opposing them was impossible. To be a performance student was in this regard much easier—you were simply supposed to play more Soviet music, and who before 1948 could object to the works of Miaskovsky, Prokofiev, Shostakovich, or Anatoly Alexandrov?

Intramural competitions in the piano department were an annual tradition. As a freshman, I managed to be third after Bella Davidovich and the brilliant virtuoso Gleb Axelrod (Ginsburg's best student) for my performance in the Liszt competition; next year I shared the first prize with Isaak Katz, an older classmate, for Schubert's Sonata in D. Of course, at eighteen, I was not a mature musician with a distinct personality. My strong points were good taste, plasticity, and technical precision. I coped successfully with many études by Chopin, Liszt, Rachmaninov, the "Carnival" and Toccata by Schumann, Rachmaninov's First Concerto, and so on. In spite of some brief periods of slackness and preoccupation with the personal side of life, when I was in good shape the piano became like a part of myself, and I enjoyed these moments. Any performer who knows what I am talking about will agree that nothing else in the world can give the musician a greater sense of happiness.

In February 1948, Soviet music sustained a new and crippling blow. This time the victims were several leading composers, mainly Shostakovich, Prokofiev, and Miaskovsky, and to a lesser degree, Khachaturian. By fiat of the Central Committee of the Communist Party, their music was pronounced "formalistic," inimical to the people, and was, in effect, banned. Evgeny Mravinsky, conducting Shostakovich's Fifth—as many then thought, for the last time—demonstratively kissed the score and lifted it high above his head. Given the times, this extremely courageous gesture evoked tears and prolonged ovation.

I had the good fortune to hear the same Symphony—in the same hall—almost twenty years later, when Mravinsky was nominated for the Lenin Prize, and I was in Leningrad to give a concert. The impression was so strong that I could not resist going backstage to shake the conductor's hand, something I do not ordinarily do, unless the performers are my personal friends.

In January 1936 an incompetent and rude article in *Pravda*, characteristically titled "Muddle Instead of Music," had sent the youthful Shostakovich into a deep depression. (You see, Stalin did not like his opera *Lady Macbeth of Mtsensk*.) And now his Symphony no. 9, which was supposed to be "the Soviet Beethoven's Ninth," did not live up to Stalin's grandiose expectations, provoking his anger.

Prokofiev, in his turn, was not forgiven his temporary emigration (1918–32), his popularity in the West, his allegedly having transformed the piano into a percussion instrument, and so on. Before the revolution, his audacious, innovative work often provoked his more orthodox colleagues. His thorny and sometimes arrogantly independent personality had also earned him many enemies.[2] And now not even his glorification of Stalin in the captivating cantata *Zdravitsa* (1939) could help the man who had created *Romeo and Juliet* (1936), the piano sonatas nos. 7 and 8 (1942 and 1944), and the powerful music for the patriotic films *Alexander Nevsky* (1939) and *Ivan the Terrible* (1942–45).

As it soon turned out, the creative future and well-being of nearly all composers and musicologists, from the outstanding to the mediocre, were threatened. These were the last Stalin years. Any musical work, article, or even statement that did not follow the simplistic, dogmatic lines from above might be branded as a manifestation of alien antidemocratic tendencies. All nonstandard paths of expression and means of development were proclaimed "formalist perversions," a "putrid influence of the West," and could be dearly paid for.

We, the students, did not realize at first the devastating consequences of this party concern for "euphony" and "easily understood" Soviet music for the people. We were amused to watch honorable and semi-honorable professors flinging mud from the stage of the Grand Hall, accusing one another of a notorious formalism, a bending down before the West, or former membership in RAPM (All-Russian Association of Proletarian Musicians [1923–32]).

Gradually, however, it became obvious that something shameful and frightening was happening before our eyes. People often settled a score by trying to whitewash themselves and ruin a colleague before the representatives of the ideology department of the party's Central Committee and the superior functionaries of the Committee on Art Affairs, who presided at a huge table onstage. Soon, all the mutual accusations and squabbling poured out publicly. Newspapers and broadcasts were full of "the wrathful responses of the simple people" (oh, that unforgettable vocabulary), like "When I hear a symphony by Miaskovsky, I quickly turn my radio off," and so on.

Speeding up the revolution, the sanctioned campaign expanded in time and space. We were told that Stravinsky had always scoffed at Russian folk song, that Medtner had established the rotten aesthetics of the moribund gentility he represented in his book, published in Paris in 1935. Of course, nobody had read the book, *Muse and Fashion*, but it was sufficient then to declare, in Stalin's style, "It is well known that . . ." and then go on to lie and slander from one's paunch, as Russians say. The names of Arnold Schoenberg, Allan Berg, Paul Hindemith (or, in the graceful pronunciation of the superior bureaucrat, "Handemith") were spoken with repugnance. No matter they usually had no idea who or what they were talking about. Simply: "It is known that the buffooning formalist Schoenberg produces his works by the social order of the bourgeoisie." And that was that.

The rage for obscurantism did not fade away. In fact, the next year it degenerated into an openly antisemitic campaign against cosmopolitism. The worst human qualities—baseness and ingratitude—flourished. Former pupils, trying to advance their own careers, took part in hunting their teachers. "Gray begins and wins"—this twist on a chess adage was heard at the end of the 1940s, when it was safer to be mediocre. The next step was general ostracism, which started with mass firings of prominent scientists, professors, and workers in art and literature (at the Moscow Conservatory, Shostakovich, Lev Mazel, and Maria Yudina, among others). Many tried to get a job in remote cities in order to make a living. Only a few artistic directors dared to save the professionals they needed in their organizations—among them the conductors Nikolai Semyonovich Golovanov (of the U.S.S.R. Radio Symphony Orchestra), Evgeny Alexandrovich Mravinsky (of the Leningrad Philharmonic), and Mitrofan Kuzmich Belotserkovsky (of the Moscow Philharmonie concert bureau).

A lesser-known example of the incompetence and cruel unfairness of the decree of 1948 was the persecution of Nikolai Yakovlevich Miaskovsky, an honorable person and outstanding musician. For some reason he found himself among those whom the order treated especially harshly, and in his case, unlike those of Prokofiev and Shostakovich, it is hard to find an explanation. A composer and teacher, Miaskovsky was a tireless toiler all his life and never made program statements, nor had enemies nor enviers. Among his many works are twenty-seven symphonies, some of them masterpieces (nos. 6, 21, 22, and 27). To study under him was the dream of every young composer, and he brought up a whole pleiad of outstanding composers, including

Kabalevsky, Khachaturian, and Shebalin. His almost half-century friendship with Prokofiev was free of ambition or jealousy, a beautiful example of the noble creative bonds between two great musicians. A highly decent man of principles, Miaskovsky inspired deep respect among all who knew him.

The basic accusation against Miaskovsky's monumental work was the genuinely tragic concept of many of his compositions, which was interpreted then as "a pessimism devoid of ideas." At an open meeting of the composition department in 1948, several pert, unscrupulous, and well-instructed speakers mouthed this terminology while having nothing professional to say; it was maddening to watch. In this oppressive situation, a short statement by Neuhaus came as a kind of grim comic relief. Neuhaus, who was slightly tipsy, considered it a debt of honor to stand up for a fellow musician. He made his way onstage from the audience of the Little Hall and said, "You see, comrades, it's not the sort of pessimism to condemn—it is our healthy Soviet pessimism!" Here he even stamped his foot. And really, what could one say about these clumsy allegations, justifications, and excuses? My chamber ensemble professor, Pavel Lamm, a close friend of Miaskovsky, said to me, in a highly unusual manner, "What kind of country is this, where a composer cannot write the way he wants?" Miaskovsky, profoundly insulted, shrank into himself and passed away two years after this trauma, in the summer of 1950.

It is now impossible to tell whether the more conservative, traditional musicians had drawn up a response to the party's Central Committee in 1947, which allegedly called for a simplification of harmonic language, a return to folk sources, more programmatic music, and so on. If such an event did take place, it played right into the hands of ideological obscurantists and predatory careerists. All this eventually led to the sinister witch hunt in our arts and sciences, which hindered their development for a long time.

In the concluding deliberation in the Central Committee, the Conservatory director, Vissarion Yakovlevich Shebalin, mentioned his long and unsuccessful petition for funds to repair the building's roof, to which Zhdanov[3] replied, "You'd better introduce proper order *under* your roof." Naturally, Shebalin was removed. In the summer of 1948, he was replaced by the choral conductor Alexander Vassilievich Sveshnikov, who held the office until the early 1970s, the most lasting director in the Moscow Conservatory's history.

Let us briefly recall the history of the board of directors of the Moscow Conservatory, from the day of its foundation in 1866 by Nikolai Grigorievich Rubinstein. (It is profoundly unfair that neither of the two Russian conservatories bears the name of its founder. You may raise an objection: "Well, did not Rimsky-Korsakov and Tchaikovsky deserve it?" And probably you will be right.) Unlike his legendary brother Anton, who had founded the St. Petersburg Conservatory in 1862, Nikolai's life was firmly bound to Moscow. His loyalty to his brainchild was so complete that though he was according to some evidence not inferior to "the great Anton" as a pianist, he virtually did not leave Moscow for concert tours, reluctant to break his ties, even briefly, with the Conservatory. The only exception was his prolonged tour through the cities of the Ural region and Siberia in the 1870s, which he was enticed to make by an imperial promise of ennoblement. Tchaikovsky wrote of this in a letter to his longtime correspondent Nadezhda von Meck: "I wonder what kind of title our friend will be granted, maybe a Jerusalem one?" (both brothers were converted Jews). Now that the reader has digested this quotation, let me add that Tchaikovsky not only deeply respected Nikolai Rubinstein as a fellow musician, in spite of disagreements about his two piano concertos, but was his close friend. Few works of music can shake you with such despair of loss as "Trio to the Memory of a Great Artist" (1882), written after Rubinstein's death. I think it is not for us to judge nor even to comment on such contradictions in the lives of the immortals.

Among the pupils of Nikolai Rubinstein—they were not numerous, for he overworked himself with his administrative duties—was Alexander Ilyich Siloti, a pianist, conductor, and teacher (and incidentally, an older cousin) of Rachmaninov, and my teacher's professor. He left a very interesting memoir of Liszt, with whom he had studied in Weimar shortly before Liszt's death, and later taught for almost twenty years at Juilliard.

In 1885 the directorship of the Moscow Conservatory was assigned to its young professor Taneyev, a pupil of Tchaikovsky and Rubinstein, and an outstanding composer, theoretician, pianist, and teacher. Among almost two hundred of his students in composition and theory were Scriabin, Rachmaninov, Medtner, Glière, and Goldenweiser. In the Conservatory, Taneyev continued the traditions of his great teachers—the highest professionalism and a spirit of mutual respect, to which he added absolute frankness in his dealings. He has a place in music history as the composer of the opera-trilogy *Oresteia*, a Symphony in C minor, the cantatas *Johann Damasquin* and *After Reading the Psalm*, and many chamber works. His *Convertible Counterpoint in the Strict Style* (1909; English translation 1962) remains a valuable textbook for composers and theorists.

A man of rare integrity and erudition, Taneyev was also known for his quick wit, both friendly and unexpectedly cutting. Once, leaving the Conservatory together with Leetvin (the famous Wagnerian dramatic soprano), he realized that the corpulent singer had occupied most of both passengers' seats. Quite stout himself, Taneyev walked around the cab several times looking for his seat, then finally gave up. "Pardon me, Phelia Vassilievna," he asked, "on which side did you sit down?"

Another, better known remark of Taneyev's reveals his dignity and professional pride. After the Moscow premiere of Scriabin's *Prometheus* (March 1911) one of the composer's ardent admirers asked Taneyev his opinion. Lukewarm toward the later works of his brilliant student, Taneyev answered accordingly. Scriabin's excited fan, a teacher of geography by profession, couldn't restrain himself and blurted out, "Sergei Ivanovich, you do not understand this music!" Taneyev broke the awkward silence that followed with this calm reply: "I thought until now that it was enough to dedicate your whole life to music in order to understand it. Now it turns out that one should be a geography teacher as well."

In 1889 Taneyev, who had not had enough time for his own creative work, resigned the directorship. The Conservatory art council decided to offer it to piano professor Vassily Ilyich Safonov. About what happened next Taneyev told his polyphony student and young friend Goldenweiser, who in turn shared the story with a few of his own students decades later. It seems Taneyev invited Safonov to the huge office on the first floor to tell him of his candidacy. The telephone on the desk then rang, and Safonov picked up the receiver and said, "Conservatory director speaking." "And you know," added Taneyev, "it was the first time I realized that we had picked the wrong man."

In 1915 two great musicians died in Moscow—Scriabin and Taneyev, who caught a deadly flu during Scriabin's long funeral procession. Rachmaninov, usually reserved in expressing his feelings, wrote at the time, "Sergei Ivanovich Taneyev passed away—a composer, a master, the most educated musician of his time, a man of rare originality, sincerity—the height of musical Moscow. For all of us who knocked at his door, he was a superior judge, wise, fair, accessible, and simple."

Safonov (1852–1918), who led the Conservatory until 1906, was an extremely complicated and contradictory figure. A Don Cossack by birth, he had a possessive, willful nature that tolerated no opposition. In his dislikes he could be staunch, unfair, and rude—witness Taneyev, Siloti, and Rachmaninov, whose application for a vacant position as a piano professor he succeeded in turning down!

Everybody feared his cruel tongue.[4] He managed to bite even the ingenious Ferruccio Busoni, who taught at the Conservatory for a year. At the same time, his piano studio will never be forgotten: Scriabin, Medtner, Leonid Nikolayev, Yosif Levin and Rozina Levina, to name just a few. It seems that in their memoirs, his students are talking about a different man—paternally kind, cordial, and a remarkable teacher. I am especially impressed by his words to the students who were observing his lesson with Scriabin: "Why are you looking at his hands? Look at his right foot"—referring to Scriabin's amazing pedalization. A strong and popular conductor, Safonov was the first in Russia to conduct without a baton.

His authority and reputation were so high that in 1906 he was offered a three-year contract as a conductor and director of the National Conservatory in New York (the same position that Dvořák had taken up fourteen years earlier). Unfortunately, during the interim discussions over his successor, his dictatorial style and rudeness exceeded the bounds of decorum. After a strongly worded argument, Taneyev handed the director of the Russian Musical Society the following statement, which was published in the newspapers: "In consequence of the totally indecent behavior of the director of the Moscow Conservatory, I am leaving the faculty of this Conservatory. S. Taneyev." Safonov lived on for thirteen more years, but never returned to the Moscow Conservatory.

The excellent composer and teacher Mikhail Mikhailovich Ippolitov-Ivanov (whose "Caucasian Sketches" are still popular) replaced Safonov as the director from 1906 to 1922. Kind and tolerant, he was a complete contrast to his predecessor, and that is how he is gratefully remembered by his numerous students.

The directors during the first postrevolutionary decade were Goldenweiser (1922–24) and Igumnov (1924–29), both Moscow musicians tightly bound to the Conservatory first as students and then as professors. We must thank the Fates for not having allowed some primitive Bolshevik official to head the Conservatory during this period, promoting by any means possible Lenin's policy of "Party Line in the Arts." In 1927, during the Soviet period, the Conservatory had its first big success on the international stage. Two of its disciples were winners in the first Chopin Competition in Warsaw—Lev Oborin, a pupil of Igumnov (first prize), and Grigory Ginsburg, a student of Goldenweiser (fourth prize).

In the 1920s Alexander Borisovich came to the aid of Pavel Lamm, who had been arrested after an absurd slander by RAPM, and also saved Piotr Jurgenson's original matrix plates of Tchaikovsky's works, which had been marked for destruction by the same group. By the end of the 1920s the growing RAPM took more rigid control of the Conservatory's creative freedom. The association's method of breaking with tradition and its narrow, class-oriented approach to music were the dress rehearsal for the shocks that were later to befall Soviet music. By 1932 its demagogy and striving for primitivism and vulgarization had become so intolerable that RAPM was abolished without fanfare, but its damaging effects were felt on our musical development for a long time to come.

The awful time of the Stalin terror was approaching. By the late 1930s, the directors of the Conservatory succeeded one another more often, even though, except for Boleslav Pzhibyshevsky, none of them perished in the waves of repressions. In 1939 Alexander Borisovich became the director again. His cooperation with the Soviet power after the October Revolution, the foundation of the Central School of Music in Moscow, his outstanding students—all this supported his authority in the upper strata, and I must say he always used it in the interests of music. Of course, by then not much was left of the Conservatory's autonomy, yet one could calculate the number of arrested musicians in dozens, not in hundreds and thousands, as was the case in other fields of arts and sciences.[5]

One figure in the Conservatory's history at that terrible time was Nikolai Semyonovich Zhilyaev, a remarkable theoretician, critic, and editor, who perished in 1938 due to his friendship with Marshal Mikhail Tuhachevsky, whose one-day trial and execution, with a big group of the best Soviet military men, had been staged by Stalin in 1937. Zhilyaev did not renounce this friendship when he was arrested.

Soon after the war started, the Conservatory readied for evacuation to Saratov. As I mentioned earlier, several honorable artists including Alexander Borisovich were sent to Nalchik by government order. In 1942 the post of director was assigned to Vissarion Yakovlevich Shebalin—shortish, dry, unsmiling (in any event, that is the way I remembered him in 1946–48). A prolific composer who brought up such pupils as Tikhon Khrennikov, Oleg Eiges, Alexandra Pachmutova, and many others, Shebalin was a highly professional musician, a successor to the Russian classical style of his remarkable teacher, Miaskovsky. It was difficult for him to reveal his personal integrity after the havoc wrought by Zhdanov in the field of literature in the summer of 1946. When two years later Zhdanov delivered the same blow to Soviet music, the director was naturally the figure to blame for everything (or, as the Russians say, to hang all the dogs on). At one turbulent meeting in the Grand Hall, associate professor Yury Vsevolodovich Keldysh contrived to charge Shebalin with opening paths for contemporary Western music to the detriment of the Russian, which was total nonsense. The very restrained Shebalin, while answering this absurd accusation, almost shouted, "I dedicated my whole life to Russian music and I cannot allow any comrades keldyshes to jeer at it!" The entire scene was very hard to watch.

Fear and distress seized everyone, except, of course, for the unprincipled career-makers with neither shame nor conscience. And what can one say about those who were pointed at with the leading-whip? "Tally-ho! Sic him, sic him!" Packs of enviers and scoundrels maliciously, without mercy, pounced on Shostakovich, Maria Yudina, Lev Mazel, and many others, including the brilliant founder of what was probably the first-ever chair of the history and theory of piano, Grigory Mikhailovich Kogan, defaming shamelessly their creative life-works.

The Soviet tendency to select choral conductors for high administrative positions was long-standing and deliberate (I leave Russian readers to explain this). And so in 1948 we made our way to Alexander Vassilievich Sveshnikov, an experienced choral organizer and a conductor in the rather precentor style. Notwithstanding his appointment as director of the Conservatory, I think that Sveshnikov's activity in the Academic Choir of Russian Song and in the Moscow Choral College, which he founded, occupied a larger place in his heart. Sveshnikov was a one-hundred-percent obedient executor of directives from above. Along with that, he looked out for his own well-being, eventually promoting his wife, a quite mediocre singer, to the rank of full professor.

At meetings Sveshnikov spoke pedantically, not always smoothly. Once he started a conversation on a teacher's loyalty and brought up our Old Man as an example, who, having come to his office several times outraged by some unfairness, overreacted, even threatened to resign, but of course never did. "It is impossible to imagine anybody walking out on our Conservatory voluntarily; our faculty should leave us only for the graveyard!" he added, enlivening the meeting.

As far as I remember, it did happen in 1959, after Grigory Ginsburg had taken offense at the administration for something, and sent in his resignation. The letter was unexpectedly accepted without any attempt to convince this great musician to stay, which literally struck him down. When in December 1961 Ginsburg died from cancer, his family flatly opposed the idea of holding a civil funeral at the Conservatory—they felt that the administration's indifference had shortened his life. So the ceremony took place in the Tchaikovsky Hall.

In the 1949–50 academic year, when the struggle against cosmopolitism was in full swing, a public party session took place in the piano department as well. The time had come for three of our professors to find themselves "endangered species," in spite of their merits and reputations. They were a notable pupil of Medtner, Abram Vladimirovich Shatskess; the coordinator of the concertmaster faculty, Maria Solomonovna Nemenova-Luntz; and as it proved later, since they did not attack him openly at the meeting, the brilliant pianist, Yakov Flier. Of course, the scenario had been set beforehand; I prefer not to name the party secretary of the piano department at that time, a well-known musician who fulfilled the task of conducting the meeting in the approved fashion (he died in 1976, having himself fallen victim to the same cruel political system after a student of his did not return from a concert tour of the West).

Shatskess obediently debased himself. They made him publicly repent not only for playing works by his brilliant teacher Medtner but also for including them in his students' repertoire. After a miserable Abram Vladimirovich had diligently thrown mud at himself and left the podium, the representative of the party's district committee brought him back with the question, "And how would comrade Shatskess explain the fact that he kept advocating this harmful music for such a long time?" And comrade Shatskess ascended his Golgotha again and informed the meeting in the voice of a doomed man that he could explain it solely by his "political bankruptcy." I am citing these words, as well as the following passage from Goldenweiser's statement, verbatim—one does not forget such things.

"People stayed silent" (Pushkin, *Boris Godunov*); fear hung in the air.

During the war Maria Nemenova-Luntz had sheltered in her faculty a jobless musician who resembled Tolstoy's Karenin (Anna's husband) in character, only younger. And now to our horror and shame, this no-talent, dried-up man, having risen to the rank of the Conservatory's academic secretary, was ruining Nemenova-Luntz, accusing her of allowing too much Western music to be played and sung in her class at the expense of Russian and Soviet music—and of other nonexistent sins. The stunned old lady, who had been associated with the Conservatory for nearly half the century, sat pale, unable to find any words to explain this low-down action to such a backstabbing nonentity.

Here I recall with pride how our teacher conducted himself just then. Leah Levinson and I, knowing him well, noticed that the whole spirit of the meeting oppressed him. Rising to the stage, he said in a strained voice that he hadn't intended to comment upon what was happening but was forced to make an exception concerning a previous speaker. "Instead of the Bolshevik critique promised to us, we have had to listen for fifteen minutes to a low piece of scandal!"—here his voice almost broke, again recalling old Prince Bolkonsky. The tears started to the old lady's eyes, and a spontaneous ovation broke out in the auditorium—people could not help hailing even a brief victory of esteem and fortitude over fear and corruption.

This story had its continuation, as Grigory Ginsburg told me later. Alexander Borisovich had asked him and Gilels to join him at an appointment with the big shot of the Committee on Art Affairs, to try to vindicate the three persecuted fellow musicians. With his characteristic humor, Ginsburg reconstructed the conversation, acting everyone's part. He and Gilels were standing behind the seated A. B., who argued with the official that regardless of the reasons, three such worthy professors could not be discharged from the Conservatory. He was given in response a condescending elucidation, in a tone which crossed the line permitted when one talked with our Old Man. Ginsburg nudged Gilels, as if to say "watch what happens now." And indeed, A. B. exploded, jumped up from his chair, lectured the self-important cad that his explanations were not convincing, and that he, Goldenweiser, would discuss his manners "in another place." This familiar Soviet saying had an immediate effect, and the big shot faded. He approached A. B., trying to explain that he was "misunderstood," or something like that. Our Old Man just waved him away, like an annoying fly, and walked quickly toward the door, pulling along the two younger men. The appointment was over. And not only an appointment—the shameful order was not signed, and the three doomed musicians were saved.

The official's reaction was not wholly ungrounded—Alexander Borisovich was still quite influential "above." He proved it again in 1949 when Ludmila Sosina, one of his favorite pupils, did not make the team of six Soviet pianists participating in the fourth Chopin Competition in Warsaw. I cannot assert that he called up Stalin personally, as some said at the time. The point is that Goldenweiser *could* make such a call and attempt to revoke a decision he thought was unfair. Anyhow, at the very last moment the talented Stanislav Neuhaus (Heinrich's son) was removed from the team, which, of course, traumatized him severely for a long time.

Sosina went to Warsaw and, no doubt with the cooperation of the Soviet jury members, received only an honorable mention. The big victory of Bella Davidovich—who was sent only as a candidate and shared the first prize with Galina Czerny-Stefanska of Poland—overshadowed everything else.

The fourth Chopin Competition, or rather, the rigorous selection for it in the U.S.S.R., was my first attempt at participation in such contests. The preliminary auditions for the Warsaw competition of October 1949 started in early spring—first the two rounds among Conservatory students, then two All-Union nationwide rounds. About one hundred people were in the running—including such well-known pianists as Tatiana Nikolayeva, Leonid Zyuzin (the popular blind Moscow pianist), and Tatiana Kravchenko. These three were eventually eliminated, while I, an unknown Conservatory junior, passed to my surprise through the sieve of elimination and found myself among several who were told by officials, "Go on vacation. Do not think of anything till the end of September—you will be called for the last round with the orchestra."

As a candidate for international competition I first encountered a different and no less important kind of selection over the summer. I had to fill out several detailed questionnaires, which turned inside out the whole life of one's family for three generations. Let's render progress its due—five years later, after the death of Stalin, they no longer asked you about your parents' service in the Czar's mounted gendarmerie! Then, in 1949, the double arrest of my father, whom I didn't even remember clearly, nearly canceled my chances to go abroad.

We went to the Committee on Art Affairs for interviews with workers of the so-called special department. Our fate was in their hands, these people with the polite smiles and quick looks; I was not the only one who experienced discomfort and instinctive fear in their offices. Many years later, as a concert pianist with a good name, walking up the same marble staircase to the Gos- (State) and Ros- (Russian) concert bureaus, I reexperienced the oppressive feelings of my youth.

So in the summer of 1949 I left for the same small Ukrainian town, Belaya Tserkov (White Church), where I had spent the first two-and-a-half years of my life, to take a good rest in our old friends' house. I had scarcely practiced a month when a telegram arrived at the end of August, signed by an official with the Committee whose name I still remember: "Leave immediately for participation in the third round." Even now it is hard for me to believe it, but five days later I was indeed walking out onto the stage of the Grand Hall to play the Second Chopin Concerto with the Moscow Philharmonic, not quite realizing what was happening. I looked carelessly from behind the door at the hall, which seemed unfamiliar and much larger, packed to the ceiling. At this moment my conductor, Nikolai Anosov (Gennady Rozhdestvensky's father), turned me around and said, "Now then, let's sit down and be silent for a minute." Funny—since then I have never come out onstage without sitting down for a few seconds, with my eyes closed.

The second and third movements, after I felt more comfortable onstage, went off well. As for the first movement, I simply don't remember how I played it.

I cannot say I was greatly upset by the jury's decision not to send me to Warsaw—my participation in the last round of selection was a notable achievement in itself. Nonetheless, for a couple of months I couldn't face the piano and lived a rather irregular life. Once, after another sleepless night at the card table, I went out with a friend of mine into the foggy autumn morning and read in the newspaper on the streetstand, "Soviet pianist Bella Davidovich is a winner of the Chopin

Competition in Warsaw." My friend said only, "It's even better than winning ten bridge games."

In the spring of 1950, another selection took place in Moscow, this time for a so-called Festival of Democratic Youth in East Berlin. Two Goldenweiser students tied for first place—Lazar Berman and myself—and the final decision was left to our teacher. Objectively, the title of laureate was at that time more important to me than to the younger Berman—the next year was my graduation and, of course, the *aspiranture* (or postgraduate candidacy) was always at the back of my mind. Besides, I think I've never played Liszt's Mephisto Waltz better than at that selection. Nevertheless, Alexander Borisovich's decision in my friend and rival's favor neither surprised nor pained me, unlike some of my friends and colleagues. It is difficult to imagine A. B.'s attitude toward Berman at that time. His phenomenal virtuosity outweighed for A. B. everything he would not forgive in his other students—the exaggerated tempos that sometimes resulted in a lack of clarity, a blurry pedal. When Berman brilliantly and noisily played in our class the most difficult pieces of the piano literature, our teacher, obviously proud of his favorite student, could not hide his delight.

Of course, Lazar got the first prize in Berlin. And I undertook, with special persistence, the preparation of my degree recital program. It's interesting that as an item of independent work I prepared one of Liszt's most difficult études, "Feux Folleaux," which I don't remember ever including in my concert programs (though perhaps I played it a couple of times as an encore).

The final recital went off very successfully. The state commission, chaired by Khachaturian, granted me the diploma with honors, and the piano department recommended me for the Conservatory's *aspiranture*. In the Grand Hall, at the concert of the best graduates, I played Chopin's Fourth Ballade and received a very memorable compliment from Sofronitsky (he never attended the concerts but listened to the live radio broadcast). Kind old Alexander Feodorovich Goedike, whom I came across in the Conservatory yard, spoke to me about the audition program for *aspiranture* later in the spring. "Look, don't you replace the Chopin Ballade—let well enough alone." Was that ever flattering and encouraging!—and happened to be especially important in connection with what awaited me around the next corner.

By that time the situation in the country was getting rougher and more cruel—one might say suffocating. A politically kosher biography, your nationality, your "social activity" were more important criteria than professional qualities. Nothing can erase the memory of the humiliating conditions at the Commission on the Placement of Young Specialists for our 1951 graduates. In spite of being recommended for *aspiranture*, I was assigned first to Yakutsk (ever heard of the "pole of cold," the coldest point on earth?—that's it), then to Barnaul (in the heart of Siberia), as a secondary music school piano teacher. I took the news seriously (and how!), until by good fortune a cable arrived from Barnaul, saying in effect that the school did not have a teaching position, but badly needed a concertmaster. An obvious bureaucratic snafu gave me several months' respite—a breathing space.

I have kept a snapshot from that time. My professor and I, looking preoccupied, are discussing something, leaning our elbows on the piano on the stage of the Little Hall, perhaps during some rehearsal intermission. The subject of our conversation was delicate—filling in an application for *aspiranture* (considering the circumstances of 1951, I was especially vulnerable in this respect). Clearly Alexander Borisovich sympathized with me and wanted to have me in his class for a few more years. With the form filled out and entrance examinations successfully overcome, only one thing remained to do—await the Committee's decision. And just then the personnel department of the Committee received an anonymous denunciation. We were sure that it had been sent by the neighbors in our communal apartment. The telephone in our corridor served all four families, and anyone who wanted to could be well informed of others' private affairs.

Sveshnikov called me to his office and said that a letter had come in, accusing me of critical views, a "bourgeois way of thinking," and so on. Several years later, during the short period of Khrushchev's "thaw," an anonymous letter would not be taken seriously, but then Sveshnikov looked concerned and seemed sincerely willing to help. The next several weeks of waiting were far from pleasant, for the whole business was damned dangerous. Finally, at the end of October Alexander Borisovich called me up and said, "You are confirmed—get down to work." I composed myself in order not to reveal my reaction before the loathsome co-tenants.

The Westerner with his concern for privacy can hardly imagine that up to ten or twelve families could live in a communal apartment with one kitchen and bath, and rarely two lavatories. It happened, sometimes, that even if neighbors were not exactly close with each other, they stayed human, having endured the terror of the 1930s and the following terrible war. Our case was unfortunately more typical: one family in the apartment continually poisoned the lives of the others. Therefore, when the state later allowed semi-private housing (the so-called cooperatives), millions were ready to pay any price to get a separate apartment and feel themselves independent, at least in their own home. My family had to wait until 1957, and the years drained away our health and endurance.

So one of the miracles of my life had happened—I became an "aspirant" of the Moscow Conservatory in somber 1951. I did not meet often with the director of the Conservatory, but when I did, Sveshnikov would invariably ask me, "Dmitry, do you remember how we helped you then?" I do remember, Alexander Vassilievich, rest in peace. I remember, and thank you.

Fifteen years later, in 1966, near the Moscow Historic-Archive Institute, my wife ran into one of her former classmates, who was then working in the Conservatory archive. She told my wife that a record of the proceedings of a bygone meeting of the Conservatory art council had once come into her hands. The subject in question involved the admission of new "aspirants," and a familiar name drew her attention. Alexander Borisovich had informed the council in a short remark that if Paperno were not accepted into *aspiranture*, he, Goldenweiser, in token of his dissent, would leave the Conservatory.

Thank you, my dear teacher. I did not have a chance to thank you for these words in time—I've learned of them only after your death. *Thank you!*

For better or worse, in the Soviet Union a young performer who had not won a competition had virtually no access to the concert stage. No Moscow concert bureau would hire a soloist without this mandatory "laureate's hat" above his name. The sole exception was Stanislav Neuhaus, who had never received this title and yet was one of the most popular performers of my generation. I could name many who for different reasons did not make it to the "laureate elite." In the best cases, they became associate professors of the provincial conservatories, or excellent concertmasters to their more fortunate colleagues—the violinists, cellists, singers. So, during my three postgraduate years I faced an overwhelming task of vital importance—namely to make it through one more selection and become a prize winner in an international competition.

For obvious reasons we decided to concentrate on the fifth Chopin Competition in Warsaw. It meant that during the first year and a half I had to pass the Ph.D. candidate requirements: at least one full recital, the history of piano, a foreign language (which for me was German—if only we could see twenty-five years ahead!), and you guessed it, Marxist-Leninist philosophy. Then I could start work on my dissertation, "The Polonaise-Fantasy, op. 61, as the Height of Chopin's Work in the Polonaise Genre."

In those gloomy years, when the country's atmosphere was stifling with fear and the expectation of the worst, it wasn't easy to be steadily and efficiently productive. Nothing remained of the optimism of the first postwar years. As in the late 1930s, people were estranged and tight-lipped—a careless word might have fatal consequences. Music, books, and a narrow circle of close friends were among the few escapes. Another, tucked away on one of Arbat's old lanes, was the Conservatory opera studio, which staged Mozart's *Don Giovanni* and *The Marriage of Figaro* with a combined force of students and a few professional singers (exactly as we did at DePaul's School of Music forty years later). The unbelievable music, the sincere performance of the young singers, the whole spirit in the small hall, carried you far away—and you simply did not want to return. Once a companion asked me something during a performance, and deep in my enjoyment of the music, I couldn't speak. I had never experienced this priceless feeling before. Another time, during an intermission, I ran into Neuhaus, who said, "This is the best music one can hear now in Moscow; I've already lost count of how many times I've been here." For him too it was a way of escaping reality.

A very few guest artists visited from Western countries. I remember the strong Austrian conductor Josef Krips (especially the Strauss waltzes) and, of course, the brilliant Willy Ferrero, who had already conquered Russian audiences as a phenomenal conducting prodigy at the beginning of the twentieth century. A world-class musician of comprehensive mastery and charisma, he radiated music so intensely that the orchestra seemed to react to even his most casual movements, as when he quickly sleeked his hair or set his cuffs. His sparkling performance—of Beethoven's Symphony no. 4, Strauss' waltzes, and

shorter orchestral works by Rossini, Liadov, and Richard Strauss—
was a festive but brief occasion, after which real life looked even more
somber.

In 1952 a group of Jewish writers and poets was shot in secret. In
January of the next year the foul, nefarious Doctor's Plot[6] broke out.
The country was losing its human face. It seemed that if all this bloody
cruelty, madness, and hypocrisy continued, Stalin and his henchmen
would plunge the whole country into medieval hell.

And here, Providence at last turned her eyes on our homeland.
The monster who had ruled Russia for almost thirty years died, in solitude, at his dacha near Moscow on 5 March 1953. It would be out of
place to reason here why this death was perceived by millions of people with sorrow and perplexity. For long years our patriotism, a wish
to believe in and to be a part of society, had been poisoned by the cruel
oppressions and fear surrounding us. People tried to survive and keep
their faith in the great destiny of Russia. We were told over and over
that Stalin was the one who had made the country strong, overwhelmed the monstrous Hitler, fought tirelessly for peace, contained
the American instigators of the war. And now this bulwark had collapsed, the great leader had left us. Hundreds of thousands of people
filled the Moscow streets; many were crying.

The whole Conservatory gathered that day in the Grand Hall, simply to be together. How could we, the young ones, know that on the
same day people throughout the nation, in millions of families, both
the faithful and atheists, thanked God for what had finally happened?
By somebody's order, all Moscow streets adjacent to the city center
were blockaded by military trucks. The attempt to maintain order
turned into its opposite, and several hundred people were crushed to
death among the crowds who tried to make their way to the Column
Hall, where Stalin's body lay in state for several days. This time I was
lucky and just barely got out of what might have been the most dangerous spot, Troubny Square—the lowest point on the Boulevard circle. It cost me only one galosh and a torn coat.

In one of those characteristic twists of fate, Prokofiev's death on the
same day as his persecutor went almost unnoticed. Many musicians
could not even make their way to the Composers' Union to bid a last
farewell to their brilliant fellow composer. In the face of strict limitations prescribed by his doctors and the moral shock he sustained, the

creative intensity of Prokofiev's last years continues to amaze. Only a few hours before his death, he was working on the score of his ballet, *The Tale of the Stone Flower.*

Prokofiev's career had much in common with that of Shostakovich. They both graduated from the Petersburg Conservatory as composers and pianists. With the years and before abandoning concert appearances altogether, they limited themselves to their own compositions. Performance was an especially important part of Prokofiev's life in the West. The best preserved recording of his Third Concerto clearly presents his pianistic potential—logic, precision, brilliantly worked-out technique. Many recollections of Prokofiev after his return to the U.S.S.R. in 1932, and especially during and after the war, describe him as a kind, sociable person, tenderly loving to relatives, friends (especially Miaskovsky), and children. And so he is in his music—logical, assertive, harsh, yes, but at the same time generous, inspiringly lyrical, and compassionate.

Chess played an important role in his life, except for his final years, when the doctors forbade him to play. He had friendly relations with two world champions, Capablanca and Botvinnik. A poster of his match with Oistrakh, another potent chess player, is preserved in one of Moscow's clubs. Both were ranked in the first (quite a high) category in chess.

When Rachmaninov was asked what percentage of his life was occupied by music, he replied that he was eighty-five percent musician, fifteen percent man. In the cases of Prokofiev and Shostakovich, I think the musician percentages can be raised even higher. Music had caused them great emotional suffering and pain, but they could not have existed without it. It was their bitter and towering destiny.

By the middle of 1953 my set task was fulfilled—I passed the candidate qualification and began work on my dissertation on the Polonaise-Fantasy. This piece, of course, was included in my program for the next Chopin Competition (February/March 1955). Since this contest would be decisive in my musical life, it added pressure to the long selection process, but this time there was nowhere to retreat. I took several lessons with the remarkable pianist Maria Izrailevna Grinberg. A favorite pupil of Felix Blumenfeld, and later Igumnov, Grinberg had been very popular among a cultured audience. Feminine, with a soft serious look, she possessed a strong willpower both as a person and as a musician. Her intellect, refined taste, and ability to narrate music in her own way, modeling the shape of large works, made her concerts interesting and sometimes even outstanding.

Her husband had perished in the 1930s, and she lived with her daughter and an old aunt. People lent their ears to her opinions, which were always expressed calmly, in a soft voice. Her lessons encouraged me a lot, which was very important then. Her candor with students was uncommon: "How can you play this passage so smoothly? I have never managed it the way I wanted." (And this from Maria Grinberg, who with her small, clever hands played such pieces as Beethoven's Hammerklavier Sonata, op. 106, and Rachmaninov's Third Concerto!)

I vividly recall one musical impression connected with her. It took place in the almost empty Tchaikovsky Hall, as she rehearsed Beethoven's Third Concerto with the German conductor Hermann Abendroth. Everything was played, as usual, with completeness and strength. But after the cadenza of the first movement, the short broken arpeggio (in the background, *pianissimo* strings and timpani) suddenly made my flesh creep. And not only mine—the conductor Nikolai Pavlovich Anosov, sitting in front of me, turned around with his eyes wide open and his head lowered between his shoulders, as if to say "ooo—scary." Even the old man Abendroth, who must have accompanied this piece hundreds of times, walked down from the podium to compliment Maria Izrailevna.

In 1954 Grinberg's sight deteriorated rapidly. Tests revealed a benign brain tumor, which required an immediate operation. In the hospital she impressed even the doctors and nurses of the oncology ward, who had seen a lot, with her dignity and willpower. Much later, in 1967, I became her younger colleague at the Gnessin Institute. She was a remarkable teacher, if maybe too sensitive and sometimes intolerant when jury discussion turned to her students. Maria Izrailevna Grinberg died in 1978 at the age of seventy, as I was informed then, of remote consequences from her earlier trouble. Like many, I remember her with admiration.

So, the selection started in the spring of 1954. At this time there was a lot of talk about the young students of the Central School of Music, the seventeen- and eighteen-year-olds Vladimir Ashkenazy, Rimma Bobritskaya, Dmitry Sakharov. One had only to listen to them to appreciate the maturity and technical completeness these young people exhibited in the "grown-up" Chopin.

The two rounds of the Conservatory selection were very tense. Not completely satisfied with my playing, I was the more pleasantly surprised when the results were announced: among the ten of us who made it to the All-Union Competition, I was the first. I cannot help citing Neuhaus' remark apropos of this: "It's a strange competition: Paperno first, and Gornostaeva tenth." (Vera Gornostaeva was then his favorite student, now the leading professor of the Moscow Conservatory.) Neuhaus' attitude toward Goldenweiser, or rather his pedagogical methods, had always been sceptical—they were so sharply, drastically different both in life and music.

The decisive All-Union selection was scheduled for the autumn. This time I asked Emil Gilels to give me several lessons. Besides the Chopin program, I also played Liszt's Ninth Rhapsody ("The Carnival in Pesht") and a few pieces from Medtner's "Forgotten Motives." As for the Rhapsody, besides Gilels and myself, in all Moscow the performers of this acrobatically difficult piece could be counted on the fingers of one hand: Vladimir Sofronitsky, Leonid Brumberg, Lazar Berman, and later Igor Zhoukov.

Perhaps Gilels wanted to listen to my Rhapsody out of a natural professional interest, as he had the Medtner pieces. That same year, 1954, Gilels wrote an article for the magazine *Soviet Music*, reviving the music of this great Russian composer. Of course, it did not mention the shameful and meaningless persecution inflicted upon Medtner in 1948. It opened in this manner: "Recently I have come across Medtner's G minor Sonata, op. 22. What remarkable music it is! It's a pity we've heard it very seldom lately. I think our music lovers would appreciate its performance in the current concert season," and so on. I quote roughly, from memory, just to show what kind of naïve hush-ups and tricks one had to resort to in order to bring back to the concert stage the music of the Russian genius, who had died in England three years earlier.

About the same time Alexander Borisovich, who had been friends with Medtner and loved his music dearly, decided to perform the complete "Forgotten Motives" cycle with his students. This concert became a joyful event for Moscow musicians, A. B. was happy, and for me a performance of three pieces from opus 38, which I later recorded twice, had an interesting sequel, which I will mention further on.

The lessons with Gilels benefited me enormously—he played himself and talked about orchestration on the piano and diversity of timbres; his advice was very practical. After one session he made me sit down on the couch, handed me the score, and performed, with a wide range of emotions, the Medtner Sonata. For him it was another public rehearsal before a concert of special importance. And what an experience it was for me!

About one hundred participants gathered from all around the country to take part in the All-Union selection, and it was a fight to the death. Except for Sofronitsky and Richter, the country's best pianists were on the jury. After several strenuous auditions from ten o'clock in the morning until five o'clock in the evening every day (in two rounds), six performers were elected in the following order: Vladimir Ashkenazy; Naum Starkman; myself; Dmitry Sakharov; Nina Lelchuk, an eighteen-year-old from the Gnessin Institute; and Irina Siyalova, the aspirant from the Lvov Conservatory. With the exception of Starkman (a soloist with the Moscow Philharmonie concert bureau), none of us had any serious concert experience. We were told that the selection process was finally over, and all six of us could heave a sigh of relief. Later in the fall we would play a Chopin concerto "for practice" with the orchestra in the Grand Hall (coincidentally, we had all chosen the F minor Second Concerto).

Precompetition selections are indeed necessary. At every competition, even the most prestigious ones (the Queen Elisabeth in Brussels, the Chopin in Warsaw, and later, the Tchaikovsky in Moscow) some participants inevitably do not meet the high requirements, simply because their countries do not have national selections. At the same time, a performance at a competition differs essentially from a concert: the jury fixes on and does not forgive those small (and not so small) inaccuracies and slips that a concert audience would not care to notice. Keys accidentally brushed against, momentary memory blanks resulting in hasty jerks, blurry pedalling, and so on, are virtually inevitable onstage, especially for less experienced or excessively nervous performers. (Such, in any event, is the prevailing opinion; others think that age provides not only experience but wear and tear on the nervous system.) The troubling thought that mistakes may fatally influence the jury's decision creates an additional burden on every participant, and in a multistep selection like ours, this burden is repeated over time. Still, five performances with such a heightened responsibility may have both their pluses and minuses.

The Warsaw competition was not far off, and to restore this expenditure of nervous energy and regain freshness was not easy. Besides, I was about to face one more troublesome situation—I would say unexpectedly, but having known my luck in these years, my good reader, it could have been expected, could it not? Several days before we were to play with the orchestra, they told us there would be one more jury, consisting this time only of officials from the ministry of culture. Yes, it's hard to believe, but there were no musicians on this jury. Of course, all this was another blow to our nerves. It was clear they intended to eliminate some of the six candidates.

In fact they eliminated two of us, both Dmitrys—Sakharov and me. The deputy minister (an amateur pianist himself) allegedly said of me, "One cannot play so softly in Warsaw." It sounds like a joke, but I was in no mood for laughter then. My long-cherished dreams of the concert stage were ruined. I was finishing my last year of *aspiranture* and could count only on a teaching job, but not in the Moscow Conservatory, of course. I felt hurt, a sense of injustice: I had been confident in my pianistic abilities and was on the threshold of musical maturity.

I am looking at another snapshot. In November 1954, after the results had been announced, I attended a small birthday party for Elena Ivanovna Grachova, my teacher's former student and an infinitely loyal helpmate who was soon to become his second wife. (The uncommon, wholehearted nature and spiritual wealth of this genuine Russian lady would bear much telling.) For the first time I had come to Goldenweiser's apartment not for a make-up lesson, but for a cup of tea, as a guest. As was customary in old Russia, a couple of elderly women bustled about. The very decrepit Tatyana Borisovna, Goldenweiser's older sister, was present, and also Leah Levinson, with whom we had been preparing the Chopin program and who was taking my failure with heavy heart.

Nobody expressed sympathy or showed me moral support. It was the Moscow way, warm, simple, and hospitable. I caught our Old Man's eyes on me, and he certainly understood, better than the others, my condition at that time. Outraged by the arbitrariness of the music dignitaries, Goldenweiser had sent a strongly worded letter to the ministry, in which he condemned the disrespect shown the honored musicians who were not even invited to the last jury. He wrote, "It is bad when the jurors are not musicians, but even worse when a man capable of fingering the keyboard considers himself competent in piano playing." Naturally it couldn't change anything, but at least our Old Man had expressed his low opinion of them.

To say that I did not want to touch the piano at this time would be an understatement. I simply could not approach it and avoided the Conservatory. The trauma had deeply affected me (I even noticed my first gray hair). I needed some time to absorb all that had happened, and to think about what to do next.

Emil Gilels invited me to his apartment and made an interesting offer, to become the full-time accompanist for Slava Rostropovich. I suppose he wanted to help me find my way to the concert stage somehow, and to work in close collaboration with such a musician as Rostropovich would have been a great solution. (I still don't know why Slava didn't address me directly, though he remembers the case.) I asked for some time to make up my mind.

New Year's Eve was quite cheerless—1955 seemed to be without prospect. And here, as in the Christmas story, an unexpected turn of events takes place. I believe it was on 6 January that Maria Grinberg called and informed me in her calm voice (as if nothing special had happened) that she had just returned from a meeting in the ministry council to which they had invited the whole jury panel that judged last summer's selection. The council acknowledged that last November's decision was erroneous; Sakharov and I were included in the Soviet team again, and I had to arrive immediately to rest and practice for Warsaw at the Composers' Union estate in Ruza, not far from Moscow. "My congratulations, goodbye."

The news was so incredible I could not take it in right away. Several more days passed before I found myself in Ruza, where the four other participants had already lived for some time. After two months without practice, my hands did not want to obey. It was hard to believe that in one month I was going to leave for Warsaw to play a long and complex program at a crucial international contest.

Great importance was attached to this competition, as the winners of two previous competitions were nominated to be jurors—Lev Oborin (the first competition, 1927) and Yakov Zak (the third competition, 1937), who had been remembered and respected in Poland all these years. Among us, only these two had been abroad. The rest of us had never even had the experience of flying. On the night of 17 February 1955, we took off for Warsaw.

The competition was an eye-opening experience, in general for those times, and especially from the point of view of six young Soviets. Upon our arrival, we were accommodated in the cozy old Hotel Polonia, where Rachmaninov stayed during his tours long ago. The state took on the expense of housing and feeding the almost 150 participants, jurors, and guests. One floor of the hotel was set aside for our practicing. The rooms were cleared of furniture, and several dozen pianos were installed.

In one room, Ashkenazy, without sitting down at the piano, let his fingers run through a passage from Chopin's Étude, op. 25, no. 6, in double thirds. A young Chinese man came up and said with amazement, "Fantastic!" It was Fu-Tsung, who later became very popular, receiving not only the third prize but a special award for the best performance of mazurkas. (He had studied in Krakow for a year with old professor Zbigniew Drzewiecki.) Yakov Zak remarked once that if there were no word *bardzo* (very) in Polish, Fu-Tsung would not be able to express himself. He practiced with true Chinese persistence, up to eight hours a day, and when asked "How are you?" usually answered "Phenomenally exhausted." His future took an uncommon shape: one of the first Chinese emigrants, he lived in London and married the daughter of Yehudi Menuhin. Later his playing lost its charisma; my Polish friends told me that they hardly recognized him when he performed in Warsaw in 1973.

Ashkenazy was my roommate, and I could not have wished for a better one. Despite his youth (seventeen), he was serious-minded, reasonable, well read, and unassuming in everyday life. Almost always, our evaluations of people and events coincided, and we trusted each other, too. When I, as the older one, advised him about something, he usually accepted it. Even today we recollect with pleasure that month when we lived in one small room in Warsaw.

For the first time since the war, the competition was to be held in the traditional home of the Warsaw Philharmonic on Yasna Street. The Nazis had bombed Warsaw into ruins, and even ten years after the war, it still hurt to see the destroyed blocks of this beautiful city. The Philharmonic had especially bad luck—shortly before the competition, the recently restored building somehow caught fire and was urgently under repair again.

Six pianos stood on its huge stage: two Steinways, two Bösendorfers, a Bechstein, and a Pleyel. Russian pianists by long tradition played primarily on the Bechstein. Unfortunately, after the Bechstein plant in

Berlin was destroyed by bombing, their postwar manufacturing followed the standards of Steinway, the world leader. In so doing, the
Bechstein seemed to lose its distinguishing qualities—a warm, singing
tone and mildly tight keyboard. This caused a decrease in Bechstein
popularity, and the Soviet Union had only just begun to purchase Steinways from the United States and Germany. Our instructors decided we
would all play on the Steinway-2 (as opposed to the Steinway-1).

The participants performed in alphabetical order, and Ashkenazy
astonished everyone at the start. He was, I believe, the only contestant
who began his performance with two highly difficult Chopin études:
op. 10, no. 1, in C and op. 25, no. 6, in G-sharp minor. The program
for the first stage included any nocturne, one of the last three polo-
naises, a three- to four-minute piece of free choice (I played the Taran-
tella, op. 43), and two études from certain groups (two others were to
be performed at the second stage). Among the hundred or so pianists,
there were, as always, a certain percentage who were driven by the
Olympic spirit, believing for themselves that participation, not victory, was important; indeed, that Chopin's music was being performed
by young pianists from China, Japan, India, Iran, Chile, and Equador
spoke for itself. But Ashkenazy's performance was like a bomb explod-
ing, and the contest gained an obvious favorite from the very first day.

The jury panel was representative and very impressive. Its oldest
member, a kind of antiquity, was Émile Bosquet of Belgium, winner of
the third International Anton Rubinstein Competition (Vienna, 1900).
It is interesting that the young representatives from Russia who had
also taken part in that competition were Medtner, who received the
first honorable mention, Goldenweiser, and Goedike, who won a prize
in composition. I told Bosquet that I was a student of his old rival
(whom he hadn't forgotten during those fifty-five years) and that Alexander Borisovich would be eighty in the beginning of March. The
kind and sociable Belgian sent a telegram of congratulation to Moscow,
which brought real joy to our Old Man.

The one representative from France was the small, lively, talkative Lazare Lévy; the famous Marguerite Long did not arrive until the
competition was in its third stage—the performance with orchestra.
Another colorful figure was Magda Tagliaferro, the invariable representative of Brazil since the second competition in 1932. I still remember her recital—her bright red hair, lots of Spanish music—a lively and
consistent performance. How astonishing it was for me when, a quar-

ter of a century later, my friend, Nina Svetlanova, called me up from New York City and announced that she had just heard an amazing old lady, Tagliaferro, perform at Carnegie Hall. As we say in Russia, "These people do live"—while the majority of our own (Sofronitsky, Ginsburg, Oborin, Oistrakh, Shostakovich, Flier, Zak) do not even reach seventy.

Similarly, the largest, Polish group had two older men: Jerzy Zhu-rawlew of Russian extraction, who had founded the Chopin Competition (held every five years) during the 1920s, and Zbigniew Drzewi-ecki, a popular teacher from Krakow, through whose hands several generations of Polish pianists had passed.

A distinguished group of laureates from past competitions also sat on the jury. Besides our Lev Oborin and Yakov Zak, there were the Poles, Stanislaw Szpinalski and Henrik Sztompka (the first competition, 1927); a representative from England, Louis Kentner; and the blind Hungarian Imre Ungar (second competition, 1932). By the way, at that competition a fifteen-point system for the evaluation of playing was used. The winners—Ungar and Alexander Uninsky (a Russian Jew who had represented France, and spent his last years in the United States) received the same score. According to the regulations at that time, lots were drawn (we are talking about first prize here!), and Ungar found himself second. After that time, a twenty-five-point system of scoring was adopted to reduce the possibility of a tie.

I still remember a funny comment regarding two 1932 participants, who played the same A minor Étude, op. 25, no. 11: "While Alexander Iokheles (who had eyes to see) missed half of the jumps in the right hand, the blind Imre Ungar hit them all six times." The late Alexander Iokheles (who, thirty-five years after the competition, was my chief at the Gnessin Institute) was a very knowledgeable musician, highly self-opinionated and temperamental. I can hardly imagine him reading this.

Another group of jurors were the popular piano teachers—Jacques Février (France), Emil Hajek (Yugoslavia), Frantisek Maxian (Czechoslovakia), Bruno Seidlhofer (Austria), and Carlo Zecchi (Italy), formerly a famous pianist who later switched to conducting—and the composers Lubomir Pipkov (Bulgaria) and Witold Lutoslawski (Poland). The youngest in the jury were the beautiful Flora Guerra (Chile) and the strange, reserved Arturo Benedetti Michelangeli (Italy; d. 1996). All we knew about the latter was that he had received the seventh prize in Brussels in 1938, when Emil Gilels won first and Yakov Flier took third place. The scores Michelangeli was giving out were frightening: ten, six, and even three points ("unsatisfactory" and "failure"). From the first stage of the competition he liked only a few performers, Ashkenazy best of all.

In short, we were surrounded by the cream of the pianistic world, close contact with which had been especially unusual for us, the Soviets. Only one year earlier, the first Western guest artist had come to Moscow after Stalin's death, Gerhard Puchelt, an average, reliable pianist from Germany. The person next to me in the audience that night said to her friend, "Isn't it strange to sit in the Grand Hall and listen to a musician from a capitalist country?"—as though this were some mysterious creature from another world.

Every participant was given twenty minutes for rehearsing onstage early in the morning of his performance. At this practice session, I realized that one of the two études I had chosen for my first round later that day (the particularly difficult A minor, op. 10, no. 2) wasn't working. With the unusually tight Steinway keyboard, I simply was not able to hold out to the end—and this just after Gilels' recent compliment, that he had not heard such a performance "since Yakov Zak's time" (Zak's A minor Étude was one of the high points of the 1937 competition). I did not allow this to upset me, since the études could be switched with any from the second stage's program, and that is exactly what I did: the A-flat, op. 10, no. 10.

An hour before your performance you were brought to a distant room with a piano in the Philharmonic building. The contestant who was to play two numbers ahead of you was simultaneously brought to the stage for a half-hour performance. You were alone, no one around. You could play, read, lie down on the sofa, or climb the walls. In half an hour they came for you and accompanied you to the dressing room, which had just been vacated by the preceding contestant. Impulsively I turned a knob on the wall, heard over a radio the live breathing of the vast audience in the hall, and turned it off even quicker.

A big bottle of valerian tincture (a popular European sedative) sat on a table; we were told it was emptied by the end of each day. I walked around the room a little, then warmed up at the piano to avoid being alone with my thoughts and the nervousness of waiting. Since then I have never arrived at my concerts too early. At last the door opened, my name was called ("*Pan* [Polish for Mr.] Paperno!"), and I was led to the stage. My impression was of a huge, overcrowded hall, polite applause, six pianos on the stage, wires and microphones everywhere.

Stage performance involves too much of the irrational to allow oneself to say in advance "this is going to be good." On this day my playing was not bad, maybe even good—it simply was not me playing. There are no excuses in our profession, even though I definitely had some reasonable ones. In any event, the applause became warmer with each piece, and as I left the stage the audience was openly friendly. Next day, the reviews in the newspapers were benevolent. I was able to relax and listen to several who were still to play their first stage.

So far, I'd heard only two favorites—Ashkenazy and Adam Harasiewicz, a Pole. In my opinion, others in the lead group were the very lyrical Fu-Tsung, the somewhat manneristic Frenchman Bernard Ringeissen, the interesting Japanese woman Kioko Tanaka, and our short, rosy Dmitry Sakharov, who won the sympathy of the audience when he got lost onstage between pianos and microphone wires. What was more important, he played his first stage just magnificently.

We were given an audience with the Soviet ambassador in Poland, Nikolai Mikhailov, who previously had been first secretary of the Central Committee of the Comsomol (the Union of Young Communists). He behaved pompously, said some trivial things about music, as they all did, and displayed "the communist concern" about our accommodations. Then, poorly hiding his exaltation, he announced that he had just been confirmed as the minister of culture.[7] I cannot remember how long he held this position, but years later I was told about the inglorious end of Minister Mikhailov by a journalist who accompanied Nikita Khrushchev on his trip to Indonesia. Khrushchev allegedly asked his expert in the arts to identify the nice music that had been played at another high-level reception. Mikhailov, having no choice, blurted out his "educated" guess—Tchaikovsky—after which a light-headed Nikita thanked his hosts for the pleasure of hearing his favorite Russian composer so far from his native land. So with the well-wishers' help it was the swan song of our cultural leader. To finish with Mikhailov, I may add that the only time he attended the competition was the first evening of the third round, when Ashkenazy played. For some reason, no one greeted the ambassador and his wife at the entrance. I came out of the radio room, where I was listening to Vladimir, stumbled upon them, and led the couple to our dressing room to take off their coats and to allow the enraged Madame to cool off: "Oh, they have yet to learn what Soviet power is!" To his credit, the ambassador did not even open his mouth.

The results of the first stage were announced at an emotional meeting. "With a heavy heart," as he put it, old Drzewiecki began his recitation of the list of participants who had made it to the second stage, but first he appealed, in very warm terms, to those who were about to learn that their participation in the competition was over, urging them not to despair, but to continue to work persistently and to perfect themselves in order to come back to Warsaw in five years, for the next competition, with great chances for success, and so forth. Strained attention had reached its peak. A good Bulgarian friend of mine, Snezhanka Barova, whispered, "Mitya, hold me, I'm going to fall down." Forty of us made it to the second round (fortunately, Snezhanka was among them); about sixty were eliminated. The competition committee generously invited them to stay as guests for several more days and go with the others to visit Chopin's birthplace in Zelazowa Wola and other sites.

I had moved into sixth place. Ashkenazy was first, leaving Adam Harasiewicz behind by one and a half points, and the next five contestants followed one another closely. Sakharov was ahead of Fu-Tsung and Ringeissen, which caused a small sensation. It was clear that the fight was still ahead.

The evening concerts by members of the jury began. Now I remember only separate pieces from the programs of Oborin, Kentner, Ungar, Zak, Guerra, and others. Eighty-year-old Émile Bosquet played his own transcription of the Mephisto Waltz by Liszt-Busoni.

One evening I was sitting with Ashkenazy getting ready to listen to Michelangeli play the Schumann Concerto. The very first phrase made us prick up our ears and, as the Americans say, that was it. One did not want to miss one note of this magic. The music, long familiar, was now filled with a new sense of wisdom and kindness. He communicated the same impression with two Scarlatti sonatas as encores. Incidentally, this Michelangeli performance was the first one he gave after a two-year break during which doctors were saving him from a galloping consumption or some other illness rare for our times (even the ailments he suffered were strange).

One could not merely say of his playing, "gorgeous sound, impeccable technique, touch," and so on. Everything was brought to an almost unbelievable perfection. But even that was not the main thing.

Later, when Moscow musicians asked us what had moved us in Michelangeli's playing, we could not find the right words. *Humanity* would be, perhaps, the closest, but it doesn't get specific enough unless you listened to this amazing musician yourself. We went backstage afterward to express our delight and gratitude for his Schumann, only to be told by Michelangeli, "You haven't heard Lipatti!"

Ashkenazy and I ran into Michelangeli again several days later in the hotel's corridor. "What do you think about Rachmaninov's Fourth Concerto?" he asked us. I do not recall how Vova answered. As for me, at the time I took great interest in this music and said so, to his obvious pleasure. Only several years later, when his amazing recording of the Fourth Concerto became available in Moscow, did I recall this conversation.

Meanwhile the second stage of the competition had started, and the duration of our programs was extended to forty-five minutes: one of the two sonatas (or a ballade and a scherzo); the mandatory piece, the C-sharp minor Prelude, op. 45; three mazurkas; and two études. Only during the morning stage rehearsal on the day of performance did I somehow quickly accommodate myself to the Steinway and get rid of the lingering anxiety about the dangerous étude. Much later, I discovered this in Medtner's aphorisms: "Do not try to tame a Steinway! Every accent or temperamental hit makes this rough animal wildly refractory. The more indifference, the better this brute works."

I managed to get rid of my nervousness right away and played the diverse program quite well. A very friendly reaction from the audience as soon as I arrived onstage, and the warm and long applause after every piece, helped me relax and give a free and bright performance. This success increased toward the end, and after the Fourth Ballade the audience did not break up for several minutes more, in spite of its being time for intermission. Excited, Oborin said in the hotel, "Oh, if only you had played like this at the first stage!" It was a pleasure to learn that Michelangeli had given me twenty-three points. Next day, 10 March, was Alexander Borisovich's eightieth birthday, and I was glad to send him a telegram with the good news. I did not go to my seat in the hall for the second half, even though Ringeissen was playing—I simply could not take more music that day. The Frenchman too had consolidated his position, for the next day's *Tribuna Ludu* ran an article entitled "History and Geography," in which popular critic Jerzy Broszkiewicz compared and praised us generously.

As a result of my second round I found myself in fourth place. This did not have practical meaning, however, because starting from second place the participants were separated only by tenths, sometimes even hundredths of a point. Two first-round favorites—Sakharov and Ta-naka—did not endure the tensions of the struggle and rolled back to the bottom of the top ten. Subsequent dramatic events finally established our places, but had the competition lasted one more round, the results might have been different again—we stood so terribly close in the score table. The situation became very tense. Before this competition, a Polish contestant had shared the first place only once: in the previous contest, 1949, Galina Czerny-Stefanska with Bella Davidovich, and in many respects this decision had been dictated by political reasons. Now, in 1955, with Stalin gone, the contest organizers felt themselves more independent and passionately wanted to see their countryman as an individual winner at last.

This goal could only be achieved by Harasiewicz, who so far had obviously not kept up with Ashkenazy in the struggle for first prize. And here, because of subsequent events, one can consider the unofficial line that was circulated about the competition's conclusion: some believed that there was an agreement between the Polish and French factions on the jury to give mutual support to each of their favorites. One can well understand that the Polish stake was highest—first prize.

By the third round, not only had jury member Marguerite Long of France arrived but also an honorary guest, Queen Elisabeth of Belgium. From that point on, all concerts were to be held in the evenings with the Warsaw Philharmonic Orchestra. People stopped us on the street, asking for help in obtaining tickets. The men were to play in tailcoats. As far as I remember it was only for the three Soviet participants, Ashkenazy, Sakharov, and myself (totally lacking any such experience) that the jury made a reluctant exception.

The long strain began to take its toll. Even Ashkenazy complained that a particular spot in an étude kept going out of his control. I became afraid of a relatively simple passage in the first movement of the Second Concerto. In short, once Ashkenazy had performed his concerto with a little less confidence, it unexpectedly poured oil on the flame of the fight for first place. When Harasiewicz's turn came, a couple of days later, agitation reached its peak. It was hard to make one's way into the packed hall. Journalists and movie and television cameramen scurried back and forth with their bulky equipment. All this unaccustomed racket and excitement became one more irritant for some of us (and you may guess who one of these was).

This time it was Adam who turned out to be up to the mark. The third stage was his moment in the sun. Living up to the audience's expectations, he ignited a burst of patriotic rapture in the hall. Of course, under no circumstances could he pass Ashkenazy in the total sum of points received for all three stages, but at that time there was much we did not know.

Another Soviet participant, Naum Starkman, who had been placed in the second five, performed very successfully. As for me, I had the same experience I had gone through previously, during my first elimination trials in Moscow in 1949—I simply do not remember how I played the first movement of the Concerto. The next thing I knew, it was behind me. The second and third movements satisfied even me. The conductor, Bogdan Wodiczko, embraced me onstage, to the audience's delight. But this was a competition, after all, not a concert. I still remember the next day's review by Jerzy Broszkiewicz. After mentioning the "charming tone" in the slow movement, and "brilliant technique" and "lively rhythm of the mazurka" in the third movement, he added, not without some humor, "But as we know, there are three movements in the Chopin Concerto."

In this highly charged situation, the competition committee gathered all the participants in the hotel restaurant after the last audition, in an attempt to ease tensions while we awaited the jury's final decision. There was much wine, sincere talk, anticipation of parting. The twenty of us who had just gone through this severe ordeal were trying not to think about what was going on in the jury room.

After midnight, a gloomy and dismal-looking Michelangeli suddenly appeared, taking his seat at a remote table with a glass of wine and the inevitable cigarette. Much later, about two o'clock in the morning, the rest of the jury began to emerge. Our two judges, Oborin and Zak, looked very displeased and agitated. One could understand why: the first prize had been awarded to Harasiewicz; Ashkenazy took second. Everyone felt the unfairness of this decision. Michelangeli, in protest, would not sign the document recording the competition proceedings (that is why he had emerged early), but the business was done.

The two winners were followed by Fu-Tsung in third place; Ringeissen in fourth; Starkman in fifth; and me, sixth, behind by a few hundredths of a point. Two Poles, Lidia Grichtolowna and André

Tchaikovsky (who died in 1982), Sakharov, and Tanaka completed the list of the top ten winners. The second ten received honorary diplomas. Among those who later became popular were the Hungarians Peter Frankl and Tamás Vásáry, and our own Nina Lelchuk.

Two days later, the ten brand-new laureates performed at the gala concert that closed the competition. The honor of concluding this special evening fell to me, because we were assigned to play in the following order: first prize, then tenth, second prize, then ninth, third, eighth, fourth, seventh, fifth, and sixth. The entire audience, including Queen Elisabeth, the Polish government, and all the various diplomatic corps, stayed in their seats until well past midnight when the concert finally ended. Feeling unfettered after our long ordeal, we enjoyed playing, and the audience asked for encores.[8] With this as background, the setback that occurred to Harasiewicz was especially unfortunate. While playing the twenty-third Étude in A minor, he experienced difficulties, even stopped for a moment. This derangement now seems symbolic, to some degree, of his subsequent concert career. The constant burden and responsibility of his position as a winner turned out to be beyond his strength. He developed a fear of the stage and not long after this, his name began to appear more often on record jackets than on concert bills, even though the most prestigious concert halls were always open to the winner of the Chopin Competition.

Next night the president of Poland, Boleslav Berut, had arranged a lavish reception celebrating the official closing of the competition. Several hundred guests, including Polish musicians, actors, journalists, and diplomats, packed the halls, where large tables were crammed with delicate dishes and beverages. A fever pitch of rejoicing was soon reached, and many roamed around, searching for the next drinking companion. Nothing shocked anybody, in spite of the presence of the queen, who radiated a sincere goodwill and simplicity to all around her. Lev Oborin could finally indulge in hearty, plentiful drinking and have a bite to eat. For the last couple of weeks he had drunk excessively, in isolation, missing his family very much: he had married for the first time in his forties, and now the tears welled up in his eyes when he talked of his little daughter.

Those who knew him remember this decent man, a musician of great talent, with respect and sympathy. His pianistic style recalled the performance of his teacher Igumnov, except perhaps that it was more consistent. Besides, Oborin's technical facility was immeasurably

higher—such peaks of pianistic difficulty as Beethoven's Hammerklavier Sonata, op. 106, all Chopin's études, Rachmaninov's Third Concerto and so on, came easily to him. Oborin conducted himself simply
but with proper pride. He was accessible and benevolent. Yakov Zak,
who never missed the opportunity to be a mentor to younger colleagues and demonstrate his extensive musical knowledge, somehow
effaced himself in Oborin's presence. Thanks to his special status and
authority, Oborin, like Gilels, could stand apart from all the intrigues
and squabbles at the Conservatory. Even during the period of "ideological campaigns" I never saw them at any meeting. He would never
take part in anybody else's persecution, and at that gloomy time one
could hardly condemn such a position of noninterference.

I continued to feel Oborin's friendship with me after the competition. I met with him later in Moscow and in 1958 we happened to be
together in Brussels. The last time I saw him was after his Japanese
concert tour in the late 1960s. I found him much less agile; his familiar smile was tired. I think his last years were not happy. Oborin became a powerless witness to the departure of his vital and creative
forces. He suffered a severe stroke, after which concert activity was
out of the question. It is difficult to say what role past luster and glory
plays—Lev Nikolaevich Oborin had a lot to recollect, starting with
his triumph as a nineteen-year-old at the first Chopin Competition. He
will be remembered.

After this official ending, all the participants who remained in
Poland were entertained with a trip to old Krakow, one of Europe's
most beautiful cities. There Michelangeli repeated his Warsaw recital
program, although he had a temperature and the concert had to be
delayed one hour. Again, as in Warsaw, the audience was bewitched.
After the concert, the ovation did not quiet down for about fifteen
minutes. Michelangeli took few curtain calls, and bowed without smiling. He appeared displeased with the old piano and seemingly with
himself, for being persuaded to play at all. (For several years almost
every performance he gave, especially during his American tours, was
marked by eccentricity and escapades.) Suddenly, responding to the
audience, he sat down at the piano and repeated as an encore Brahms'
Paganini Variations with the same degree of brilliance and perfection.
At this, Oborin finally admitted, "Yes, this young man *can* play the
piano," and from his lips such praise meant a lot.

Finally the time had come to return to Moscow, after a month and a half's absence. All eight of us in the train had mixed feelings of relief and sadness. The city was in the throes of early spring, with its special light air and streamlets of melting snow. Days were full of joyous reunions and hopes. Among the presents I brought back to my teacher was an album of autographs of famous nineteenth-century musicians and writers, which had been collected by Countess Maria Szimanowska of Poland. After we'd leafed through its pages, Alexander Borisovich brought out an antique leather album with stamped cover and curved metal clasps. I guessed it was the famous album of the Russian Princess Golitsyna, which he had bought in the 1920s.

It was hard to believe that these pages had been touched by the hands of Pushkin, Balzac, George Sand, Liszt, and many others. I had wanted to surprise our Old Man with the same autographs but had only come up with lithographic signatures from a popular publication! Seeing my reaction, my teacher with obvious pride produced two original letters of Dostoevsky and a proofsheet for Tolstoy's novel *Resurrection*, filled completely by the great writer's small illegible handwriting. Then followed several personal belongings of Tolstoy's: the famous wide belt, a porcelain cup from which he had once drunk tea at Goldenweiser's dacha in 1908, and a common cherry-wood pen. Tolstoy had written with it the last words of his life as he lay dying in a small railroad station at Astapovo in 1910; it was Alexander Borisovich who opened the window that cold morning of 6 November and announced to the silent crowd of people who had gathered outside, "Lev Nikolayevich just passed away. . . ."

These priceless items can now be seen at the Goldenweiser museum-apartment (Tverskaya Street, 17), and for me that unforgettable evening in the spring of 1955 has remained one of the most vivid evidences of a connection between our generation and Russia's great past. Thank goodness for people like my teacher who, despite the obstacles they encountered throughout their lives, did not let time get "out of joint," in the words of Hamlet. And now we can proudly consider ourselves as the next link in the endless chain of the great traditions of Russian art.

In the first month after our return from Warsaw, life and the future seemed to be cloudless: my first recital under the marquee of the Moscow Philharmonie, the offer to enter Gastrolbureau (later Mosconcert), the purchase of my own grand piano (we had always rented before). There was also a telephone call from the House of Recording:

the recently anointed minister of culture had given instruction to issue records of all four Soviet laureates. These records quickly sold out and soon became collectors' items. One memorable episode in this connection: in the studio, I learned that I could not play one of the two planned études (op. 10, no. 8, in F), since Ashkenazy just made a tape of it earlier that day, and our programs were not to coincide. I had practiced for some fifteen minutes while they set the microphones, and decided to try another one—C-sharp minor, no. 4—from the same opus. It had not even been a part of my competition program, even though I, of course, knew and played it by heart. To our surprise, it went off so dashingly and assertively that it became one of the best pieces on the record (musicians will understand my satisfaction).

I still had two dreams left: to break away from our damned communal apartment and to become Goldenweiser's assistant in his Conservatory studio, which he too wanted. The first became a reality after two and a half agonizing years, the second remained but a dream forever.

My two "moms" and my father—Ida, Alexander, and Roza Paperno.

In front of the Moscow Conservatory during the war, winter of 1943. Left to right: Professors Oborin, Goedike, Igumnov, Shebalin, Miaskovsky, and Oistrakh.

"To dear Mitya Paperno from the loving A. Goldenweiser—Do not forget my advices! Moscow, 8 June 1949"

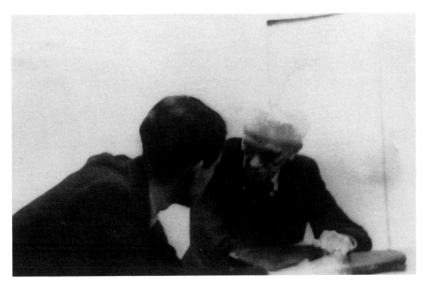

Alexander Borisovich and I discussing my application for *aspiranture*, at the piano on the stage of the Little Hall, 1951.

On the stage of the Little Hall after the Goldenweiser studio recital, 1954. Ludmila Sosina is to the left of our teacher, Leah Levinson to the right. In the back row (from the left) are Elena Ivanovna Goldenweiser (fourth), Lazar Berman (fifth), Tatiana Nikolayeva (sixth), Dmitry Bashkirov (eighth), and I, with my hand on the piano.

One of our last lessons before leaving for the Chopin Competition, January 1955.

My participant's ID for the fifth Chopin Competition, February/March 1955.

Warsaw jurors Arturo Michelangeli (left) and Lubomir Pipkov.

A relaxed moment at the fifth Chopin Competition; I am at left, with my fellow participants (left to right) Adam Harasiewicz (first prize), Günter Kotz, Fu-Tsung, and Annerose Schmidt.

Award ceremony of the fifth Chopin Competition, March 1955; with me (at right) onstage at the Warsaw Philharmonie are (left to right) Vladimir Ashkenazy, André Tchaikovsky, and Bernard Ringeissen.

In Queen Elisabeth's box at the World Expo, Brussels, August 1958. I am on the queen's right; others pictured are (left to right) Sergei Kaftanov, the deputy minister of culture; Ambassador Avilov; Klement Voroshilov, chairman of the U.S.S.R.; concertmaster Isaak Zhuk; and conductor Konstantin Ivanov.

In recital at the Little Hall of the Moscow Conservatory, 1963.

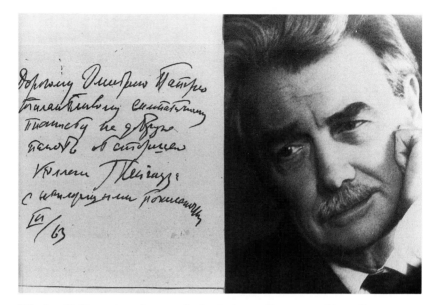

"To dear D. P., a talented, sympathetic pianist . . . from your older colleague Heinrich Neuhaus with best wishes, March 1963."

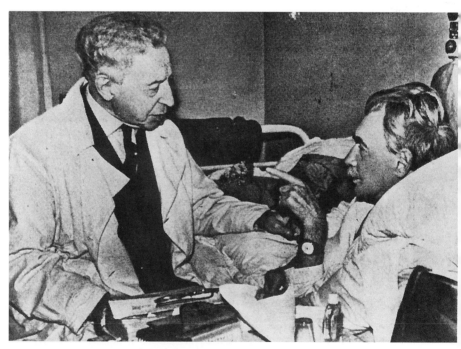

Arthur Rubinstein visiting Neuhaus in the Moscow hospital, shortly before the latter's death, October 1964.

A few days before our emigration, Red Square, Moscow, March 1976.

Vladimir Sofronitsky in the 1930s.

Grigory Ginsburg in the 1950s.

Emil Gilels and his warm inscription to me, Chicago, 1979.

With Slava Rostropovich after our recital in Pasadena, California, February 1989.

Shostakovich (second from left) at a press conference at Northwestern University, Evanston, Illinois, 1973.

Conducting a master class in studio 42 at the Moscow Conservatory, 1996. The marble plaque on the wall behind me commemorates my teacher's nearly fifty-six years of teaching there, from January 1906 to November 1961.

CHAPTER 3

Encounters of a
Concert Pianist

On the night of 11 November 1955, after playing an all-Chopin program in Tchaikovsky Hall, I took off for Odessa—the first city in my long concert career. The next day, the Odessa Philharmonic Hall (formerly the Exchange) was packed: at that time there were not so many international competitions, and our Chopin was still fresh in music lovers' memories. Unfortunately, I played the first half of the recital at such a level of nervous tension that my only thought was to finish it decently as soon as possible.

Since fighting nervousness onstage has always been a problem for performers, let us stay on this topic a little longer. It seems to me that the remarkable musician and theorist of pianism, Grigory Mikhailovich Kogan, first defined its two kinds: one, "an agitation within the image," that is to say, an inspiration; and the second, its opposite, "an agitation outside of the image," or simply a state of panic, which paralyzes the personality, sometimes beyond recognition.

One cannot explain the age-old complex of stage fright in a straightforward manner; it is too irrational, it acts in defiance of common logic. It might seem that you had practiced sufficiently, were in good shape, had enough sleep, and so on, and yet the concert or at least its first fifteen minutes goes "under the piano." Of course, your steadiness of nerve, your ability to allocate your attention with a "cool mind" (one of the most frequently used phrases in our class) between more and less significant moments on your way, are crucially important. And so are your professional skills, both motor and auditory. If they work in concord, interacting in case of the most minute disorder during the performance, then all is well. But just as there is no more comprehensive joy in our art than to share one's gift with others, so this agitation-panic can poison it all.

One need not look far for examples; they are all too common. Igumnov, Goldenweiser, and Poliakin have been already mentioned in this connection. During his last tour in Moscow (in 1964), Arthur Rubinstein could not scramble out of the middle section of the Scherzo from Chopin's Sonata in B-flat minor, which he had played hundreds of times. About the same time, Claudio Arrau got lost in the first movement of Beethoven's Moonlight Sonata and did not recover from this shock till the end of his Moscow recital. It did not prevent him, though, from making a great impression with both Brahms concertos two days later, especially the D minor. About fifteen years later, Rozhdestvensky, who had accompanied Arrau that evening, confirmed that it was, in his memory, perhaps the best performance he had ever heard of Brahms' First Concerto. (I am not a fan of Arrau, who, though he preserved his technical abilities until late in life, seemed to me too academic, sometimes approaching boring.) And how about the young Richter, who left the stage after a heavy memory slip in César Franck's Prelude, Choral, and Fugue, or the "Iron" Gilels, who stopped in the fugue of Liszt's Sonata?

In general, such cases of derailment happen relatively seldom onstage. My point is just to show that nobody is insured against them. Mainly, as noted in *Robinson Crusoe*, "Fear of danger is ten thousand times more terrifying than danger itself." And what possible danger do we have in mind, speaking of the most natural and harmonious of all arts?

The great Busoni said early in the twentieth century, "Ninety-nine percent of our stage fright comes from the fear of forgetting." It sounds so elementary that many nonmusicians would surely cry, "What? With your memory, pitch, technique? You can't be serious." But that's what it is—the natural coordination of musical self-expression onstage can get damaged, or even broken, by over-concentration—an initial cause of agitation-panic. You find yourself no longer a master of your technique, but rather its slave. The mind, instead of leading with dignity the whole harmonious process of performance, tries to keep pace with the fingers, sending out scattered, desperate impulses as it attempts to maintain order in its kingdom. A dramatic actor who suffers a memory slip during a performance may pause to catch a lost thought, phrase, or single word, and continue as if it had been his intention; but the musician is not given this opportunity.

Neuhaus often quoted Liszt's favorite pupil, Hans von Bülow: "If there were a musician's bible, it would start with the words 'In the beginning there was rhythm.'" Music, as if voluntarily, partitions itself into frames of rhythm, without which musical speech does not exist. The violation of rhythm does not necessarily stop a performance, but results in a kind of stumbling, which may trigger more serious distortion."Freedom is realized necessity"—here is another philosophical thesis that looks more attractive in the arts than in real life.

To put it briefly, if after the beginning of a concert, a musician cannot get rid of the humiliating thought, "What's next?"—meaning the development of the melodic line, harmony, texture, or whatever—things don't look good. The spontaneity of the creative process is damaged; what was supposed to develop by itself becomes an agonizing problem. And until a performer gets strong enough to overcome this evil question, one cannot speak of a creative process; the problem is to survive.

I do not think that I suffered stage fright more often than most of my colleagues—for a long time I had even had a reputation as a "reliable" pianist. Simply, unlike them, I did not avoid talking about this painful problem, and quite often received bitter confessions from my friends, whose professional lives had been poisoned by the constant anticipation of danger. Some of them felt sick the day of performance, and of course the sensation of cold, wet, cottony hands onstage is familiar to us all. It happens when music that you can play at any time, even half awake, becomes unfamiliar, nearly hostile. In 1964, during one of my tours to Poland, I discussed this topic at length with the excellent pianists Lev Vlassenko and Adam Harasiewicz, who also knew the subject from experience. After my recital in the Warsaw Philharmonie, a good-looking young lady asked, "What can I do to get rid of my nervousness? You look so balanced onstage." The three of us just exchanged glances.

There is only one answer, and all musicians are unanimous in it. About two weeks prior to the public performance, play your program for a narrow circle of acquaintances, first at your friends' houses, then in more unfamiliar and official situations. It's better to have the last of these public rehearsals one or two days before the concert. Of course, we are talking here about the same program—the repetition should be exact. (One of Igumnov's pupils quoted him long ago: "I would always play well if only each concert were the fifth in a row.") One reason for my troublesome concert in Odessa is that the first half of the program was made up of pieces I had not played for a long time (Rachmaninov's Six Études-Tableaux, Prokofiev—several pieces from *Romeo and Juliet* and the short but tricky Third Sonata, and others). As soon as it came to the Chopin, which I had played a few days before, everything settled into place. But, I repeat, there can be only attempts to explain, not excuses, in our profession: a performer onstage is like a soldier in combat.

In our harsh struggle for survival on the concert stage, the quality of reliability or stability became a legitimate criterion in the evaluation of a performer. It is hardly possible to captivate an audience with one's "creative personality" if a performance suffers a lot of gaps or gets shaky. But when outstanding talent, personality, and technical perfection are combined with reliability, we are fortunate to listen to a musician of the highest class.

After Ukraine (where I'd also played in Kishinev, Chernovtsy, and Lvov), a long tour through the cities of the Transcaucasian Republic and the North Caucasus (from Erevan to Rostov) followed. Ever since then I have been in love with the inimitable beauty of Tbilisi and Baku. I remember my first meeting with the colorful Azerbaijani conductor, Niyazi. He was the only man who could keep the noisy, irrepressible Baku Symphony Orchestra in line. After he was transferred to the Baku Opera, discipline in the symphony descended almost to the beer-garden level. A popular conductor from Russia came to Baku during one such period. He was about to quit the first rehearsal, outraged by the constant chatter in the orchestra. "But why, dear Nathan Grigorievich," the concertmaster said with good-natured surprise. "It is only out of respect for you we are sitting so quietly."

With Niyazi, tricks like this just didn't work. He was like an *ataman* (chief) in this brilliant conglomeration of Azerbaijanies, Armenians, Russians, and Jews: he had only to turn toward the noisemakers and raise an eyebrow and mustache to restore silence. They were a little afraid of him. I recall him as a skillful poseur and braggart—a kind of Azerbaijani Khlestakov (see Gogol's *Inspector General*). The main thing for him was to make an impression, especially on touring musicians. Once during a noisy party at his home somebody spilled wine on the tablecloth. The Maestro (his favorite nickname) immediately did the same with his goblet, according to the old Russian saying, "Where they drink, there they spill"—and glanced at me soberly, obviously not in vain, as I still remember it. He was a genuine musician, an intense one who loved a rich style, and at the same time worked seriously on the fine details. I played with him several times, always with a high-quality, creative result.

The most outstanding personality in Azerbaijan music was Uzeir Gadzhibekov, above all a composer (the opera *Leyly and Medzhnun*, the popular comic opera *Arshin Mal Alan*) and longtime director of the Baku Conservatory. He died in 1948, but Baku musicians still revere his name. He established himself forever as Azerbaijan's pride—the first highly professional musician, a man of authority and fairness. Possessing a peculiar and ironical mind, he knew well the real price of the mandatory promotion of their own national personnel in the arts and sciences. Once, those in power expressed their wish to see the popular old folk singer Bule-Bule (Nightingale) receive an honorary doctorate. Gadzhibekov, chairing the Conservatory art council, noted Bule-Bule's absence. The secretary replied that he was working on a doctoral dissertation. "Doctorate?" Gadzhibekov growled. "I wouldn't even give him a 'nurse.'"

Apropos, Bule-Bule once told me that during a big reception at the Kremlin in 1938 he was given a seat of honor between Stalin and Voroshilov. The leader said, "Bring in the tambourine, and our Nightingale will sing for us and toss it up like they did in Baku in my day!" The tambourine appeared right away; Bule-Bule, still in his place at the table, had no choice, but managed to recall his youth successfully, to everybody's delight. The old man then added, glancing around (our conversation took place in the winter of 1956—before Khrushchev's explosive anti-Stalin speech at the Twentieth Party Congress), "Do you realize what would have happened if I'd dropped the damned tambourine?"

A month later, in March 1956, I began a long tour through the cities of the Far East, with the last concert on Sakhalin Island. Since then loneliness (the separation from my home, the many hours of time difference with Moscow) has oppressed me. Nonpianists cannot fully understand it—there is always an accompanist next to them, with whom they can wander about the streets, or at least squabble.

My first impression of the old merchant city Chita was depressing, especially after an exhausting twenty-four-hour flight (Soviet-made jets started flying later the same year). But it was here, exactly one year after the memorable second round in Warsaw, that the unbelievable beauty of Chopin's Fourth Scherzo opened for me anew. Not many works in music literature embody so perfectly the principle of "infinite melody," a dream of Wagner's, with the utmost economy of means.

And that was the start. In the late 1950s Soviet performers played around seventy concerts per season. The cities, halls, orchestras, audiences, acquaintances succeeded each other endlessly. It was not a bad period in the history of the country's concert life. The spirit of old managers was still alive, and their experience and opinion was respected by the administration. Some of the more intelligent Philharmonie directors often voluntarily ran the risk of less profitable concerts to keep classical music available for its fans (and later defrayed the precalculated deficit by scheduling numerous "light style" or "pops" groups and soloists).

By the end of my second season, I'd played in almost all the big cities of the U.S.S.R., including Leningrad, Kiev, Sverdlovsk, Novosibirsk, Tashkent, the Caucasian and Baltic capitals. In the spring of 1957, I played for the first time my newly learned Schumann Concerto with the Vilnius Symphony Orchestra. The conductor, a peculiar man and excellent musician, Balis Dvarionas, also a composer and pianist himself, had been a notable figure in Lithuanian culture ("national in form and socialist in content," a Soviet slogan about our cultures). The authorities had tried their best to "domesticate" him, but I witnessed an incident at the Philharmonic control post that showed how little they succeeded. Dvarionas made no attempt to restrain his bilious hate for caddishness or "thick skin," which for him personified the cruel alien force that bent his small country to its will. The orchestra musicians seemed to like him, respecting him as an older, authoritative colleague; they forgave his drastic shifts of mood and sarcastic tone. Despite his ironic comments and both professional and political remarks, our rehearsals remained creative and businesslike. The concert went off well, with no need to make allowances for the first-time performance (for the maestro as well, which he mentioned in his friendly inscription on my score).

Later in October, I came for the first time to Sverdlovsk (formerly and currently Ekaterinburg, capital of the Ural region), and played the

Schumann with their very strong orchestra under the baton of another high-class musician, Mark Izrailevich Paverman. At that time, to play on this stage was an honor for any soloist.

As always before an important performance, I did not feel especially comfortable, in spite of a smooth rehearsal. In the evening, I came out onstage and gave the conductor the signal to start, but instead of the first *forte* unison E from the orchestra, I heard Paverman exiting, grumbling in his distinctive hoarse voice. It turned out that they had neglected to place the score on his stand. With this, something clicked, opening my eyes to the nature of stage fright. The brief, bustling to-do that followed was such an everyday, humdrum event, in such dramatic contrast to the concert situation, that I almost felt the tension leaving me. I could breathe freely again and was inspired to play—that is to say, using Kogan's terminology, agitation-panic had switched to a higher stage, the "agitation within the image." I played the Schumann Concerto dozens of times; several times I was satisfied with my performance, and the Sverdlovsk 1957 was the first in this series.

With this orchestra I performed virtually my whole concerto repertoire (with two exceptions, Liszt's First Concerto and Arno Babadzhanian's "The Heroic Ballade"). We played not only in Sverdlovsk but on the orchestra's tours in Moscow, the Caucasus, in many Siberian cities. Most of the time it was with Paverman's accompaniment, and every time, recalling our first meeting, the warm and attentive Mark Izrailevich would say playfully, "If you want, Mitya, let us play the same joke with the score."

Despite his rare kindness, Paverman could not tolerate any disorder and often lectured somebody without listening to responses and excuses, like a black cock during a mating call. This often happened during rehearsals, when he could deliver a long-winded talk without interrupting his conducting. Once our rehearsal coincided with a nearly total solar eclipse in the Ural area. When there were only a few minutes left before its beginning, some orchestra musicians (I am sure, more out of naughtiness than curiosity) asked the conductor to break the rehearsal for a short time to watch the eclipse. "What eclipse?" Paverman wheezed, outraged. "You'll watch it next time!" Since the "next time" was expected for this part of the globe in about a hundred years, such a burst of laughter followed in the orchestra that nobody was able to play any more. Paverman himself, infected by the general hysteria, joined us as soon as he realized what he had just said.

I felt somewhat uncomfortable with him once. After our summer concert in the North Caucasus, I shared with him some of my impressions of Europe, and Mark Paverman, the honored musician of the older generation (as early as 1938, the laureate of the first All-Union conducting competition), said to me with bitterness that he could only dream of performing anywhere abroad.

One more significant concert from 1957: my second performance in Tbilisi, when for the first time I appeared onstage in a long tailcoat. But another circumstance attached to this concert was much more important and totally unexpected. Neuhaus, who was visiting friends in Tbilisi, attended the concert and came to my dressing room afterward. He was very benevolent ("Really good playing—well done! We don't hear such a Spanish Rhapsody too often. And your Medtner!"). In a few minutes, not without his help, I managed to compose myself, and he stayed awhile, to the delight of those present, talking in his unique, animated manner about music, the stage, composers. Can one forget such an evening?

For a long time after, my friends, his postgraduates, kept telling me that Neuhaus was pleased to find that my playing had changed a lot, had become more diverse, mature, and so on. Considering his reserved, sometimes ironic attitude toward Goldenweiser's students (the clarity of our "sanitary pedal" and so on), it goes without saying I was flattered.[1] He had obviously started to mark me out among those who were not his pupils. I went to his studio from time to time to observe his brilliant lessons. He loved it when outsiders visited his class, would grow inspired, make jokes, share recollections about his teachers and friends—Felix Blumenfeld, Leopold Godowsky, Karol Szymanowski (his cousin), Arthur Rubinstein. But aging started to take its toll on this brilliant personality. I remember somebody once played for him Beethoven's D minor Sonata, op. 31, no. 2. Neuhaus, looking quite tired, was sitting deep in his leather armchair. Several times he tried to stop the student, then, with a wave of his hand, he sighed, took a cigarette, and moistened it with the glass stopper from a small bottle of perfume, as he often did. The first movement ended. Silence in the studio; we all await "high revelations" from the Master. Something flashed in Neuhaus' eyes and turning toward me suddenly, he began, "When I was sitting in jail . . ."! I was so unprepared for such a switch that, frankly, I can't even remember what analogy he went on to communicate.

Undoubtedly, Neuhaus possessed vast physical and spiritual stamina. Though there were reasons enough for depression in his turbulent life, he never appeared weak, or evoked pity. Hard as it is to imagine, he attempted suicide in his youth, disillusioned in himself as a pianist after attending a concert by his friend, Arthur Rubinstein, as the latter states in his book. In his mature and elderly years he was a strong, animated man of medium height, with a shock of beautiful ashy hair and uncommonly lively, expressive eyes. A mix of German, French, and Polish blood created this unique musician and person, so full of intellectual and spiritual energy. Music, women, alcohol—these three forces maintained his spirits and prevented his yielding to evil and obscurantism. For all that, he was by no means a fighter; his *Fronde* never exceeded light irony or a swift smile. But in spite of all his articles about "thousands of workers and peasants who are in love with classical music," the constant quotes from Marx and Engels, and so on, Neuhaus was amazingly not a Soviet but rather a nonstandard, bright emissary from an eternal world of art. Besides his 1944 recital, mentioned above, other concerts of his were memorably festive occasions (the Liszt Second Concerto, the First Chopin, Scriabin). And this despite his generosity with unfortunate slips (in his own words: "Please, less Neuhausity, more virtuosity").

I have already written how much Neuhaus and my teacher differed, and yet along with their sharp divergences, there were periods of closeness in their lives. Another quote from Goldenweiser's diary (3 June 1928, after the finals of Neuhaus' students): "They played wonderfully yesterday. . . . He is a fine, delicate musician. I felt keenly his superiority to me. I am very glad for him and for the Conservatory." Neuhaus had been invited to Moscow from the Kiev Conservatory in 1922, during Goldenweiser's directorship. Something happened at the All-Union Competition in 1937 that darkened their relations and estranged them from one another forever. Not long before his death, our Old Man confessed to me that Neuhaus' behavior (too free, in Goldenweiser's opinion) and the wordy, speechlike style of his book *The Art of Piano Playing* were alien to him. Nonetheless, here is one more excerpt from Goldenweiser's diary, this time from 24 February 1954: "I have read Neuhaus' book. Its style is objectionable to me. But many of the ideas in it are proper and valuable. It is amazing—with such a drastic difference in style, so much, in essence, coincides with my thoughts."

November 1961. Neuhaus, gloomy, all in black, with his hands and head on the handle of his walking stick, sitting alone in the foyer of the Grand Hall during the civil funeral rites for Goldenweiser. One could only guess what he was thinking and remembering. . . .

So for three years after Warsaw, until 1958, I had an active and successful concert career in the Soviet Union, but not abroad. To knock on the door of the ministry of culture and remind them of your existence would be both humiliating and senseless. A preposterous story involving Emil Gilels dates from this period. He was invited to Paris to receive the Diapason d'Or (Golden Disc Award) for Saint-Saëns' Second Concerto, but refused to perform there. One of the ministry's leading ladies asked him to change his mind, in the following way: "Emil Grigorievich, just in case, please would you take along your violin?"[2] It's incredible that the "person in charge" didn't know she was talking to the superlative pianist. What could a young performer expect should he have an appointment, possibly with the same official, as an applicant? Besides, the subject of concerts abroad for young musicians was many-sided and sensitive then. I don't mean, of course, the first-prize winners of the big competitions, like Leonid Kogan, Rostropovich, and Ashkenazy, but even in these cases reservations concerning nationality, ideology, or morality could seriously complicate their careers.

The year 1958 began in a promising way. In the winter I received a telephone call from the director of Gosconcert (from his business trip here in the early 1960s some Americans still remember the energetic, impulsive, and bald-as-a-knee Gavrila Vladimirov, a musician and an intelligent man): "Hello, Dmitry, I heard your recent recital and liked it. Give me two of your programs for recitals and a concerto with an orchestra—right now. I have Sofia on the other line." Just like that. So I did, and not only went on my first concert tour to Bulgaria but thus found myself in a group of those eligible for touring the "brotherly" Socialist countries.

I played there with pleasure; besides, several friends of mine from Moscow and Warsaw were in Sofia. I shall take the liberty of giving a quotation from *Peoples Culture*, in which the critic traced a quality that was then becoming, for me, most important in my playing: "Paperno's striving for a clear and expressive declamatory line is especially impressive in his art." Besides several recitals in Sofia, I also played Chopin's

Second Concerto with a West German conductor of the older generation, Helmut Tierfelder.

Shortly after I returned to Moscow in May, the manager of the
U.S.S.R. State Orchestra called me up with an interesting offer. They
were preparing for concerts at the World Expo in Brussels in August,
and one of the four programs was dedicated to Shostakovich, including his recently written Second Piano Concerto, with the composer as
soloist. After the author and his son, I was its third performer, and the
orchestra's music director, Konstantin Ivanov, had invited me to play
the Concerto several times in the Moscow parks to familiarize the
orchestra with the work. Shostakovich himself came to one of our
rehearsals, and the next day Ivanov told me unexpectedly, "You know,
Dmitri Dmitrievich gets very nervous onstage now and might seriously jeopardize our overall success. If the opportunity arose, would
you play with us in Brussels?" I was convinced that such an invitation
could have come only from Shostakovich himself, who knew better
than Ivanov what a torture public performances were for him then.
Of course I said yes. A performance with the State Orchestra that was
to play for the first time in a capitalist country, and moreover, at the
Expo, seemed nearly a fairy tale.

A few months earlier, I had withstood pressure from the ministry,
which was gathering young, approved Soviet performers to participate in the first Tchaikovsky Competition. They let me alone this time,
accepting my refusal only with my promise to take part in the selection
for the first Enescu Competition in Bucharest, later in the autumn,
and now the time was coming to keep my word. The classical part of
the program was not a problem—I could simply select pieces from my
recent repertoire. But to prepare a very long and unknown Enescu
suite as well as a technical piece by a contemporary Romanian composer would be time-consuming. Besides, not one work in the program was in common with my Bulgarian recitals, not to mention the
new Shostakovich Concerto. In this sense, the performance in Brussels
would surely take time away from the strenuous repertoire work. But
again, to refuse to go—a chance that could never occur again—would
be insane. Funny, but Shostakovich thanked me sincerely for consent-
ing to replace him in Brussels.

The Tchaikovsky Competition concluded with the brilliant victory
of the young American Van Cliburn (or as we pronounced his name

then, Kleebern), who we knew had studied at Juilliard with Rozina Levina. In the beginning of the competition I left for a Ukrainian tour and do not remember all those I had heard, but I do recall that Rachmaninov's Third Concerto, which Cliburn had included in his program, drew our smiles—Texan self-assurance.

I returned from Uzhgorod (in western Ukraine) one day before Cliburn's third round with the orchestra. He was already the obvious favorite. They were saying that there was something in his Mozart Sonata and the études of Chopin, Liszt, and Rachmaninov that compensated for his relatively unfortunate Tchaikovsky Sonata. To get into the third round, when Cliburn played, was impossible; those who somehow managed it will never forget this evening. Before it started, I found our Old Man in the crowd of people, who as usual were strolling up and down the semicircular foyer on the main floor of the Grand Hall, and asked him about his impressions. "Pollack first, Cliburn second," he replied briefly. (Daniel Pollack, the second American finalist, was logical and splendidly organized, perhaps more suited, say, for Prokofiev's Third Concerto than for the Rachmaninov Second·he chose to play, which resulted in the eighth prize, lower than anyone could have expected.) Well, let it be Pollack; both names meant little to me.

The audience greeted Cliburn with warm, long applause; they obviously sympathized with him. When he finally sat down, complete silence ensued, as if in anticipation of something significant. A short, soft orchestra introduction (the Moscow Philharmonic with Kondrashin) gave me enough time to ask myself, "Isn't it a little too slow?"—and the piano started to hum the first immortal theme of the Rachmaninov Third. There are not many such openings, where the piano captures the audience from the first note with its disarming sincerity, the very timbre of the instrument (the Mozart concertos in D minor and C minor, Beethoven's Fourth Concerto, the first of Brahms). Michelangeli achieved the same effect in César Franck's "Symphonic Variations," music on a much different scale.

This time the beginning of the Rachmaninov and all that followed reached even the worldly-wise Moscow musicians. Some of them later, as if ashamed of their involvement in the general and spontaneous reaction of the entire audience, talked about a group hysteria that was too hard to resist. I remember the elderly woman sitting next to me, after the first culmination and abatement before the second theme, brought a handkerchief up to her eyes stealthily. It did not seem embarrassing then.

A lot has been said and written about this evening, at the time and later. I can say that the striking sense of time in Cliburn's playing became for me in some degree a revelation. I mean here not only the more restrained, as against common, tempos but also a music-making itself, with its stretched pace and heightened intensity of phrasing. Not many pianists are given this lofty and humane gift of communicating their music to others. (The Russians Gilels and Ashkenazy, the Italian Michelangeli, the Englishman Clifford Curzon, the Romanian Radu Lupu, and maybe a few more.) It assumes an absolute possession of all the components of piano playing.

By the end of the third round, Goldenweiser had fallen in love with Cliburn's playing unconditionally ("the brightest performance of the Third Concerto after Rachmaninov himself!"). I'll repeat something I heard attributed to him—a funny response to Oborin, who was always restrained in his estimations, especially as the leading juror. "Good, really very good, Alexander Borisovich, but you know, he's shaking his head a lot, rather sentimentally." "But you see, Lev Nikolaevich, he is talking to God; we are not given that gift."

Anyhow, Cliburn made a tremendous impression, then and later during his several Soviet tours. Along with the less convincing performances, there were always the creative revelations as well. In 1972 the prestigious magazine *Soviet Music* commissioned from me a review of Cliburn's concerts in Moscow. Since the scale of marks had fluctuated between "Pianist of the Century" and "A Sentimental Provincial," the reviewer's opinion had to be objective and conclusive. I hope I managed it—for months after, many people in different cities of the country approached to thank me for the article. Here is a little extract from it:

> Having been for a long time and not without foundation cautious of sentimentality, haven't we gradually equated sensibility or feeling in music with "sentimentality"? The essence of the creative process for Cliburn lies in a moment-by-moment discovery of music and a vital need to share it with us. This is his aesthetic and ethical credo. Was it born in the mind or heart—is it really so important?

It has become fashionable in this country to attribute Cliburn's retirement from the concert stage to the alleged loss of his former enormous
attractiveness. If it's really so, it seems to me a pity; he brought so much
to us in 1958. I would prefer people speak of it in the way a sensitive
friend of mine once did: "There have been three tragedies in the postwar development of piano art: the two untimely deaths of Dinu Lipatti
and William Kapell, and what happened with the concert career of
Van Cliburn."

Before leaving for Brussels, I passed the selection for the first Enescu
Competition, scheduled for September. The year 1958 was living up
to its promising start.

In the beginning of August, a very large Soviet delegation, including the State Symphony, the legendary Moyseyev Ballet, and the Circus Company, as well as several dozen soloists in different genres, took
off for Brussels to participate in the Soviet National Days at the Expo.
For economic reasons we were accommodated in a second-class motel
on the outskirts of the city. There were no honorariums for anyone.
We were all given a more-than-modest daily allowance, sufficient for
· buying sandwiches and souvenirs at the exposition. True, we were
entitled to two meals per day in our motel, but not all of us returned for
it by public transportation, wasting valuable hours on a long ride.

Because of our linguistic ignorance, lack of money, and the "pre-
ventive" instructions about the constant danger of "provocations," our
people preferred to keep to themselves and felt inferior amidst an animated, mixed international crowd. "Keep together, don't walk alone"
is an important part of the manual for all Soviets in a capitalist country.
I should mention for the sake of fairness that this rule did not affect the
leading actors and soloists.

One day I missed my stop on the way home, got lost, and showed
up at the motel very late, when the chartered buses with the orchestra
had already left for the rehearsal. An energetic landlady, while serving
my dinner, found out that I was "the soloist" and that I had to leave
immediately for downtown. It was fun to watch the sudden change in
her attitude: I was offered a lift and asked for an autograph.

Finally, the day of the concert arrived. As we approached the Palais
des Beaux Arts, we noticed a considerable commotion and a lot of
black police uniforms. The audience looked elegant in formal dress.
Once backstage, we learned that Queen Elisabeth and her honored

guest, Klement Voroshilov (the president, or rather chairman, of the U.S.S.R.), were expected, and here, right before our eyes, the tension overwhelmed some orchestra players. Somebody from the string group came up to me to say how nervous he was, even though I was obviously not the best man to share it with, since in half an hour it would be time for me to play the Concerto.

The concert started with the national anthems. The "Festival Overture" followed, and then it was time for the Concerto. I remembered only the sweaty face of Konstantin Ivanov and the sensation of a remarkable piano under my hands—reasonably tough, with a rich and clear tone. True, it is hard to call the Shostakovich Second Concerto a difficult piece, but it has quite a few of its own specific tricks for both a soloist and an orchestra. Besides, the piano part of the first movement is written without rests and if, God forbid, something happens, you can hardly "collect your bones" (an old Russian expression).

We managed it without a single hitch: it was a bright and cheerful performance. The audience enthusiastically called us onstage many times for several minutes. Afterward, the anxious head of the delegation, longtime director of the Moscow Philharmonie Mitrofan Belotserkovsky, ran into our dressing room—the queen had invited the conductor, the soloist, and the concertmaster into her box. So we set off to visit the queen, led by somebody from the court and picking up on our way Nina Kovrigina, the Soviet minister of health, and Sergei Kaftanov, the deputy minister of culture, who was enquiring at the last moment "What's the name of our pianist, again?"

In this swift sequence of events, I forgot that the queen spoke a little Russian and was completely stunned when she said to me, "You were at the last competition in Warsaw, were you not?" It is still hard to believe she remembered my name—the competition had taken place three years before, and I was not the first-prize winner. While I was collecting myself to answer, Belotserkovsky forestalled me; moving forward, he urgently shared with Her Majesty a joyful message, "Yes, he remembers you." Wow! That was a good one. Some forty years have passed since, but I still feel awkward, remembering this scene. For a long time this phrase was the subject of great enjoyment for the Moscow wits.

Champagne was served; I've never drunk one like it. The queen, whose manner was simple and friendly, reacted smilingly to Voroshilov's remarks, delivered in the style of a slightly merry Russian merchant. Turning serious for a moment, he asked me the length of Shostakovich's Symphony no. 11, which was to be performed in the second half. I said that it lasted about one hour. "Oh, my God" moaned he, grabbing his head.

Apropos, in two days I was invited to fly back to Moscow in the same plane with him. I thanked him but refused; as an award for a successful performance, the ministry of culture allowed me to stay in Brussels for a few more days. Some friends later criticized me for this decision, saying that my entire career could have developed very differently. Even if so, there are too many other things in one's life to regret.

The other piano soloists with the State Orchestra were Alexey Nasedkin, quite a boy then and now a professor at the Moscow Conservatory (Andrei Balanchivadze Concerto), and Lev Oborin (Khachaturian Concerto), noticeably unhappy that the Tchaikovsky Concerto was to be played by Van Cliburn.[3]

In September 1958, the first Enescu Competition took place in Bucharest (in the piano, violin, and violin-piano sonata divisions). Reverence for the outstanding Romanian musician, who had passed away three years earlier in Paris, attracted to the jury panels several musicians of the highest authority, like Claudio Arrau, Carlo Zecchi, Monique Haas, Yehudi Menuhin, and David Oistrakh. The Soviet member of the piano jury was Pavel Serebriakov, the longtime, all-powerful director of the Leningrad Conservatory—a talented musician, but much too despotic and controversial. The competition opened with Enescu's opera, *Edipus*. I remember the dramatic contrast between the lively, spontaneous atmosphere in the Atheneum Hall, and the stagnant, unsmiling faces of the Romanian government ministers.

For me, the competition followed a familiar pattern: a reliable first round, a very successful culmination in the second, after which I was placed first in the score table, and a last stage (the Rachmaninov-Paganini Rhapsody) distorted by nervousness, earning me the bronze medal (third prize).

The young Li-Min-Chan, the latest splash in Chinese fashion, very typical for those years, got first prize, and another Soviet participant, Mikhail Voskresensky, took second. Among the concerts of the jury members were two remarkable performances by Oistrakh—the Beethoven Concerto with Constantin Silvestri and Bach's Double Concerto with Menuhin and Georges Georgescu.

During the huge closing dinner given by the government, the Romanian Folk Orchestra played, dressed in national costumes. A solo violinist was managing unthinkable variations on the traditional "Skylark," obviously inspired by the presence of the great Menuhin, who, in his turn, left his table and approached the musicians closely, watching his fellow violinist with interest.

Of the American participants the actively concertizing Jerome Lowenthal from Juilliard was best known. He told us later that he was slightly upset when he drew number four, immediately following both Soviet participants. A pianist of a logical, urbane style, somewhat similar to Pollack's, he was perhaps not at his best when he played Chopin's B-flat minor Sonata in the second round, but Serebriakov's behavior in the jury was almost obscene: he nudged his colleagues at the table, pointing at the young American.

Two friends of mine won the violin competition: in second place was Evgeny Smirnov, a charismatic young man and musician. (When the Moscow Chamber Orchestra, founded by Rudolf Barshai, recorded Vivaldi's *The Seasons* with Evgeny as soloist, Oistrakh allegedly half-joked, "Well, I have nothing to do in this piece any more.") Semion Snitkovsky shared first place with Stefan Ruha.

Also the second-prize winner at the Queen Elisabeth Competition in Brussels, Snitkovsky had a warm, vulnerable "Odessa-esque" heart for friends, but at official meetings he was a skilled speechmaker and did not spare himself in making a successful career in Moscow. He struggled for advancement of any kind, including foreign tours. From time to time we seemed to become closer, but when we decided to emigrate, I did not want to disturb his peace of mind, and he did not call us either. In the spring of 1981, in Chicago, we were horrified to notice his name in the obituaries of *Moscow Evening*, to which we then subscribed. He did not make it into his fifties. Shortly before his death he had been promoted to full professor at the Moscow Conservatory.

So I returned to Moscow as a laureate of another international competition. After Brussels my standing in the Soviet musical hierarchy had become high enough, and the third prize in Bucharest could add very little to it. It did not bother me, frankly. The only thing that puzzled me somewhat at the time was that even Moscow Radio could not get from Romania the tape from the second round of competition, with possibly my best performance of Schumann's "Symphonic Études."

This life on wheels went on like a long train. In 1958, I made my second recording with Melodiya (Bach-Busoni, Debussy, three pieces by Nikolai Medtner from the first book of "Forgotten Motives," op. 38). Soon after its issue, an old friend, a musician and radiologist, Lev Tarassevich,[4] called me up and told me that Anna Mikhailovna Medtner, the widow of the great Russian composer and a relative of Lev's wife, wanted to visit with me. She had recently returned from England to spend her last years in her native Moscow. (Incidentally, Gilels' authority helped to make her dream come true.) I met the small, active old lady, filled with the memories of her brilliant husband. She made me a very flattering compliment as regards my Medtner recording (she liked especially the "Danza Silvestra," op. 38, no. 7, a very refined piece with an unusual rhythmical structure). Later the same evening she offered me the chance to do the Russian premiere of Medtner's Third Concerto. I asked for some time to think it over and finally turned the offer down several days later, causing some chagrin on her part, and real displeasure to Goldenweiser, who had always loved Medtner's music dearly. Indeed, my reasons were practical rather than artistic—work on this very long and complicated Concerto would have taken no less than half a year. So, I was wrong again. The Third Concerto was recorded and played a few times by Tatiana Nikolayeva under conductor Evgeny Svetlanov, a 1951 Gnessin graduate from the studio of Maria Gurvich, herself a student of Medtner.

Nowadays, Russian music lovers know a lot about the difficult immigrant life of the Medtners (mainly in England). But then, Mrs. Medtner's stories about their warm friendship with Rachmaninov, or the fairytale appearance of the Maharaja of Maysoor, Jaya Wuadiarz, during the harshest times of the war, were extremely interesting. By the way, the third Piano Concerto-Ballade, op. 60, which Medtner began composing in Birmingham during the cruel Nazi air raids, was commissioned by the Maharaja and dedicated to him.

On 5 January 1959 we repeated the Brussels Shostakovich program in the Kremlin Palace. Dmitri Dmitrievich came backstage to shake hands and was friendly, very benevolent, having approved several of my dynamic changes in the final movement of the Concerto. With his nervous, angular handwriting he wrote down on the program several warm words (many years later, leaving the U.S.S.R., I was very upset to realize that somehow I had misplaced it). I was told soon after that Shostakovich had kindly recommended me to play his Quintet with our popular Beethoven Quartet in Poland.

My own concert tour of Poland also took place in 1959. I was pleased that the Poles remembered the last Chopin Competition and its participants so well. In Gdansk we played the Rachmaninov-Paganini Rhapsody with my good friend, conductor Bogdan Wodiczko. During the performance, a powerful floodlight burst deafeningly on the gridiron above our heads, and glass fragments poured down on the musicians. We were told later that only the conductor and soloist seemed to ignore it.

I learned from my translator that the oldest Polish vocal teacher, the famous singer Belina-Skupiewsky, was living in Gdansk. I knew this name from my mother's stories; she had been his fan in prerevolutionary Kiev, where he was a starring tenor. I asked for an appointment and the next day we came to his home. *Pan* Belina-Skupiewsky turned out to be a fragile old man about seventy-five, literally doubled up by some bone disease. The flowering of his career had come in the 1920s, when he had sung in many European opera houses, including La Scala. In his words (we spoke Russian), while changing once for the part of Radames in *Aida*, he noticed that his leg could hardly go into the tight military armor. It was the beginning of an irreversible deformation of the bones, which soon ended his brilliant career and turned a heroic tenor into a cripple. He had survived this terrible blow, and subsequently dedicated himself to teaching—many leading Polish singers had asked him for coaching. When I told him that I had seen among my mother's souvenirs several of his photographs in different roles, the old man, on the verge of tears, left the room for a few minutes and brought in one more of his old pictures as Radames. Asking my mother's name, he put down several moving lines to "My dear young Idochka." Upon my return home, it was my mother's turn to shed tears over it.

I played my concerts with the Warsaw Symphony in the familiar Philharmonic Hall as well as the huge, five-thousand-seat Palace of Culture with Nikolai Pavlovich Anosov, a decent and highly intelligent man. Somehow I was less tense than usual, and everything went off very nicely. In general, the personality of a conductor plays a critical role for me. Human sympathy is very important in musical collaboration.

Next year, in honor of the 150th anniversary of Schumann's birth, I played the Schumann Concerto at his birthplace in Zwickau, with the famous Leipzig Gewandhaus Orchestra under the direction of the venerable Franz Konwitschny. Despite outward courtesy, there was no real, personal touch between us—he looked tired and distant. Unfortunately, this aloofness somehow affected my attitude and playing (not to my credit as an artist, of course). It was one of the most unfortunate performances in my foreign tours. As in my very first concert in Odessa, I kept fighting haste and crumpling. Not till the end of the Concerto did I manage to get rid of the damned, panicky question, "What's next?" In the short seconds of relaxation, I could only think, "God, I wish this torture would end soon, please."

In such bad cases, seeming success cannot alleviate a feeling of deep dissatisfaction and disappointment in yourself. I could not take seriously the inscription Maestro Konwitschny made on my Schumann score: *Eine grossartige Leistung* ("a big creative achievement"). I felt better about the cautiously disapproving review in the next day's newspaper. I am ashamed of this concert, but unfortunately it happened with me more than once and not only in performances with an orchestra.

I've always been comfortable playing under Mark Paverman, Abram Stassevich, Gennady Rozhdestvensky, and several friends who conducted in the Russian provincial towns. Maybe the first in this list should be the late Karl Ilyich Eliasberg, a loyal and selfless musician. It was Eliasberg who premiered Shostakovich's Symphony no. 7, the "Leningrad," in that besieged city. They preferred not to mention this very often in the Soviet Union, even though the occurrence of this historic and one may say heroic concert is widely known—there was even a movie on the subject that never mentioned Eliasberg's name. The despotic nature of the outstanding, longtime music director of the Leningrad Philharmonic, Evgeny Mravinsky, and his intolerance of anybody else's independence, coupled with the straightforward personality of Eliasberg, who was incapable of flattery, made their cooperation in the orchestra impossible.

For a long time Eliasberg led the Leningrad Radio Orchestra. In his later years he performed in his native city sporadically, having become in essence a visiting conductor who helped to raise the musical level of many provincial orchestras around the country. He would stay up late at night in his hotel room, proofreading scrupulously every orchestral part for the next day's rehearsal. His exacting demands never aroused the displeasure of the orchestra players, at least in my memory. They sensed that behind his dry manner lay a genuine sense of the cooperation of colleagues participating in the same important business.

In the late 1960s, I played the Beethoven Fifth ("Emperor") Concerto with Eliasberg in the huge Palace of Culture in Omsk, the large old Siberian city. We were given one small closet of a dressing room backstage for both of us, where young and energetic organizers constantly ran in and out. Eliasberg was nervous, and since they did not let him concentrate before the concert, I decided to tell one of them about the conductor who was about to perform for them; I was pleased to see how much respect and attention they immediately showed toward him.

We had met for the first time in Voronezh (an old city in central Russia with good musical traditions), performing the Shostakovich Concerto. I had not played this piece for a while and naturally felt tense. After a very smooth rehearsal, Eliasberg told me, "Good, we're going to have no problem this evening," but I dampened his optimism a little. So he started to recall how he played long ago with Igumnov, who as always was "extremely nervous" and how he, then a young conductor, cheered him up by driving confidence into the great old musician. Then he said categorically, "OK, so now you stay onstage to practice for an hour, then you go to the hotel, have your dinner and go to bed. At six o'clock I'll wake you up, you'll come over to me, we'll have a cup of coffee and head for the concert together." That was what we did, all right, but just before the concert, after I'd heard the hum of the packed hall, all the good things started to fade away. So I went out and strolled around in the freezing weather for about twenty minutes, trying to convince myself that I was crazy about playing. I returned to the Philharmonic Hall as the orchestra played the finale of a Haydn symphony. The excited Eliasberg showed up; we sat in silence while they placed the piano. The manager called us onstage. Eliasberg said, "Let's go and show them what we can do." This time, he was right: indeed, we had no problem—I came to myself almost immediately. After we had finished dashingly, the audience reacted with loud cheers. I thanked my partner wholeheartedly, and he expressed his feelings right onstage in very informal terms. We burst out laughing and became friends forever. I cannot help quoting his nicely pompous inscription on the program: "To a superlative pianist, and, what is more important to me as a conductor, an excellent player with the orchestra—Mitya Paperno. K. Eliasberg with respect and kind feelings. Voronezh, 24.12.1966."

I do not even remember where I played Chopin's Second Concerto with him—the work which requires the utmost blending of the freely flowing piano part with the orchestra. Eliasberg's accompaniment turned out to be nearly the most comfortable for me ever, and I told him so. "I'm glad you appreciated it," he replied. "I consider it merely a matter of honor for the conductor to memorize the music he is to accompany."

Perhaps some would be surprised to hear how this man with his serious and dry appearance enjoyed jokes and anecdotes. One of his favorites was a word play that traced the last names of two of Leningrad's popular conductors in the title of Debussy's only opera, *Pelleas and Melisande*: "P-*eliasberg* and Meli-*sanderling*."

I was deeply saddened to learn that Karl Ilyich Eliasberg passed away in February 1978.

In 1959, I also played in Hungary, in a joint tour with the excellent Georgian violinist Marina Yashvili. This was one of the contacts that were supposed to improve the attitude of the Hungarian people toward us after the sinister events of 1956. The next year, I was booked for concert tours in East Germany (the ill-fated performance with Franz Konwitschny in Zwickau was a part of it) and Yugoslavia. From the German impressions I would like to share one more with you, albeit of a completely different nature. While in Weimar, I was honored by a once-in-a-lifetime opportunity to practice at Liszt's house on his piano. It was an old Bechstein, one of the very first instruments with a double action, which the firm had presented to the great musician. I was alone there for about two hours, as if in a dream. Liszt's bedroom recalled, in its nearly squalid modesty (without a speck of dust, though), a monk's cell—a very simple quilt, maybe even with patches, the worn-down soft slippers, a crucifix above the head of the bed, a washbasin on a tripod. And, as though to make up for it, in the next (dining) room there were innumerable orders and medals, paintings and portraits of friends and splendid women, extremely valuable presents from wildly enthusiastic fans, including monarchs. A spacious living room or rather his study was divided by a heavy, floor-to-ceiling portiere with horizontal stripes. Everything bore the marks of the unique personality of the master, who seemed just to have stepped out for a moment. When the curator—a small, decrepit German man with fading eyes—returned, I told him about this impression. "No wonder," the old man replied. "First, we try to maintain the house in that condition, and second, he passed away not too long ago." (Franz Liszt died in 1886!)

In the early 1960s, the piano faculty of the Moscow Conservatory lost several leading professors, one after another. In 1961 alone, Shatskess, Sofronitsky, Ginsburg, and my dear teacher, Alexander Borisovich Goldenweiser, passed away. The first three had been gravely ill for some time, and their deaths were a heavy but expected blow.

The unfortunate Shatskess had never recovered from the shock of the late 1940s. An expression of hopelessness and fear had frozen in his sad eyes. An excellent and refined musician, he had not been artistic in real life at all and embodied in the Conservatory a kind of walking eternal Jewish sorrow. Until the mid 1950s, the Shatskesses had lived in a communal apartment in the Arbat area. His wife, energetic and clever Esther, had tried to isolate her husband from the cruel reality surrounding them, at least at home, but it was hardly possible. For example, she turned one tragicomic event of the Stalin era into a joke. The census taker was interviewing several housewives in the communal kitchen. Answering his question about nationality (which meant in the U.S.S.R. neither citizenship nor religion, as one might think, but national origin, the famous "fifth point" in your passport), she naturally replied, "Jewish." A well-disposed crone of a neighbor—an almost inevitable accessory in the crowded Moscow apartments of those years—exclaimed, clasping her hands, "Oh God, they themselves confess it!"

Shatskess got animated only when Yakov Flier or a few friends of the Shatskesses' son Boris would drop in to play cards, bantering and mocking all around without looking cautiously over their shoulders after every word. And he was only fifty then. Sometimes he would sit down at the piano and play beautifully, mostly music of Medtner, whom he continued to worship. Even a funny sound, something like "sh-sh-y-y," which he produced inadvertently while playing, did not hinder our enjoyment of this lyrical, flexible music-making. He behaved more confidently after they moved into the new Conservatory condominium, sometimes even puffed up a little (he was not too bright), but he didn't enjoy this relative independence for long. A few months before his death, he was included on the Conservatory jury panel for the second Tchaikovsky Competition. I think I'd never before seen Shatskess so balanced, almost happy—the ministry remembered him and entrusted such responsible work to him! The poor man did not know that one of the VIPs in the ministry council had convinced the board to approve Abram Vladimirovich Shatskess' candidacy to enhance his last months.

I would like to mention this man's name here—Alexander Alexandrovich Kholodilin, a truly intelligent and cultured high-ranking official of the ministry who stood out like a white crow against the background of his cynical red-necked colleagues. If it were possible to take care of some injustice, the clever and delicate Kholodilin would do it tactfully. It is surprising that such a man could perform his complicated job for decades, trusted from above and respected from below, that is, by the musicians: among all the big shots in the ministry of culture my teacher took seriously only Kholodilin and the deputy minister Sergei Kaftanov. Kholodilin's parting words at funeral services were always marked with his personal feeling of loss (as in the farewell to the outstanding violinist Julian Sitkovetsky—1958, Tchaikovsky Hall).

If only there had been more officials like Alexander Kholodilin, and they'd sat higher up.

I wrote earlier about a great musician and artist of the pianoforte, Vladimir Vladimirovich Sofronitsky. His cruel and untimely death in the summer of 1961 was an irreplaceable loss for the whole music world. The far-from-perfect monophonic recordings cannot convey the real image of this powerful musical personality. His rare combination of architectural clarity and logic with a spontaneous, improvisatory manner of playing remains unique.

Another exemplary artist in the history of Russian pianism was Grigory Romanovich Ginsburg, who died late in 1961, after several months of suffering. But the similarity of these two men, little known and subsequently undervalued in the West, virtually stops here. Giants like Sofronitsky and Ginsburg do not appear often; the young Evgeny Kissin is perhaps the only personality in Russian pianism who could be compared with them.

Ginsburg's creative personality was completely opposite to Sofronitsky's. He worked out a plan for every performance, right down to the most minute details. I did not hear his concerts in the 1930s, but they said that like some great performers with phenomenal technical ability, Ginsburg went through a period of being keen on fast tempos, playing in an openly virtuosic manner. In due course his pianism reached such a height of craftsmanship that even abandoning "extra tempos" forever, his performance still made a dazzling, masterly impression.

His repertoire was not wide. He did not play many works by Russian and Soviet composers (only the Rachmaninov Preludes, Balakirev's "Islamey," the Sonata in G and pieces by Tchaikovsky, Medtner, Prokofiev, Miaskovsky, and a few younger authors), nor much French impressionistic music (fantastic Ravel Sonatina). And although it is true that his performance of Busoni's transcriptions of Bach, and several Mozart and Beethoven sonatas, amazed with their completeness and clarity, Ginsburg's obvious propensity was for the romantic music of the nineteenth century. He was one of the winners of the first Chopin Competition in Warsaw, 1927 (B-flat minor Sonata, Polonaise in A-flat). His highest achievements, however, are connected with the music of Liszt. In fact, I am ready to contend that Grigory Ginsburg was and still is one of Liszt's very few perfect interpreters. Those who listened to his performances of the second, sixth, and tenth rhapsodies, the First Concerto, "Danse macabre," "Années de pèlerinage," "Consolations," études, and so on, would agree with me. And of course, Liszt's transcriptions—a genre unfairly and almost arrogantly treated in the West: Ginsburg's interpretations of *The Marriage of Figaro*, *Don Giovanni*, *Rigoletto*, *Norma*, and the Waltz from *Faust* remain unsurpassed. The highest technical skill, the silver tone of the piano, the human intonations of flexible phrasing—all compelled the listener irresistibly. The characters appeared and took over, true to life.

Once, in the late 1940s, a few of Ginsburg's students and I were at his rehearsal in the empty Grand Hall for the next day's recital. He had finished everything except Liszt's transcription of *Don Giovanni* when the timpani player from the State Orchestra showed up and started to tune his kettles onstage, ignoring Ginsburg's presence. The situation became increasingly heated, so much so that we ran onstage to prevent a disgraceful scene. Finally the fumbling troublemaker left. Never before had we seen Ginsburg in such a state—he was shaking with agitation, his usually gentle features were distorted, he was on the verge of a breakdown. After we had managed to calm him down, we returned to the hall. He started the difficult transcription again, and I'll never forget what we then heard. The whole age-old struggle between the blossom of life (Don Giovanni himself; Leporello; the naïve village girl, Zerlina) and the fatal inevitability of death (embodied in the character of the Commandant) appeared so vividly that we just looked at each other in silence. I still remember the return of the ominous theme of the Statue of the Commandant at the height of joy. There are not many such musical impressions in our lives—I feel lucky to have preserved this one in my memory.

Ginsburg had been brought to Moscow from Gorky (Nizhny Novgorod) in 1910 as a six-year-old prodigy, and until he was twelve, he lived with the Goldenweisers, virtually as a foster son. The professor took a personal interest in little Grisha's music studies, taught him theory and *solfeggio*, played four-hand piano with him, and cultivated his love of Russian classical literature. This solid musical and general education, combined with an uncommonly balanced and charismatic personality, resulted in a unique phenomenon named Grigory Ginsburg.

I often sat in his class to witness the progress and growing maturity of his students, the most gifted of whom was undoubtedly Gleb Axelrod (first in Prague, 1949; currently a professor at the Moscow Conservatory). After one of Goldenweiser's studio concerts, Ginsburg said to me, laughing (he rolled his *r*s charmingly, in the French manner, and in general could be irresistible when he wished), "Formerly, Safonov used to give students a ten-kopek coin after a successful performance; now we've become cheap, so have a sugar-candy for the jumps in the Mephisto Waltz." He seemed to like me, and I sometimes felt that not many people had been close to him, if he was so candid with me, a student.

Nevertheless, in the mid 1950s an unpleasant incident occurred, which dampened our relations for a long time. At another selection, in our mutual teacher's absence, Ginsburg—in alliance with a "gray cardinal" of the piano department, a dry career-maker, a typical "influential" Soviet figure—made an effort to push his own student through at my expense. In doing so they tried too hard and unpleasantly surprised some other jury members. Yakov Flier told the story to his student Rodion Shchedrin (soon one of our most gifted composers), from whom it made its way to me, and really, I would have been better off not knowing. There was only one person with whom I could share this distress and ask for advice on how to take it—Elena Ivanovna Golden-weiser, my teacher's wife. This fragile, modest woman of uncommon nobility decided to have it out with Ginsburg. In her words, he looked dismayed, and tried to describe it as a misunderstanding, kept saying that he wouldn't act like that, and so forth. Thus, the incident was set-tled; Goldenweiser luckily did not learn of it, but I could not behave toward Ginsburg as I had. Only a few years later, if I remember cor-rectly, in the summer of 1959, spending our vacation in Palanga (Lithu-ania), we both pretended that nothing had happened between us.

The last time we met was in the spring of 1961, in front of the Bolshoi Theater. About two years earlier, Ginsburg, whose feelings had been hurt somehow, offered his resignation from the Conserva-tory. It was accepted with incredible indifference, which cold-heart-edness undoubtedly demoralized him; one might say that his legs gave way under him after this hard blow. But now, just returned from a tri-umphant tour of Yugoslavia (until his last years, they did not send this great pianist to any foreign country), Ginsburg was joyfully excited, could not stop talking about his unbelievably successful concerts, the reviews, his preparation for a forthcoming tour of Poland. Still, in his eyes were the sadness and perplexity of a mortally sick man. He invited me to come over, to talk as in the old days, asked what new pieces I had learned lately. It was the Liszt transcription of *Rigoletto*, which I hadn't yet dared to perform publicly because of a risky passage in double sixths. Grisha got animated. "You know, I've played *Rigoletto* my whole life, and every time I approach that cadenza, I turn green with fear." These improbable words on his lips are my last recollection of him. Already doomed, he thirsted for activity and set about learning the Schumann Concerto and the Second Shostakovich Sonata. He passed away on 6 December 1961.

The realization of this loss has grown with time. It took more than twenty years to publish a memoir of Grigory Ginsburg, but his unique gift and contribution to the history of pianism deserve much more. Sev-eral of his monophonic recordings are left for posterity—let those who have ears, hear! A quotation from Grigory Kogan's obituary, amazing in its insight, reflects in a few words the creative substance of the brilliant pianist, Grigory Ginsburg: "A poet of pianistic craftsmanship."

On 18 November 1961, I played the Schumann Concerto in the Col-umn Hall with the Berlin Radio conductor Rolf Kleinert. I had two reasons not to invite Alexander Borisovich to this concert. First, he was very busy with selections for the second Tchaikovsky Competition (however much of a workhorse, our Old Man was now eighty-six). Besides, to be frank, I had not adopted some of his instructions in the Schumann and did not want to provoke his displeasure. The concert went well, even though such circumstances as its setting in one of the oldest and most popular Moscow stages, a foreign conductor, and live nationwide radio broadcast certainly increased its importance, and therefore my tension. Afterward, to my surprise, Alexander Borisovich and Elena Ivanovna, who accompanied him everywhere, showed up in the dressing room, which really touched me. He looked pleased, though tired after another day's service as a juror. Besides, it was especially hard for him to await the approaching death of Ginsburg, whom he loved dearly. In a couple of hours, I had to leave for three cities in central Russia to play an all-Liszt program, so we made arrangements to meet upon my return to talk at greater length.

Returning on the morning of 27 November, I called up Rosconcert (the bureau in charge of concerts in the Republic of Russia; Gosconcert controlled our engagements abroad as well as in other Soviet republics). A pert young business manager (of the "nothing's sacred" breed) said suddenly, "Oh, by the way, Goldenweiser has died." Everything went dark before my eyes, and I asked, "You mean Ginsburg?" "No, no," he confirmed impatiently, "Goldenweiser," and went on to our usual business, but I could talk no more. In an hour I was in my teacher's apartment, and the first thing that struck me, painfully, was seeing the lid of his coffin, standing on the staircase at the front entrance, according to the old Russian custom.

Alexander Borisovich Goldenweiser passed away in his dacha on Nikolina Gora (Nicolas' Mountain) late at night on 26 November from a heart attack at the age of eighty-six. With his death, the last of the Old Guard of the Moscow Conservatory, who had taught in the same classroom, studio 42, for nearly fifty-six years, had gone. The fifteen-year friendship with Tolstoy, personal contacts and even in some cases friendly relations with Tchaikovsky, Chekhov, Rimsky-Korsakov, Taneyev, Scriabin, Rachmaninov, Medtner, and many others made his life a legend in the history of Russian art in the first half of our century.

I'll list only three events from Goldenweiser's life that with the passage of time assume greater importance and historic interest, though at first they might not seem very significant. In July 1910, three and a half months before Tolstoy's death, Goldenweiser, at Tolstoy's request, became one of three witnesses who signed Tolstoy's last will, secretly drawn in the woods near his famous estate, Yasnaya Polyana. In the very beginning of the century, Maxim Gorky asked Goldenweiser to trace and write down a prisoners' song, "The Sun is Rising and Setting," which he used in his most popular play, *The Lower Depths*. And not many musicians associate one of Rachmaninov's best chamber works, the Second Suite for Two Pianos, op. 17, with my teacher, to whom it is dedicated. They spent many hours making music together, playing two pianos and four hands.

Dozens of photographs fill the walls of the music room in Alexander Borisovich's apartment, with friendly inscriptions from such different people as Rimsky-Korsakov and Scriabin, Egon Petri and Eugène Ysaÿe, Gorky and Chaliapin. His extraordinarily comprehensive archive, gathered over almost three quarters of a century, includes among other things an extensive library collection begun with Pushkin's first publications (A. B. once stated proudly that even during the famine years he had never sold a book), the programs of *every* concert he ever attended, and hundreds of letters, representing his correspondence with the outstanding cultural figures of twentieth-century Russia.

Yet, standing at the coffin and looking at our teacher's calm and wise face, we thought only that here has passed away a man with whom the greater part of our lives had been connected. Never again would we enter his class and hear his high-pitched voice with its warm and ironic intonations.

With all his physical fragility, Alexander Borisovich possessed a spirit of great power, having constantly taught himself to "make efforts" (his favorite expression from Dickens) to overcome difficulties, periods of doubt and weakness, the loss of his beloved first wife in 1929, and so on. Only three times in a quarter of a century did I see tears in the eyes of this complex and vulnerable man. In 1940 he received a telephone call at the Conservatory informing him of the death of his favorite sister, Maria Borisovna. I can still see how Alexander Borisovich packed his threadbare briefcase with trembling hands and, without looking at us, all but ran out of the studio.

In 1956, Goldenweiser lost one of his closest pupils, Vassily Vassilievich Nechaev, a professor at the Conservatory, with whom he had been connected for more than fifty years. While bidding his farewell to the deceased, Alexander Borisovich, before kissing his forehead, as always crossed himself once[5] and then stepped back. Soon after, the Andante from Tchaikovsky's Symphony no. 5 began to sound through the speakers in the Little Hall. It was too much for him. And again, so that no one would see him crying, he rushed from the hall, pushing away, almost with hatred, those who lingered in his way.

In the spring of 1958, Van Cliburn had just ended his third-round performance. Once again, Goldenweiser left the hall quickly, this time with tears of happiness in his eyes—he had the gift of perceiving music with uncommon sharpness and strength.

For us he will stay alive forever, with his outward sternness and authority, with his soul open to all the truly talented, and intolerant of the vapid and banal, with a spontaneity of response even to shortness of temper and sarcasm. The great man and musician, held in esteem by all who met him over many decades, passed away. For the rest of our lives we will often ask ourselves, "What would our teacher say? How would he act in this situation?"

Eternal and grateful remembrance to him from the hundreds of his pupils, all whom he ever helped by word and deed.

With Alexander Borisovich's death his faculty—one of four piano faculties at the Conservatory (the others were chaired by Igumnov and later Oborin, Neuhaus, and Feinberg)—virtually ceased to exist. Its members had included professors Nechaev, Argamakov, Ginsburg, and Shatskess.

The very reserved Nechaev only felt comfortable with his old friends and colleagues, all remarkable musicians—Miaskovsky, Prokofiev, Feinberg, Lamm. His death left us with cherished memories of a noble, intelligent man and excellent musician, a composer and pianist. Although they are now forgotten, his romances and piano pieces were marked by taste and perfection of the highest order. In 1948, when a wave of meetings took place in the Conservatory under the notorious badge of "criticism and self-criticism," Nechaev, then the dean of the piano department, called upon the participants "to confine themselves to pedagogical ethics." I still remember our perplexity when the conservatory newspaper defined this noble phrase as "suppression of criticism."

Old Vassily Nicolaevich Argamakov was a very distinct figure: short, humpbacked, and wrapped up in a oversized, long-fringed scarf that made him look like a sinister dwarf. It would be difficult to call him a great teacher—his best students were primarily indebted to Kliachko for their successes. To talk with him, however, was very interesting—he had been in love with Schumann's music and even translated into Russian the texts of many of his *Lieder*.

Argamakov, lonely and neglected, had lived a strange life. Descended from an old aristocratic family, he was highly educated, but some failures and traumas in his young years, probably the result of his unattractive appearance, and later the revolution, robbed him of all his hopes. Somehow he managed to stay in the Conservatory, which allowed him to exist in relative comfort. So the whole of his dissatisfaction and jaundice was manifested in a bitterly caustic, sometimes malicious wit that was feared by all. His only friendly colleague was the spontaneous and kind Anna Ostrovskaya, the oldest female professor of piano, but not even she was spared his sharp tongue.[6] I met Argamakov for the last time in the summer of 1963 at the Vnukovo airport—he was leaving to visit acquaintances, I for Sochi to play the Schumann Concerto with Natan Rakhlin during the State Orchestra's summer season. Argamakov was alone, already decrepit, but as tirelessly bilious as ever. To reproduce what he vented upon anyone to whom our conversation turned is hardly possible. I can only say that it was, as always, elegant and malicious. He died a couple of years later. The neighbors found him on the floor of his neglected room; apparently, he had been trying to reach the telephone.

Formally the chair of another piano faculty, but closely connected for six decades with my teacher, the highly intelligent and gifted Samuel Evgenievich Feinberg, a most interesting composer and an exceptional pianist, died in 1962. I didn't know him as well as I knew his colleagues—with the face and manners of a refined French aristocrat, he was close only to his students. And he brought up many of them, including Victor Merzhanov and Nina Emelyanova (of whom Neuhaus once said, in an excessively biting fashion, "Nina is a beautiful woman, almost a Venus, if only she had her arms broken off."). Great intellectuality combined with a stormy temperament and emotional tension always made his performances dynamic and very interesting. His unbounded repertoire completes the picture—Feinberg is perhaps the only pianist to play the whole of Bach's *Well-Tempered Clavier* (in 1961 *Musical America* declared Feinberg's recording of it to be one of the most beautiful examples of piano playing ever heard), all

the sonatas of Beethoven and Scriabin, the complete works of Schumann (some pianists rated his recording of "Humoresque" higher than
Richter's), and most works by Chopin, Tchaikovsky, Rachmaninov,
Prokofiev, and Miaskovsky. He said one day jokingly that his only
problem when performing the Beethoven cycle was not to mix up the
slow movements of different sonatas.

"The phenomenal gift of Feinberg never ceases to amaze me. His
mental organization and technical skills are really phenomenal. . . .
Feinberg plays like a devil. . . . His fabulous talent strikes me fresh each
time. . . . Musically his brain works significantly better than mine, and
I always have the feeling that I am behind him." These lines about his
great pupil are from Alexander Borisovich's diary (1926). Alien to any
career-making or intriguing, Feinberg, like his friend Miaskovsky,
enjoyed everyone's profound respect. His brief and concrete praises
after a successful performance meant more to me than the wordy com-
pliments of others. "Artistry and mastery are inseparable," the title of
one of his articles, was the creative credo of this unique musician.

October 1962, the Grand Hall of the Conservatory—the civil
funeral of Samuel Evgenievich Feinberg. The last visual impression
of him—the frozen noble features, the aquiline nose, imperial: Cardinal Richelieu. It seems only a lace jabot is missing for a complete
resemblance.

With the passing years, the Conservatory had gradually ceased to be my
second home. I stopped by less and less often—only to the library to
pick up an orchestral score and parts for an upcoming concert tour, or
to observe Neuhaus' lessons. A couple of times I went up to the fourth
floor and glanced into "my" room, studio 42, but the new faces looked
so unfamiliar and (my apologies, gentlemen) out of place that I gave up
this longtime habit. The unforgettable quarter of a century spent in
this studio, where everything had reflected Goldenweiser's personality,
receded into the past. In the present were long strings of concerts tours;
evenings filled with nervous tension; planes, trains, hotels; interesting
new encounters; striking contrasts of all kinds—from the Column Hall
of the Leningrad Philharmonie to the small school of music on Sakhalin Island or an exotic Middle-Asian republic. But a few days after
returning to Moscow, everything settled down into the same monotonous track—not always smooth, as we all know.

I thought more and more about pedagogy. With Alexander Borisovich's death, my assuming a position at the Moscow Conservatory was out of the question. Over the last several years a new generation of "titled" graduates, who had won numerous competitions, had emerged. And practically every first prize opened a path for the winner to teaching in the Conservatory—Rostropovich, Leonid Kogan, Nikolayeva had for some time been notable teachers there. From my generation Dmitry Bashkirov, Lev Vlassenko, Bella Davidovich, Rudolf Kehrer, Evgeny Malinin, and others had been raising their own students, who in turn were achieving similar success.

Only Ashkenazy found himself in a special situation. Having won the Queen Elisabeth Competition in Brussels, he consolidated his worldwide reputation once and for all with the gold medal at the second Tchaikovsky Competition (sharing first prize with John Ogden). He did not long to teach, however, neither in Moscow nor abroad, where he soon moved with his Icelandic wife (not without significant complications, however, resolved only with Khrushchev's intervention). A fantastic concert career opened before him. Only his modesty as the author of the Foreword to this book made me cross out from this part of the manuscript several lines dedicated to this outstanding artist. I will mention only that I am proud of our longtime friendship, which has resumed in the years of my emigration.

It would be wrong to say that my own concert work did not bring me satisfaction—very often, quite the reverse. Hundreds of successful concerts—in big cities and packed halls, in Moscow, Leningrad, Kiev, Baku, Tbilisi, Tallinn, Sverdlovsk, Novosibirsk, and abroad in Belgrade (where I got ridiculously enthusiastic reviews), Brussels, Warsaw, Brno, later the English tour, Havana, and so on—continued to strengthen my name recognition and my self-confidence.

For different reasons I remember two of my many concerts in Novosibirsk, the largest city in Siberia, with an excellent, discriminating audience and a very strong orchestra. At the first, I do not even recall what we were playing (perhaps Tchaikovsky's Second Concerto), but as we were about to enter the stage, I asked the conductor, Arnold Katz, to hold it for a minute. "You know who you remind me of?" he responded. "Dodick." (He meant David Feodorovich Oistrakh.) "We played the Mendelssohn with him recently, and he did exactly the same thing—'Excuse me, Arnold, let's wait for a minute,' turning pale from nervousness. And this from Oistrakh, who has played the Mendelssohn Concerto perhaps a thousand times!"

The other memorable concert occurred in the severe winter of 1962—minus 40 degrees Celsius (which is actually the same as Fahrenheit; but of course I didn't care about Fahrenheit back then); after five minutes outside in the dry Siberian cold, ice formed in one's nostrils. In the first half of the program, I was to play a not-too-familiar Haydn C minor Sonata and the ingenious Schumann "Humoresque," op. 20. A few minutes before the beginning, the happy local manager runs in. "Seven hundred and fifty tickets are sold! Where else would you find such an audience!" Where indeed? Next day I repeated the program at the famous Siberian Scientific Town, where I was struck by the number of beautiful, intelligent faces in the hall, both young and old, and enjoyed the feeling of immediate connection between the stage and the audience.

Many memories from these years are still touching and flattering. Like every performer, I had a few cities and concert halls I could call my own, where I almost always played unfettered and therefore with pleasure from the very beginning; several of them became like home to me. Once my plane from Moscow to Perm (a big regional center in the Urals) was delayed, and the recital started two hours late, at ten in the evening. I couldn't believe my eyes—almost every seat in the hall was still filled.

Of course, there are memories of a different sort—like two emergency landings, many hours of waiting for the weather to break in airports where a hotel bed was out of the question (my personal record is twenty-seven hours spent on a wooden bench in the Blagoveshchensk airport), and the recital in Khabarovsk (in the Russian Far East) that started an hour after we landed (Beethoven's D minor Sonata, op. 31, no. 2). Much worse, an indifference to classical music was spreading gradually over an ever-increasing number of local philharmonies. Concert organizations that had been solid until quite recently were turning into breeding grounds of low taste, spawning "semi-official" Lilliputian ensembles and Gipsy groups. The old cadre was giving way, replaced by people who often had nothing in common with art.

The Schumann Concerto in Sochi took place in 1963, with the famous Natan Grigorievich Rakhlin. He rehearses his program with the State Orchestra, leaving only thirty minutes for the Concerto. We play with frequent stops; he does not raise his head from the score. It is obvious that he had not worked on the accompaniment. "Don't get upset; we'll do it in the evening," says the concertmaster—the traditional line of orchestra players after a not-too-encouraging rehearsal. Rakhlin comes up to me. "You know, *detochka*"—something like "kiddie" (each of the younger soloists is *detochka* to him)—"let's stay another hour and check the tempos." Uh-oh, this doesn't look good. In Rakhlin's vocabulary to "check the tempos" means that he simply does not know the music well. A couple of years earlier, he had given Cliburn a hard time in the Schumann Concerto in Kiev, where he was music director for many years.

The orchestra left. We stayed, two of us, on the huge bandstand of the Sochi Summer Theater. The tired and sweaty Rakhlin seemed ready to doze off when suddenly he exclaimed, "My God, what divine music!" An unbelievably gifted artistic nature had awakened in his untidy heavy body, he got animated, started to sing for the orchestra, gasped with delight. In short, we really "did it" in the evening. I realized happily that he could "swim" along with all my tempo rubato and dynamic deviations. We were called onstage many times, his eyes shone with joy, we even embraced backstage. Then he said, "Now look what one can do with these hands." Spreading wide his short, sausagelike fingers, he emerged onstage again and bombastically played his old war horse—the "Rakoczy March" by Berlioz.

And yet I did not escape him. A couple of years later we played the Rachmaninov-Paganini Rhapsody in Baku. The story repeated itself: first, a prolonged rehearsal with the orchestra, including of course the "Rakoczy March"; next, the half hour remaining for the complicated accompaniment; then the "*Detochka*, let's check the tempos"—but this time it helped a little. After a difficult, nervous concert (as they say in Russia, it was like riding a tiger—scary and not a bit enjoyable), a pale concertmaster came to my dressing room. "He did not give us any cues, you know. We were lucky the orchestra knew the music. It's hard to understand how a conductor can allow himself to do such things."

Interestingly, I was scheduled to play the Rhapsody with Rakhlin in Leningrad the next month. He told me after the "Rakoczy," drying himself off noisily with a bathtowel, "*Detochka*, I'm sorry, I am leaving for [somewhere abroad] soon, and I canceled several concerts, including Leningrad." I expressed my regrets. We played in Leningrad with Boris Emmanuilovich Khaikin, a dryish but very precise and cultured musician.

The same Schumann Concerto went somewhat better several years later in Kazan, where Rakhlin had settled toward the end of his life. Most people said that he belonged to that group of conductors who simply didn't like accompanying. And yet I keep in my memory mainly that first concert with him in Sochi, and his friendly inscription on my score. My brightest impression of Rakhlin is, I think, the Tchaikovsky *Manfred*. In big romantic works with high emotional levels this spontaneous musician, even though not of the highest culture, ignited and overwhelmed everyone.

Moscow, 1964. Neuhaus was recovering from a massive heart attack. His longtime close friend Arthur Rubinstein, who was playing concerts there, visited him nearly every day in the hospital. The photograph of the two gives an excellent impression of old Neuhaus' personality. I was playing in Poland again, coincidentally at the same time as my friend, the pianist Lev Vlassenko (d. 1996); his performance of Liszt's First Concerto caused a Warsaw reviewer to remark that he had "the best octaves of the socialist camp." (Joking aside, Lev really did have outstanding octaves.)

The concert manager of the Warsaw Philharmonic and I were having lunch one day when her anxious associate approached our table. There had been a cable from Moscow to Rubinstein concerning somebody's death. It did not occur to me that Rubinstein could have stopped in Warsaw for a day, and I simply did not take this seriously. Later that evening I visited my Polish friends; we watched the Tokyo Olympics on TV until late, and in the end I stayed overnight. As soon as I got to my hotel room next morning, the telephone rang and Vlassenko said, "Where did you disappear to? I have been calling since last evening. Heinrich passed away in Moscow." It was a heavy blow. We knew that Neuhaus had overcome the first attack, and hoped for his recovery, but a second bout, the day after Rubinstein's departure, killed him. He died exactly twenty years after the unforgettable recital of 1944.

Together with several Polish musicians who knew Neuhaus personally, we sent a cable to his son Stanislav in Moscow and said goodbye in our hearts to the man who had become for us the symbol of artistry and lofty spirituality in music. This loss virtually severed my connections with the Conservatory, which even out of habit had still meant a lot to me.

I had never studied with him but I knew him well, and his influence on me, in spite of our sporadic encounters, was profound and long-lasting. Neuhaus' beautiful photograph with his warm inscription, as well as that of my teacher, are inseparable from my home and classroom in Chicago.

In 1966 I talked for the first time with Alexander Iokheles about my aspiration to teach. He and Theodor Gutman were in charge of the piano department at Moscow's Gnessin Institute. I was introduced to old Elena Fabianovna Gnessina, the last representative of the remarkable family of Russian musicians who had founded the music college in Moscow in 1895. Since then it had grown into a prestigious music institution, similar to the Conservatory. Getting a teaching position at the Gnessin was almost as difficult as getting one at the Conservatory; besides, when there was a vacancy, their own alumni were given an obvious preference. Gnessina, who was then over ninety, simply charmed me with her lively mind, kindness, and humor. She told me that in some cases she would favor having new young teachers from the Conservatory, and she would support my candidacy should the opportunity occur.

A pupil of Safonov and of Busoni (for one year), Gnessina cherished in her memory the whole history of musical Moscow. Among the Gnessin's graduates in the Soviet period were such great musicians as Khachaturian, Oborin, Svetlanov, and many others. Like quite a few outstanding workers in science and art (the physiologist Ivan Pavlov, the director and actor Konstantin Stanislavsky, the composer and organist Alexander Goedike, the soprano Antonina Nezhdanova) who reached the apex of their work before 1917, Gnessina could hardly adjust herself to the new social relations brought by the October Revolution, so she had her assistants, people whom she could trust, handle basic dealings with the communist bureaucracy. Nobody but Gnessina herself, however, could settle more complicated affairs. In these cases she would call upon the "very top" and with her brittle voice obtain their OK for the new art building, extra funds, whatever was required. One such delicate call to Chairman Voroshilov captures in semi-anecdotal form her kind and spontaneous personality: "*Tovarishch* (comrade) Voroshilov, please help. A great misfortune has befallen my friend: her grandson is being drafted into the Red Army!"

Also in 1966, I married Ludmila Gritsay (my second marriage), with whom my whole subsequent life has been connected. Lucya and I rented a semi-basement apartment from my old friends the Tarassevichs, who had temporarily gone abroad. The next two years were one of the happiest periods in my life. For the first time I was a real candidate for a teaching position, my next recording was in preparation at Melodiya, and in addition, I found myself in Gosconcert's plans for concerts in England. Along with Rozhdestvensky, the outstanding music director of the famous Hallé Orchestra of Manchester, Sir John Barbirolli, was booked to conduct in the United States in the winter of 1967 with the London Philharmonic. In order not to interrupt the concert season, the Hallé management had invited the Soviet conductor Arvid Yansons and a soloist for seven performances.

The Moscow branch of the Composers' Union extended its hospitality. To assist me in my preparation for this important tour, they invited my wife and I to spend two weeks in the winter cottage at their estate in Ruza. Marvelous weather, freedom from home chores, and several pleasant people among the composers helped me recover from the preceding annoying scrapes and get into good shape.

In late February, Arvid and I took off for London. The Manchester Orchestra indeed lived up to our high expectations; the atmosphere was very friendly, and I frequently regretted that I spoke no English. Incidentally, several months before our concerts, England had carried off the World Championship in soccer. The leading British player, smart and skillful, was the popular Bobby Charleton from Manchester United. When the orchestra administration heard about my longtime enthusiasm for soccer, they arranged for me to meet Charleton in the locker room of the famous stadium. Next day, the caption accompanying our photograph in the *Manchester Guardian* read, "Russian pianist knows only two English words: Bobby Charleton."

Arvid Yansons, with his Western appearance and manners, found himself much better prepared; he conducted his rehearsals in English, with charisma and humor. He was a very decent, communicative man, as well as an artistic and experienced musician.

The only thing that bothered me were the huge concert halls. We started with Bradford (more than fifteen hundred seats), followed by Leeds, Sheffield, and Manchester. After the gigantic Warsaw Palace of Culture, the concert hall in Sheffield, at 3,600 seats, was the most spacious of all I've played in. Strange as it may seem, there were no dressing rooms backstage; for the conductor and soloist only, they fenced off two small spaces downstairs. "Our Sir John has his scotch here during intermission," they said (Barbirolli liked to have a couple of drinks). When the orchestra upstairs started "God Save the Queen," and three and a half thousand people stood up simultaneously, the ceiling and walls shook.

Both our programs were Russian (I played the Shostakovich Second and Rachmaninov Rhapsody) and excited quite a bit of interest—several hundred seats onstage were always packed, and we played surrounded by a sea of humanity. In spite of the considerable tension, all the concerts were successful. I was very comfortable with Arvid, and we presented a high-quality concert series. Besides, we played frequently—every other day—which also helped psychologically. A couple of times the press slammed the music (the Prokofiev "Cinderella" Suite and the first movement of the Shostakovich, for instance) but not the performance—one review was titled "Bravo, Russians." The audiences listened very attentively, and their reaction after the last chord was impetuous. For the first time I witnessed the spontaneity of the "prim" Britishers. By the way, on the day we arrived in London, Arvid and I went to see a stupid comedy with endless misunderstandings, chases, and so on. The people in the movie theater laughed literally until they cried, almost slipping from their seats.

On one of my free evenings in Manchester, I went to hear the Swingle Singers, a very popular group, who sang old instrumental music (Baroque, French Renaissance, Mozart) in jazz style, with great mastery. Many seats in the hall were empty, and I couldn't help thinking how it would be in Moscow if the group performed there. People in the Soviet Union already knew about the Swingle Singers, but I think I was one of the first to bring their record *Rococo* to Moscow. After some reflection, Moscow Radio invited me to do a half-hour broadcast about the group, with musical illustrations, on the late-night program "The Time." For a change, there was not a single abusive response after the broadcast.

After we had finished our performances and sighed with relief, the BBC invited us to tape a full-length concert in their studio: "Your ministry of culture has already given its OK." (Sure, why not get a few hundred pounds more from your artists' pockets?) Arvid and I did a good job with very few extra takes—I played the Rachmaninov—but never happened to listen to it.

When I returned to London I went to our English manager, the well-known Victor Khokhauser, expecting to receive the rest of my honorarium in cash, and to give the lion's share of it, as usual, to our ministry, keeping the smaller share for myself. About ten years earlier, Khokhauser had established mutually profitable relations with Gosconcert by taking a risk and booking the Red Army Alexandrov Ensemble after the Hungarian events of 1956, in spite of another "boycott" on the part of Western concert agencies, and made a good profit on it.[7]

Instead, Khokhauser writes a check—and I don't know how to react: in the ministry of culture, they usually warn us not to mention this custom—one of "four hundred honest ways to take away money" (from the popular Soviet satire *The Golden Calf*)—when we are abroad. Nevertheless, foreigners are well informed of it, shrug their shoulders, and sympathize with the Soviet performers, who, having been paid decent fees, in reality find themselves with a miserable amount of money, especially in comparison with their Western colleagues. Khokhauser, seeing my hestiation, hands over the check, saying, "Don't worry, the Soviet embassy takes my checks," and winks. Once again, I'm in an embarassing situation. Why do they make a "Punchinello secret"[8] out of what everybody knows?

And finally, the spring—slushy Moscow again, the two-room semi-basement apartment in the ramshackle small house, a true home, sweet home. My financial report to the ministry was several pounds short due to the unscheduled BBC taping, but along with Arvid, we worked out a joint statement that was accepted by the notorious accounts department: "For the mouse there is no stronger creature than the cat." A deficit in your report is a scary thing: they fine you five times over in rubles for it (which is exactly what happened with me several months later, after my Cuban tour). But so far everything was fine; our tour was considered successful, and moreover I was soon informed that in September I would have my own studio at the Gnessin Institute as a part-time faculty member. At last! Outwardly, the year 1967 looked like a second peak of my career, after 1958.

Who would have thought that in nine more years, not only this damned "career" but my whole life would go to the devil, and approaching my fifties, I would have to start all over again on the other side of the globe . . . ?

CHAPTER 4

Last Years in Moscow

In September 1967 I was touched when Elena Gnessina, who was seriously ill by then, congratulated me upon my beginning work at her Institute. My first students (all girls) were mediocre, the miserable wages of a part-timer; but it did not matter—I was teaching. Among my colleagues were several notable musicians—Maria Grinberg, Theodor Gutman, Alexander Iokheles, and Konstantin Adjemov—and the younger teachers were highly professional as well. Interesting and even hot-tempered discussions often followed the closed student auditions.

Gutman and Iokheles, the two chairs of the piano faculties, were clearly a pair of rivals. Perhaps it had started years before, in 1932, when both of them, talented and bright, participated in the second Chopin Competition in Warsaw. The well-balanced Gutman, after a vigorous struggle, took eighth prize, placing after another excellent student of Neuhaus, the inspired, lyrical Emmanuel Grossman (whose highly promising career was later tragically interrupted by Parkinson's disease). The ambitious Iokheles achieved only an honorable mention but left Gutman behind the next year, in the 1933 All-Union Competition in Moscow.

Even though I was not his student then, I associate the two unforgettable years of the war evacuation in Penza with Gutman. From his several concerts there I remember the very noble sonatas (including Beethoven's "Waldstein", Chopin's B minor, and Scriabin's Third) and the First Liszt Concerto. Soon after returning to Moscow in 1943, I took several very fruitful private lessons with him. Gutman lived with his family in a small, two-room apartment, which seemed the height of well-being at the time. I still remember his keen powers of observation and profound practical sense. Once, unexpectedly for myself, I started some technical piece in a very fast tempo, and Gutman asked with interest, "Can you keep it up till the end?" Excited, I replied without interrupting my playing: "Alive so far!" No wonder he burst into laughter.

Very unfortunately, something that happened to him onstage in the late 1940s made this remarkable musician discontinue his concert performances. At the Institute, Gutman conducted himself with simplicity and kindness, never giving away too much or breaking out in anger. Gnessina and her associates valued him highly, which helped him to remain a faculty leader even after, in his fifties, he left his family and married a student. With his slightly inclined head and attentive eyes, he had the aura of one of the last representatives of the Neuhaus school; his personal charisma, restraint, and ability to listen to others created around him an atmosphere of calmness and trust.

The head of the other piano faculty, Alexander Iokheles (pupil of Igumnov), was his complete opposite, impulsive and sometimes unable to contain himself. Not many performers knew piano music as he did. In his last years Bach became his specialty, but whoever's works were in question—Schubert, Brahms, Ravel (whom Iokheles had seen and listened to in Warsaw), Scriabin, Prokofiev—his knowledge was impressive. Finding himself in Tbilisi during the war, the young Iokheles settled into the conservatory there, premiered many piano pieces by Georgian composers, got a professorship, and thanks to his indomitable energy, managed to move to the Gnessin Institute in the 1950s. Always in the middle of the inevitable behind-the-scenes activities, he committed himself to teaching, administration, and the promotion of his pet (and mainly female) students. With his great musical talent, knowledge, and energy, he could have been a strong leader of a large music institution. As it was, the gloomy atmosphere of the Institute in the 1970s was a continual oppression to him.

After our emigration, he was not afraid to write me long, friendly letters to Chicago. His last recording (pedagogic comments to Bach's "Capriccio on the Departure of the Beloved Brother") came shortly before his sudden death in 1978—a fatal heart attack overtook him on the bus. This man, whose life was still filled with all kinds of activity, died at sixty-six—about the same age as Oborin, Oistrakh, Shostakovich, Zak, and Flier.

At the time of my joining it, for the 1967–68 academic year, the Institute seemed to be quite healthy and creative, at least on first impression. The first term had not yet started when Gosconcert told me that I must leave immediately for a two-week tour of Cuba. One of my colleagues, Eduard Miansarov, having at last got his first concerts abroad, contrived not to submit his exit papers on time, while my official British visa was still in force. I had so little enthusiasm for the trip that I called up Venedict Boni, the director of Gosconcert (and later, of the Bolshoi Theater), in an attempt to dodge the tour.

"Are you out of your mind? Do you want to lose your foreign concerts forever? Don't you realize that it's timed to the fiftieth anniversary of the revolution, and approved by Furtseva[1] herself? Don't even think about it!" No one could withstand this kind of argument, and besides, he meant it for the best.

It was November, but stiflingly hot in fabulous Havana, and sure enough, the air conditioner the Americans had built and left behind in the rambling contemporary Hilton was out of order. Not being used to one hundred percent humidity, my good colleague from Gosconcert and I found it difficult to breathe, play, even shave. And something else dampened this bright and handsome violinist's enthusiasm even further: the Soviet embassy official made an agreement with the hotel management that I would simply sign my restaurant checks. Since all my hotel expenses were taken care of by Cuba, my three daily meals in Havana thus became free. I don't know why my pal was not extended this same hospitality; three times a day, he walked several blocks to the embassy's canteen, where the meals were much cheaper. (I mention this insignificant episode because it had an unexpected but unfortunately typical sequel.)

On 5 November I played the Shostakovich Concerto with the Havana Symphony at the Amadeo Roldan. The beautiful old concert hall was full to overflowing. Almost half the orchestra was made up of musicians from Bulgaria, for a large percentage of the local intelligentsia emigrated after Castro came to power. At one of the rehearsals the popular, respected conductor, Enrico Manticci, showed up in a police uniform with a holster at his belt—it was his day on duty.

Let's not forget that Old Havana used to listen to Rachmaninov, Rubinstein, and many others, and the city boasted two or three conservatories. For me the word *conservatory* itself meant a lot—so I was surprised to find, during a meeting with Cuban students, that their professional level was more in line with our music college or high schools. (Ten years later I found, to my even greater surprise, the same situation in the United States.) Our animated conversation clearly revealed their amicability, spontaneity, and curiosity—a quality that I consider a real pledge of progress—yet at the same time, their modest knowledge of music and its history. For instance, one of them asked, "Who in the U.S.S.R. is considered the best pianist—you or Richter?" Unbelievable! Incidentally, Sviatoslav Richter had long put up with such nonsense. Back in the mid 1940s, when his enormous popularity was just beginning, he asked a doctor from the district clinic to make a house call. In filling out the medical report, the old man learned that his patient was a pianist with the Moscow Philharmonie and remarked respectfully, "Aah, the next Bryushkov." (In the 1930s, Yury Bryushkov had enjoyed some success among older Muscovites as a sentimental Chopin performer.) In the early 1980s, during one of my master classes at the Manhattan School in New York, I was approached by a Cuban pianist in his early thirties who had attended and remembered my concert and meeting with students in Havana about fifteen years earlier—very flattering to hear.

The remaining concerts in Cuba were arranged literally "in transit." For example, all plane tickets to the town of Olgin were sold out, and we had no choice but to spend a sleepless night crossing the island by car. At eight o'clock in the morning the heavy, damp air made it hard to enjoy the subtropical landscapes, royal palms, and ancient fortresses. Havana itself is unforgettable, its proud Spanish spirit preserved in white marble staircases, the luxurious patios of the old buildings, and dozens of monuments and equestrian statues. Big waves broke noisily against the high parapet of the embankment, and in the afternoon the city was almost deserted, the stores closed—siesta time. But as soon as the heat abated, and the skies darkened, a different life began. Music poured forth at every turn, people sang and danced, forgetting their troubles—the rationing of the most basic necessities, the impossibility of spending earned money. Hundreds of restaurants and bars provided a needed escape.

A visit to the home of Hemingway, who had died only a few years before, was particularly memorable. Crowds of tourists had pilfered so many books and bottles from the museum that nobody was allowed in any more—but for us, the Soviets, an exception was made. A young-looking black man, who had been taken in long ago by Papa (as he called Hemingway), was our guide. As in the Liszt museum in Weimar, this was for me another example of treating the illustrious dead as both idol and commoner.

After a difficult fourteen-hour return flight we landed for a short time in subpolar Murmansk, where a huge snowstorm raged. Once home, Gosconcert's bookkeeping showed that I owed them a significant sum—a quintuple penalty in rubles for my three daily meals in Cuba. My friendly colleague (who I'm sorry to say died in the early 1980s from a neglected case of appendicitis) had sold me out in typical Soviet style. (As one 1960s dissident remarked, "Never mind that I didn't make it; the main thing is that the other didn't either.") The cellist Daniel Shafran, who was about to leave for Cuba, agreed to pay off my debt to Gosconcert in Cuban pesos after his return, taking from me a corresponding amount of hard currency left from my English tour.

Daniel Shafran (d. 1997) was one of three Leningrad prodigies in the 1930s—the two others were the composer and pianist Oleg Karavaichuk and Lazar Berman. Handsome, neurasthenic, and ambitious, Dania was for a time considered a rival of Rostropovich, although I think only a lack of objectivity, or poor judgment, would put him even in his best years on a level with Slava.

A musician of the very highest class, intelligent and refined, Shafran gradually became a slave to his instrument. Practicing many hours a day, he not only sought perfection but attempted to fix it in the most minute details. Only his great talent postponed, for a time, his wasting away. Neither did he take pity on his accompanists, demanding long, exhausting rehearsals, and thus damaging the spontaneity of the ensemble performance. Besides, some musicians did not like his rapid vibrato, which gave his open, light tone a touch of bleating. Some of Shafran's personality traits—qualities shared by almost all former Soviets, such as a reserved disposition and utmost caution in speaking out—brought him eventually to the inevitable sad result: he could hardly cope with stage fright. It is difficult to say now whether Shafran was happy in his scrupulous service to music. Maybe the divine gift had been placed on too-narrow shoulders. And yet, what a talent.

In late 1967 we moved into the long-awaited two-room apartment in Khimki, a remote northwest section of Moscow. This faceless five-story condo by the Melodiya firm was destined to become our last Moscow home. The following August delivered, to me and a great many people in the country, the cruellest blow: the "Prague Spring" was crushed. I discussed this in my Preface, and I would not like to describe again the bitter disappointment and shame that so many of us lived through then. For many, our country's tragic invasion of Czechoslovakia meant the end of all our hopes for a fair and democratic Russia.

The trauma was lasting, still palpable when I performed in Czechoslovakia five years later. Indeed, what a tragic destiny this beautiful country and its people had been fated to suffer—the horror of Nazi occupation, the Stalinist terror, and after a brief taste of freedom and hope, the returned force of the brotherly boot. Dvořák's Cello Concerto, in the ingenious interpretation of Rostropovich, became in these years a page of Czech history.

By the early 1970s, the steady degradation of our concert life became more obvious. The process developed in several directions, and all those involved explained it from their own points of view. Many more competitions, of all kinds, were taking place in the world every year. Unequal in significance and prestige, as a rule they produced several new Soviet laureates each year. These young musicians were almost automatically included in the touring plans of the federal and republican concert organizations, which worked amidst growing tension. On the one hand, the ministry of culture demanded that the local philharmonic managements increase the quota of low-profit classical music. On the other hand, the finance departments constantly reduced their state subsidies, compelling them to pay their own way. As a result, planning conferences in both state and republican ministries arrived at the same solution: the philharmonies tried to take fewer classical performers and grab more pop and folk singers and groups to guarantee sold-out halls. In many big cities, attendance at classical concerts decreased noticeably. Over the last dozen years the audience had become fed up with more-or-less standard performances of more-or-less standard programs. It was strange and sad to see how this indifference spread among the new generation of music students.

One should not forget, though, how much the years of terror and war had thinned out the ranks of the genuine Russian intelligentsia—the main source of classical music lovers. There was a lowering of taste; the very idea of fine arts was in jeopardy. Societal shifts alone—such as the monotony of our stagnated life, the public's indifference, and so on—could not explain the change. Something was wrong in the concert business itself—in brief, the philharmonies were transforming into purely commercial institutions, whose budgets had to be balanced by any means necessary.

The directors' chairs at the philharmonies were now occupied by people who hadn't even an idea of the semantic origin of their establishment: *philo* ("love") and *harmonia*. Retired colonels, business executives, leaders of the "amateur talent activities" at best—with all the differences in their personalities, whether haughty red-necks or glad-handed extroverts, whether idealists or liars, all had, to some degree, one quality in common: incompetence in the fields of classical music and concert management.

The younger generation of touring performers were insulted by the local bosses' indifference and the humiliating belt-tightenings made at their expense, in trifles like shabby hotel rooms, out-of-tune pianos, their transport to the next city, and so on. By this time even in such an exemplary city as Sverdlovsk, a chamber performer played, as a rule, only one of the two scheduled concerts on the main stage—either a recital or with the orchestra. For the other he might be sent to the "region," which meant a sleepless night (four to five hours) on the train, sometimes right before a performance in Sverdlovsk. This would be OK if it were a town with a music college and therefore an audience, but sometimes this mandatory "service to the region" turned into a brazen sham. The performer arrived from a faraway city only to have his papers stamped for a concert that would not even taken place—a practice called, in a Soviet joke, Press Day, since the terms for *stamp* and *the press* are the same. After the retirement of the respected director (who formerly managed a municipal food-market, a brilliant example of the exception to the rule), squabbles broke out in the orchestra. The Sverdlovsks' favorite, Mark Paverman, decided to leave, and attendance at classical concerts dropped drastically. In short, the musical capital of the Ural was rapidly losing its reputation.

The situation was similar in many cities in Ukraine, the Transcaucasian republics, Middle Asia, and Kazakhstan, where my generation still remembered very receptive audiences filling the concert halls in the 1950s. Even in those better years, an intense concert life had not been easy for me, with its constant travel, loneliness, and my nervousness onstage. My most sociable fellow musician, the excellent violinist Eduard Grach, once went to Baku to play two concerts with the orchestra, that is, without an accompanist. Returning in a few days, he told me with compassion, "What a terrible feeling to be always alone! I had nowhere to escape from the loneliness." And now on top of all this a professional unhappiness began to take its toll. There was no choice: more and more often, you shut your eyes to such things as two or three hours of riding in a bumpy, cold philharmonic bus to some remote provincial town, there to play a "facilitated" program for an unprepared audience on an upright piano—an outrage for the solo recitalist. And the day after such a "concert" you were to play your major solo program or with the orchestra on the big concert stages in Minsk, Lvov, Erevan, or Sverdlovsk, which required a difficult adjustment both professionally and psychologically.

I could bring up more examples of this kind without laying it on thick at all: incompetence and indifference, overlayed with cynical demagogy, was penetrating ever deeper into our concert life, creating irreversible damage. And, sure enough, corruption flourished, the only difference being that on the top they called it a "present" and at the lower level a "gratuity." For the sake of fairness one must note that between the managers and the light-style performers it had been an everyday routine, while in our classical department it came much later due to the intensified competition, and happened more sporadically— this was still High Art, you see.

And yet, in spite of everything, in the gloomiest, most remote tour one could find something bright, connected first of all, of course, with the brief hours of those concerts where one was expected, where a connection with the audience was established from the very first minutes. After all, by 1970 I had spent fifteen years onstage; I had already caught the best years, and the shortening of concert plans never threatened me.

Much worse was the situation for the next generation, the performers of the 1960s and '70s. Still flushed with their success at some competition, they left for their first concert tours with sparkling eyes, only to collide with sobering reality. Several years later they were different—some wandered between the desks of authorized agents of the different concert regions, like applicants, others were pushing their careers politically, joining the Communist party, speaking at meetings, "approving and condemning."

Both types were performers of a high enough professional level; it's simply that different human personalities act differently in their struggle for success, and it is hard to condemn those who happened to be more often than others at the right place at the right time, and as a result, got booked for more concerts. Purely disinterested people in the artistic world of our time are rarities, and so long as your career-making did not reach a "zoological scale," you remained an equal member of the "friendly body" of the Moscow Philharmonie or Mosconcert.

I played an average of three concerts per season in Moscow under the marquee of both the Moscow Philharmonie and Mosconcert, including performances with the orchestra. Anosov, Ivanov, Kondrashin, Nebolsin, Niyazi, Rakhlin, Rozhdestvensky, Stassevich, Svetlanov, Yansons; and from the younger ones, Yury Aranovich, Neeme Jarvi, Yury Temirkanov—these are only a small fraction of the conductors I played with at least once. I shall speak later about Rozhdestvensky, a remarkable conductor and lively person with whom I have had many years of friendship.

Now a little about the other outstanding Soviet conductor of my generation—Evgeny Svetlanov. An extremely gifted musician, he had managed to work awhile in three capacities—as composer, pianist, and conductor, like his lifelong idol Rachmaninov. I cannot judge the merit of his compositions, and just vaguely remember his postgraduate piano concerto; it's a pity he stopped performing as a pianist so early. Neuhaus, who happened to chair the state commission at the Gnessin when Svetlanov played his degree recital, spoke enthusiastically about him. Later I remember him and Alexander Labko in Medtner's violin sonatas (the Little Hall, 1960s). For all his well-grown appearance, with smallish eyes and distinct nose in a bony-cheeked face, Svetlanov made a big impression with his refined suppleness combined with typical Russian scope. Many people who came backstage to thank him were sincerely moved. ("Ahh, the Medtnerist came," he said upon seeing me.)

Yet the real mission of his life has been conducting. A graduate of Alexander Gauk's studio, he replaced Alexander Melik-Pashayev as the music director of the Bolshoi Theater at the age of thirty-four. Unfortunately, Svetlanov since his youth has tended to despotism, which was not easy for his partners to take. Since 1965 he has led the State Orchestra, and his magnificent artistic achievements come along with outbreaks of neurasthenia and petty tyranny.

We performed together many times, starting in 1960 with Tchaikovsky's Second Piano Concerto in the Column Hall. He accompanied beautifully, especially music that was close to him. True, his amazing musical insight and later his vast experience allowed him to be fully in charge of a greatly expanded repertoire (Brahms, Bruckner, Mahler). But in Russian music for the last thirty years there have been none equal to him. The clear, supple gestures, expressive hands, and powerful culminations have always captured audiences both at home and abroad.

We have never been close, even though we did "thee and thou" each other after young pioneer camp in the summer of 1940. In the winter of 1965 we played the Rachmaninov-Paganini Rhapsody (I could hardly believe my eyes when I noticed from the stage Emil Gilels with his daughter, holding the open score in their hands), and next morning left with the State Orchestra for Riazan without even rehearsing Beethoven's "Emperor" Concerto. In the train, Svetlanov with a cunning smile wrote down for me his epigram on Boris Khaikin (another colleague whom he could not stand), who was then conducting *The Sleeping Beauty* at the Bolshoi. I still remember the eight clumsy lines of verse and their fabricated wit; they were hardly funny, but Zhenia chuckled over them with childlike glee. Later that night, after the concert, we were sitting in my hotel room with a bottle of wine (apparently they did not sell hard liquor after eleven o'clock in the evening then). *The Nutcracker* was on the radio. During "The Dance of the Snowflakes," Svetlanov stopped in midsentence. "Listen to the choir." He gave the cue, and the children's voices began to flow like heaven, as always. Suddenly the eyes of this usually ungracious man filled with tears.

Those who have not heard his "Symphonic Dances" by Rachmaninov cannot fully appreciate the tragic force of this music, nor Svetlanov's enormous gift. A difficult, despotic, uncommonly talented man.

Our oldest and most popular harpist, Xenia Alexandrovna Erdeli, attended one of my recitals in the Little Hall, in the early 1970s. She had distanced herself from any social activity in the Conservatory for the last fifty years, so I was both surprised and pleased to see her entering my dressing room after the concert. (She had always deeply respected my teacher, who was only three years her senior.) She began, "I am so glad to come here and listen to you, because I am going to die in a few days." Stupefied, I asked her not to think or say it, but she interrupted me calmly. "Oh no, I know it, and please do not try to calm me down." Old ladies over ninety may say all kinds of things, so I just kissed her hand and thanked her warmly for coming. Imagine my feelings when about a week later my old friend Dora Levenstein, who had witnessed this conversation, called me up. "You know, I've just been told Erdeli passed away."

They say in Russian villages that God tells old people who have lived a long and righteous life when their time has come. Perhaps that was the case with Xenia Alexandrovna Erdeli.

Since 1955 I had recorded about fifteen hours of music on Melodiya LPs and master tapes for the so-called Golden Fund (that is, preserved forever in the Moscow House of Recording archive). Recording is a special field of performance, which seems at first not to require as much expenditure of nervous energy as a public performance. You may do as many takes as needed to capture a stubborn spot (a group of measures, one passage, whatever) faultlessly, and then an experienced audio-engineer will splice it into a master tape, which will sound over the air for many years (at least this was the common recording practice before the digital method revolutionized it in the 1980s).

On the other hand, a recording session requires you to sit at the piano in a huge, empty studio (meaning the Moscow Recording House), "face to face" with the microphones. There is no audience, none of those creative impulses that only a concert hall can provide. And yet the tape should not only be perfect in a technical sense but emotionally bright as well. Sometimes it takes long hours to make the spirit and the letter of the performance conform, its expressiveness and precision, emotions and logic. I mentioned earlier how hard recording sessions were for Sofronitsky when he got nervous, and desperate, sometimes would leave the studio. Ginsburg was his antithesis in this as well; he loved to record, did it quickly and in masterly fashion.

The first several years I preferred to work with the confident, somewhat conservative Vassily Vassilievich Fedulov (the only sound producer with whom Sofronitsky felt comfortable). In the summer of 1955, simultaneously with my Chopin LP, the Moscow Recording House commissioned several more pieces. After the competition and all it had brought, I was exhausted, and a taping of the ten-minute Ninth Rhapsody of Liszt, difficult though it may be, took six nervous hours. Sometime later, Fedulov, having spent nearly twice as long on the complicated process of editing, called me to listen to the master tape he had assembled. Everything seemed to be clear and correct, but the spirit and life were not there. I felt guilty—so many hours of hard, tedious work had been spent practically in vain—one would not want to present such a tape to the audio council. But not for nothing did performers love to work with Fedulov.

"You know what," he said, "I can see you don't like the tape. Me too. Let's try once again in autumn; and I'll save this tape, just in case." I returned to the studio in September, and we taped the Rhapsody for three hours and edited for six. The tape was accepted by the audio council with honors.

In 1958 we were making a second recording with Fedulov, which included the Bach-Busoni Chaconne. Close to midnight, when our time was up and everybody was exhausted, I risked telling him through the mike into his audio room, "Vassily Vassilievich, give me five more minutes. I want to try the beginning one more time. There is something I still do not like." Without saying a word, Fedulov sat down heavily at the control panel, and then one of those things happened that makes the performing arts so unpredictable. The same first five pages, which we had re-taped several times, due to wrong notes or emotionally flat tones, sounded unexpectedly in one wave, bright, strong, and without the tiniest blot. As soon as I hit a wrong note, I stopped. "Well done," Fedulov's voice came over the speaker. "Five minutes ago, it was hard to believe, but it seems now we can use it whole, without editing."

At the end of the 1960s, Moscow Radio commissioned several performers to make master tapes of light instrumental pieces (no longer than two minutes at most) to fill in pauses on the "Lighthouse" channel. I was offered an interesting task, one that was not as simple as it may sound—the twelve études of Czerny (from opus 740) and Moszkowski. In my school years, before switching to Chopin's études, I had played them often and, to Alexander Borisovich's satisfaction, quite dashingly. Coming back to these pieces after a twenty-five-year break, I spent a lot of time and effort to make them not only masterly but more imaginative, for all their unassuming nature. The simple and salutary music of Carl Czerny—a student of Beethoven and teacher of Liszt—captures the essence of classical piano technique and will benefit many generations of pianists. This unusual tape was also accepted by the audio council with honors.

My biggest disappointment was what happened in the mid 1960s to a recording of the Schumann "Humoresque," op. 20. An excellent audio producer, Yury Kokzhayan, and I had worked on it with great excitement. When we listened to the master tape, it was rewarding to watch the creative, temperamental Kokzhayan enjoying every phrase as his own brainchild (and in many respects, it was so).

While some of my 1950s recordings eventually came to disappoint me and yet were still aired (Beethoven's Thirty-two Variations, Scriabin's Waltz op. 38), the council this time did not approve our "Humoresque" for the Golden Fund, but only for the so-called limited one. Kokzhayan cursed so sincerely that to watch and listen to him was a comfort. In five years this, the best of my Soviet tapes, was probably demagnetized, according to regulations. My friend, the composer Victor Kouprevich, who was then serving a term in the council, told me with outrage that before the thirty-five-minute "Humoresque" they had listened to some even longer piece, quite monotonous, and part of the panel simply got bored.

Harsh budget cuts had spread to both the Moscow Recording House and the Melodiya firm. By the beginning of the 1960s the honorarium for one audio minute had been cut by two-thirds. To be a recording artist was still honorable, but the remuneration for it now seemed more symbolic than real. Musicians expressed their outrage, especially among themselves. An excellent pianist and real gentleman, Anatoly Vedernikov, a friend and colleague of Richter[2] in the Neuhaus studio, had even threatened to refuse all future recording offers. All this was sincere but naïve, and could not go beyond words.

That is how our life went on, monotonously, through sheer inertia, with some joyful moments but more disillusions and disappointments. During my travels around the huge country I often met my fellow graduates. Only a few were satisfied and happy. Those who taught in the local conservatories, driving themselves to teach up to twenty or more students, at least made their lives more meaningful.

A few hours spent together, even late at night after a concert, helped us forget for a while what had happened since our graduation in 1951, when we found ourselves scattered around the country. Irkutsk, Saratov, Tbilisi, Gorky, Lvov, Stalingrad, Baku, Donetsk—from these and many other cities arise images of the dear friends of my student years. So much had changed in our lives—we had acquired apartments and titles, rejoiced and suffered, got married and divorced, lost those near to us, already began to grow older—but as soon as we found ourselves together after the years of separation, all this receded. We remembered in detail our Conservatory, its studios, lectures, our professors and friends—both alive and gone—parties, affairs, quarrels, the somber witches' sabbath of the 1940s and '50s.

At one such meeting, my fellow student and good friend Boris Koloyan, a soloist and concertmaster of the Stalingrad Philharmonie, a former frontline soldier, a man subject to melancholy but far from sentimental, said to me with sadness, "You know, I was listening to you last night with my eyes closed, and it seemed to me that I was sitting in the balcony of the Little Hall during a student recital. My old friends are all around, listening to this music, and the thought just struck me: weren't those the best years of my life! How short they were. And I didn't want to open my eyes and come back to all these hypocritical squabbles and party meetings. Now I have to wait several months till Bella's [Davidovich's] concert to experience such an evening again, after which I'll have a kind of bitter hangover."

I remember all my old friends and can visualize each of them. Not the way we are now—shabby, worn out by life, heavy, and sentimental—but the way they remain in the photographs of those years—young, talented, full of hope. . . .

The third (1966) and fourth (1970) Tchaikovsky Competitions produced a few new names. In 1966 the Americans looked very strong: Misha Dichter (Schubert, the big posthumous Sonata in A; Stravinsky's "Petroushka") and Edward Auer (a superb Tchaikovsky Variations in F; Prokofiev's Seventh Sonata). On the third round, however, Dichter, aiming for the first prize, played Beethoven's "Emperor" Concerto limply and even got a little lost in the Tchaikovsky Concerto, in the slow octaves in the transition after the majestic first section. The highly gifted though not athletic Auer could hardly cope, psychologically or physically, with the two huge B-flats—Tchaikovsky and Brahms. Nikolai Petrov, a student of Yakov Zak, was then considered a Soviet favorite. Entering the competition at the second round (a privilege the regulations allowed first-prize winners of previous contests), he could not overcome the tension, and his performance was tight, almost dull (sounds familiar, doesn't it?). Even before the announcement of the results, he withdrew, officially due to an injured finger.[3]

Nervous tension and fear radiated palpably, especially during the third and last round—from all but one participant, that is: the childlike sixteen-year-old Grigory Sokolov (an excellent Saint-Saëns Second Concerto). Several days before, after his second round, the newspaper *Sovietskaya Kultura* had awkwardly, as it turned out, spoken before the authorities did, calling him in effect a good boy with an outstanding gift but not ready to compete on equal ground with the more mature participants. Fair enough, but as soon as it comes to prestige (the question is, whose? or what?—the music's? or the state's?), fairness has never been the first priority in the U.S.S.R. In the words of one of the ministry bosses, "the secret Soviet weapon fired a shot," and the boy got the first prize.[4]

The story did not serve the competition well, but we were accustomed to such affairs. The Westerners growled a little but then swallowed it as usual. After all, who would not want to return to Moscow in four years for the next competition, and judge it again at the same table with Gilels and Oborin? Nevertheless, from then on, Gilels refused to chair the Tchaikovsky jury.

Among the winners in 1970 were the not-always-interesting but very talented virtuoso Vladimir Krainev and a classically balanced Englishman, John Lill. Victoria Postnikova (third place) was a typical Flier student—bright and assertive. After the competition she married Rozhdestvensky, and her playing became more versatile. Of course, one could hardly expect personalities on the level of Cliburn and Ashkenazy to emerge, and I am not overly optimistic about the future.[5] (I am not speaking of violinists; the 1970 competition gave us Gidon Kremer.)

Having its pick of the best graduates from music schools and colleges across the country, the Moscow Conservatory wanted to see in every entrant a potential winner of future competitions. It takes five years of studying under highly competitive conditions. No wonder that technical reliability becomes crucial, sometimes to the detriment of the creative personality of the young musician. I don't completely agree with the Americans who consider the Soviet performers very much alike; still, something gives rise to this opinion. Perhaps it is the high technical standard now possessed by a growing number of performers.

The standard of evaluation in our art rose dramatically in the twentieth century. In one of his rare articles (1910), Rachmaninov could write of "the great Anton," "When Rubinstein was too precise, his performance lost some portion of his delightful charisma. Rubinstein was truly incomparable, possibly even because he was full of human passion, and his performance was far from the perfection of a machine."[6] Thirty years earlier, von Bülow had come up with this famous phrase: "I would like to give a recital from Anton Rubinstein's wrong notes." Well said, but since then more than a century has passed. Nowadays a concert performance that falls short of technical perfection is doomed to failure, to say nothing of a competition.

The truth is that our natural aspiration for technical perfection should serve to reveal whatever creative individuality is present. Only then will a talented student develop harmoniously toward a promising future. If the best Conservatory in the country turns into "a factory of laureates," however, and begins to see technical reliability as of paramount importance, some standardization, even if of a high quality, is unavoidable.

In the summer of 1970, we vacationed again in Päarnuu, one of our favorite spots. There we met more and more often with David Feodorovich Oistrakh, spending several hours a day playing chess and preference (an old Franco-Russian card game, something like bridge), and talking with ever-increasing candor. Oistrakh's lifelong love of chess is widely known. Officially ranked in the first category, he actually played at the level of a master's candidate, was friendly with many leading grandmasters, including a few world champions, and never missed an opportunity to attend chess tournaments and world title matches. It was a real pleasure to play casual games with him (he always brought a chess clock to Päarnuu)—his graceful manners and unaffected chess style made him the best possible partner.

Though frankly he was not as strong at preference, he sincerely enjoyed the whole process of playing. Every evening by seven o'clock we used to come over to his place with Leningrad pianist Lidia Pecherskaya. Oistrakh always openly looked forward to another enjoyable evening. Once, approaching his dacha (the Oistrakhs had rented the same home for nearly twenty years), we heard muffled violin sounds. "Let's wait," Lidia said, "the king is still practicing." At that moment the window opened slightly and Oistrakh called out, "Why don't you come in?"

"We did not want to disturb your practicing."

"No, no, I was giving a lesson to Valerick"—his seven- or eight-year-old grandson. Then, suddenly, with humorous anxiety, "Do I already sound like him?"

His unobtrusive, calm manner of speaking, hidden humor, intellectual charisma, and gentleness made personal contact with Oistrakh unforgettable. He told a lot of amusing stories about Soviet officials, Western managers, and other musicians around the world. Once, returning from his vacation in Sinay (the best Romanian resort), Oistrakh decided to pay a courtesy visit to the Soviet ambassador in Bucharest. The ambassador was not in, but the guard at the entrance contacted the deputy and informed him that "the violinist Oyster" wanted to see him. "On what matter?" asked the deputy. Oistrakh, who was already regretting the whole embarrassing affair, replied that as a matter of fact he had no special reason to see the *tovarishch* (comrade). The guard, hearing the answer over the telephone, smirked and said, "Neither does the *tovarishch* deputy." Oistrakh added, "I turned around and walked back to my hotel feeling like an idiot."

Oistrakh did not hide how much it hurt him personally that an important concert tour abroad had been taken from his son Igor and handed over to Valery Klimov (a very good violinist, also Oistrakh's graduate). Igor's marriage had naturally distanced him from his adoring parents, which obviously upset Oistrakh, who in general was very much involved in everything concerning his son.

It often seemed to me that Oistrakh simply needed to open himself up a bit, to be more than usually frank. With a touch of bitter humor, he told how he was reprimanded by Madame Furtseva (the cultural minister) for accepting "without asking the ministry first" an invitation from his old friend Yehudi Menuhin to come to the latter's summer festival somewhere in western Europe. "Did you not know, David Feodorovich, that he is a well-known Zionist?" Oistrakh, humiliated, sent Menuhin a letter of refusal. In his later years, his everlasting loyalty to the regime gave him the sense of "selling his immortal soul."

I will never forget one of our last days together. We had agreed that Oistrakh would drive to our place to pick us up and go to the beach— one of those amazing northern beaches with sand dunes drying quickly between frequent showers and the gentle sunlight, which only the Baltic countries can offer and which Oistrakh loved so much. Shortly before his arrival I heard on the BBC that his close friend, the conductor George Szell, had passed away in the United States. Oistrakh had often spoken of him with unusual warmth. Getting into the car, I shared this news with him as delicately as I could. His countenance changed, and he asked as if in disbelief, "Did you hear it yourself?" He was obviously shaken. Once at the beach, silently, we spread out a blanket, and having taken off our clothes, got slowly into the water. At this moment he said something which struck me so forcibly that I still recall it, though I never shared it with anyone during his lifetime.

"You know, Mitya, today is such a marvelous sunny day, we are standing in warm, calm water—and one almost forgets what kind of shit we live in."

Those who knew Oistrakh better and longer than I will find it un-believable that this phrase crossed his lips—which never uttered crude words. Nonetheless, it was said—while dozens of people, standing around staring at him, might have been thinking to themselves, "There he is, one of the happiest people of our time."

We parted as warmly as we had spent that month in Päarnuu. When we came over to say goodbye to the Oistrakhs, he embraced and kissed us both and wished us good luck in everything (my wife was then expecting our child), and expressed his wish to see us in Mos-cow. But as often happens, our relations did not continue. We met accidentally only a few times more (for the last time, I believe, at the funeral service for Isaak Tchudnovsky, the husband of one of Ois-trakh's former students, Nina Beilina, and a very good musician and decent man).

In October 1974 the whole music world mourned Oistrakh's sud-den death after a concert in Amsterdam, a heavy and unexpected loss. Having lived through two serious heart attacks during his last year, he seemed to feel better, but the third proved fatal. The next day, in one more twist of fate, Minister Furtseva died, having spent, it is rumored, a lot of effort to get permission (!) to bury Oistrakh in the most presti-gious Moscow cemetery, the Novodevichy Monastery.

Looking back, Oistrakh's art appears truly eternal, Olympian. Per-fection, natural substance, humanity—these three qualities, I think, describe him best. His tone, pouring like fluid silver, and his intimate yet natural phrasing made Oistrakh's playing uniquely noble. Those deviations from good taste to "please the gods," which many per-formers are too generous with, were absolutely alien to him, and his audience paid him back with admiration and respect. In the 1940s, during and after the war, Moscow Radio often broadcast Oistrakh's first recordings of the concertos of Tchaikovsky, Khachaturian, and the unfortunately half-forgotten Miaskovsky (possibly, all three with Alexander Gauk). What a vital supply of energy it was for us then!

As I have already mentioned, apart from Miron Poliakin, who died before the war, nobody in the country could come close to this magician of the violin. Later, the popularity and flourishing career of Leonid Kogan seemed to make him Oistrakh's one real rival; in any event, it is impossible not to mention him in the history of postwar violin performance. (Kogan in fact gave the formal farewell at Oistrakh's civil funeral, inexcusably reading from a written text.) A rich, sensual tone, a natural and magnificently worked-out technique of both hands (he was a longtime student of Yampolsky), and a bright artistic temperament made Kogan's great public success virtually inevitable. His career peaked in the 1950s: the victory at the Queen Elisabeth Competition in Brussels, and his first concert tour of the United States, when Sol Hurok said that he could not remember such a triumph since Chaliapin's time.

Perhaps there is something to the old saying, "Everyone plays himself"—that is, personality is revealed in playing. Some musicians of the older generation, who had known Kogan since their school years, were not among the great violinist's fans, more for personal reasons based on childhood impressions than on musical grounds. It seemed, besides, that toward the end of Kogan's intense and short life, his health became more fragile, which would inevitably affect his artistic career, even though he was much younger than Oistrakh. Life itself made its arrangements, providing the long perspective. Oistrakh's clear and lofty art stands alone, hardly comparable with other bright stars.

Two of my pals, former students of Oistrakh, are inclined to blame him for the fact that their careers did not reach full bloom as expected. For me, it doesn't change anything, even if they are right. I hope this does not require an explanation: Oistrakh was human, with all the contradictions that entails. He always displayed nobility and tact in delicate situations, trying never to hurt anyone. He was a truly great musician and an outstanding person, and all who were privileged to know him remember the association with pride.

To finish the conversation about musicians who had been for different reasons subject to arguments and comparisons, I'll give an example from the long-lasting rivalry of the two most popular tenors of the Bolshoi Theater, Ivan Kozlovsky and Sergei Lemeshev.

Sometime in the 1960s Kozlovsky arrived at the Radio House without his passport—which we Soviets were supposed to carry with us at all times as a mandatory ID. The security system was tough, and the guard simply would not let Kozlovsky in. Finally, after a long and fruitless discussion, Kozlovsky grew angry. "Don't you understand, after all, that I am Kozlovsky?!" To which came the cool and devastating answer: "So what? I wouldn't care even if you were Lemeshev."

In October 1970 our daughter Anna was born. Naturally, my life became even more private, limited mainly to concert tours and teaching at the Institute. Besides, every trip to the city took about an hour. Now in Chicago we think about our walks to the grocers, the cleaners, the pharmacy, and so on, with a kind of nostalgic tenderness. Our developing community in the outskirts of Moscow was undergoing nonstop construction in the long and careless Soviet fashion—you walked on temporary street surfaces, evading big puddles and piles of trash and waste. By that time a general indifference to everything had spread within us so much that I took advantage of every chance to walk unshaven, like the plodders around me, looking shabby as only the Soviet workmen could look. My colleagues and students would perhaps not recognize me in such a guise, and the people in the lines and buses would not have believed that their fellow commuter was a teacher and concert pianist. At home there was my family and music, and at night, my books and broadcasts of the Voice of America and BBC.

Although our circle of friends had narrowed, we had a few close friends, fortunately, for without them our life would have been too gloomy. Muscovites of that time will never forget those kitchens, their tables laid—as the old Russian saying has it—with what God had provided. After several shots of vodka (we were not spoiled with a great diversity of hard liquor, and frankly did not suffer for it), everybody got animated and slightly sentimental, talking openly about everything, remembering and laughing. Such evenings are possibly our best memories from the last several years in Moscow. Millions of people in my country lived a similarly dual life, being truly themselves only with friends and family.

Concert touring was becoming harder for me to take. Two winters in a row (1972 and '73) brought me for the first time to the cities of Norilsk and Magadan (in remote northern Siberia, and the Far East).

They both made a harsh impression on me, beginning with a very uneasy feeling when nobody met me at the airports. This had been happening more often lately (another example of the growing indifference), but after a long, exhausting flight it was especially discouraging. The shamelessness of the officials—my hosts and co-workers, so to speak—shocked even a touring artist with my experience: it was the vilest impression of the past twenty years. But this is not the main thing—after all, everything passes away, even lies. But not the following. . . .

For the several days I spent in each of these cities, walking on crunching snow under the low, indifferent sun, it was impossible to rid myself of the thought that I was literally walking on the bones of hundreds of thousands of people. From the end of the 1930s until Stalin's death, their terrible destiny threw them to the ends of the earth, where they settled their scores with this severe life. I happened to talk with several old people from "the first wave"—a cloak room attendant at the Magadan theater, taken as "a daughter of an enemy of the people," a watch repairman in Norilsk. They had nobody and nowhere to move to; here they had at least their "sub-polar bonus"—both were, of course, "rehabilitated" long ago.

They had been so ruthlessly crushed that neither malice nor heartbreaking reminiscences remained with them—only the calm fatalism of hopelessness. It was hard to comprehend how they survived in these dreadful places, saving in their memory only scraps of images from their bygone youth, but somehow they had—unlike millions of others, who were rudely snatched from their old lives. These others—after the hell of "intense" interrogations, the so-called troikas[7] and overcrowded prison cells, the stopping-places on the way to the camps—had died many years ago.

Pedestrians and loaded buses scurried through the streets; schools, stores, offices, and clubs were working; smart operators were making big money—in short, our "Soviet life was seething all around." But the nightmarish burden of the past constantly reasserted itself, and washed or rubbed off it will never be. . . .

I toured Czechoslovakia a second time in 1972. This country and its people, history, culture, and music have always been so near to my heart that I enjoyed strolling along even the smoky streets of industrial Ostrava. I can hardly find the words to describe astonishing Prague and could not bring myself to visualize Soviet tanks on ancient Vaclav

Square. Also in this year we made a videotape of Chopin's Second Concerto with the All-Union Radio and TV Symphony Orchestra under Rozhdestvensky, and a video of my solo recital (Schubert, Chopin, Rachmaninov) was shown twice nationwide on the first television channel. I was pleased, too, that my student at the Institute was the only one in her graduating class to be recommended for postgraduate study. And after the review on Cliburn I spoke of earlier, *Soviet Music* commissioned me to write several more articles for them between 1972 and 1974.

Although these scattered events might seem to be encouraging, by that time, given the growing and pervasive disappointment and pessimism, it was hard to expect decisive improvement in the life of my generation. The thought of emigration was far from me then, but the idea was spreading, among several of my fellow musicians in particular. They were basically younger than I. It was simpler for them to think seriously of such a break in their lives. They felt themselves unfairly treated, and a desperate attempt to make a career abroad, before it was too late, outweighed all else for them. At heart, I condemned some of them, but the resolution and strong motivation of others seemed to show their personal independence and faith in themselves. I just tried not to think how insecure my part-time position in the Institute was, since teaching by that time meant too much to me.

The longtime director of the Gnessin, Yury Muromtsev, had retired (I cannot recall exactly when, or why), and after several months of interregnum, the able choral director Vladimir Minin was appointed to the post.

The untimely death of the bright and distinctive choral director Alexander Yurlov had been a big loss for Soviet choral art. He was an innovator both in choosing the repertoire of his Republican Kappella and in its performing style, which was sharply contemporary, expressive, and sensitively connected with the text (for instance, in Sviridov's "City of Koursk Songs," and Shostakovich's "The Execution of Stepan Razin"). Minin had successfully employed this bright performance style in his Moscow Chamber Choir. In my opinion, he also paid attention to the methods of the highly talented Andrey Volkonsky, the leader of Madrigal, a popular Moscow ensemble. Minin's professional career was given a green light just as he was becoming a successful ministry official.

As a part-time teacher, I had not associated with this medium-sized, red-faced man, who was about my age. A couple of times he showed up at students' auditions and, without the trace of a smile, lectured at great length on the problems of performing, mouthing truisms in the presence of the aging Gutman and Iokheles. Sitting next to me at one such harangue was Konstantin Khristoforovich Adjemov, a highly cultured man who had known me from my student years (and incidentally, a unique example of a person and musician of principles who nevertheless remained on good terms with everyone). Our eyes met and Adjemov, leaning toward me, said, "Mitya, take it easy. We all have to sing in their choir." (Adjemov was also an associate professor at the Conservatory, under Sveshnikov.)

As a director, Minin was a complex, heartless man, alien to the more human spirit of the Gnessin. Having taken a hard line toward some influential full-time teachers, he enlisted the department heads in an underhanded campaign against them. Fear and intrigue began to creep everywhere. Once Iokheles, unable to restrain himself after yet another coaching session in Minin's office, practically ran into my class. I asked the students to leave us alone, and Iokheles began to complain about the cobra, as he called our boss. Tears even started to his eyes. The situation in the Institute was becoming unhealthy. Nothing of the kind could have happened when Elena Gnessina was still alive.

Toward the end of the 1972–73 academic year, Minin, in order to free his hands of the struggle with the several objectionable full-time professors, logically decided first to abolish several part-time positions. Two of these were in the piano department, held by Adjemov and me. Ironically, that academic year had been the most successful of my six years there.

That is how it happened—unexpectedly and heartlessly. The man did not even invite us to his office to thank us for years of productive, practically donated work. My good colleagues, decent people and high-class musicians, were upset, some even outraged. For Iokheles, it was also a blow to his self-esteem and independence as a faculty leader. My fellow victim Adjemov presented me at that time with his memoirs, *The Unforgettable*, warmly inscribed, "Dear Dmitry Alexandrovich! Keep, through your whole life, your ardent love of the Arts. I respect and value you. K. A." It was very kind of him. He, of course, retained his professorship in the Conservatory, but for me, the loss of teaching was an extremely heavy blow—with far-reaching consequences, as it turned out.

In the summer of 1973 I went to Poland for a recital in Warsaw and to participate in the oldest Chopin festival (begun in 1946) in Dushniki, my last concert tour abroad. Taking part in the festival were two well-known Polish pianists—Barbara Hesse-Bukowska and Lidia Grich-tolowna—as well as the young American Jeffrey Swan, who had been popular in Poland since the 1970 Chopin Competition.[8]

After our two recitals, Jeffrey and I played both Chopin concertos with the orchestra. I managed to conquer the bad state of my nerves, and played well. The final festival concert was to be held in the Kur-saal, or auditorium, of the oldest Polish health resort, where the young Chopin had undergone a cure more than 150 years earlier, and I was honored to close it. Before coming onstage I literally could not decide what to play at this unforgettable concert, traditionally held by candle-light. Each of the four of us was to play any Chopin nocturne and a big work. At my request, my piece had not been indicated in the program, and I (unexpectedly for myself) started the Fantasy, op. 49. I think I had never before managed to play it on such a large scale. Every festival participant received a memorable vase that featured Chopin's profile; unfortunately, mine disappeared from our luggage when we were leav-ing the U.S.S.R.

I received an invitation to tour Poland in the next year, but it was not destined to be.

The episode at the Gnessin was the last straw. I felt strongly how much I could give to my students, having had such a long experience in per-forming, and now a solid one in teaching as well. To be suddenly dis-carded, and in such a caddish fashion besides, had been both a profes-sional and a moral shock. Perhaps it was to some extent my fault, but I was not able to reconcile myself to it. All the negative sides of our life, which I, like many others, had tried for a long time to shut my eyes to, now appeared especially traumatic and irreversible. The frightening thought of emigration—which I had not seriously considered a year ago—suddenly became more real.

I shared my feelings with my mother, who was approaching eighty. She replied, "Once this thought has occurred to you, you should prepare yourself to do it. You are not young any more, but not aging, either. If it went so far, I want to believe that it is still possible for you to start all over again, even in a foreign place. And do not ask me to go with you. I will never leave this land where I have lived for so long, and gone through so much. You are the last man in our family, and I do not want you to live constantly with the thought that your country does not need what you can still give to it."

The year 1974—the departure of two giants. Lev Oborin—a superlative Russian man and musician, for whose memory I will always feel a deep respect—died in winter, and David Oistrakh, his old friend and longtime partner in chamber ensemble duets, and a popular trio with cellist Sviatoslav Knushevitsky, passed away in autumn of the same year. These two embodied the very best in Soviet performing art.

Strange as it may seem, I did not sign up for the guard of honor at Oistrakh's coffin, for by that time we had already received a formal invitation from Israel, the only way for anyone to emigrate from the U.S.S.R. Later, for the same reason, I canceled my forthcoming concerts in Poland. To avoid being pestered with questions, I let Gosconcert know over the phone, even though it would have been fun to watch their reactions. Self-cancellation was virtually unique; usually they determined everything for you.

Rostropovich's departure from the country contributed to the general pessimism. Even with his popularity, his extraordinarily active nature, his inexhaustible optimism, Slava felt hunted down, overstrained by the different interdictions and limitations. Lately he had sheltered Solzhenitsyn and signed addresses in defense of the dissidents, and now the authorities were getting even. In his last concert he conducted the Conservatory Student Orchestra. After an exceptionally emotional performance of Tchaikovsky's Symphony no. 6, the audience felt bitterly that they faced a lengthy separation from a great artist. The ovation in the Grand Hall seemed endless, and hundreds of people came backstage to shake Slava's hand and wish him happiness. I've never seen him so feverishly excited. We embraced, and he wrote several memorable words on my program in his nervous sprawling handwriting, inadvertently rearranging two letters in my nickname in a funny way. We met with Slava very rarely but always on friendly terms. It is strange that our attempt at musical cooperation in 1955 was realized almost impromptu thirty-five years later in the United States, and in general, we met more often in our first American years than we did when we lived in the same Russian city for thirty.

In the winter of 1975 I made my last Soviet record, including the Grieg Ballade, op. 24, and Liszt's Polonaise in E. So far, the letter from

Israel's foreign ministry had been kept in my secretaire without any action. Lucya and I couldn't reconcile ourselves to the thought that there was no longer another alternative for us, but finally we decided to emigrate. In May 1975, we left for my concerts in Odessa and Kishinyov, together with little Anya, which turned out to be one of the most bittersweet memories of my entire concert life. Besides several successful concerts and very warm and large audiences (primarily due to the all-Beethoven solo program and the Chopin Concerto with the orchestra), this tour coincided with the thirtieth anniversary of the war victory. We made reservations for hotel rooms with TV sets (which were not so common in the old Soviet hotels), and almost all the broadcasts were connected one way or another with this frightful and fateful time in our history. I can say only that our reaction to what we saw was particularly emotional.

Ironically, the Odessa Conservatory, through my longtime colleague Igor Sukhomlinov, offered me the position of associate professor "for the purpose of consolidating the piano department," with the requirement of moving to Odessa. But our recent decision had already taken too much out of us, and now it was too late to talk of anything else.

My own first grand piano, a "Bekker"—which I had purchased twenty years earlier with my Chopin prize—was not eligible to be taken out of the country. We sold it for a trifle and bought from Rozhdestvensky a Grotrian Steinweg (a German predecessor of the contemporary Steinways), a comparatively rare label that perhaps by oversight was not included on the taboo list.

In the beginning of August I heard about the death of Shostakovich through the night broadcast of the BBC. The next morning, I called up Rozhdestvensky to confirm that the news was true. "Unfortunately yes," he said, "and how have you learned?" In our country it was announced only the next day.

For the last ten or fifteen years Shostakovich seemed sick and worn-out, going along with the stream of life, submerged in his music, without letting anybody into his inner world except for the very few close to him, like Rostropovich, Tatiana Nikolayeva, and obviously Solomon Volkov, who later published the bombastic *Testimony* in the West. So the Americans found him when Shostakovich came to receive his honorary Ph.D. from Northwestern University in Evanston,

Illinois, in 1973. The works of the last period reflect his profound pessimism and thoughts of death, the fear of which he constantly tried to
overcome (the Symphony no. 14, the last quartets, the vocal cycles).
With the departure of this tragic genius, whose music had always been
a part of our life, all Russian musicians experienced a huge, irreplaceable loss.

Soldiers were ordered to stand guard at the civil funeral, an unusual
sight, making a living chain along the central aisle. Those who came
late were not allowed to linger on the main floor. They moved slowly
forward with the crowd toward the coffin and then could only walk
upstairs and sit in the quiet balconies.

Soviet emigration was in its first wave in 1975, and every application
handed in by a more-or-less known figure in Moscow immediately
became a sensation. The initial shock of disbelief gave way to a wide
spectrum of reactions. But not among the authorities—*Homo sovieticus*
remained true to himself. The applicant immediately became a traitor
and was treated accordingly, less obviously by the big shots, and worst
of all by small fry of every kind. So, we decided to hand in our application immediately after my last Melodiya recording was issued. On
the evening of 15 November, the scheduled day of my recording's
sale, we checked the record store next to the Conservatory, having
decided that tomorrow, no matter what, I would inform Mosconcert
of my decision. Its director, Igor Safonov, who claimed to be a descen-
dant of the famous Russian musician, was a decent and polite man,
and I thought that I should be the first to bring him this news—highly
unpleasant news for Mosconcert. The record went on sale earlier the
same day.

I would prefer not to return to all the complications and depressing experiences of the next four months. In any event, it was not Mosconcert that caused them—my scheduled concerts were not canceled,
which would have been routine practice in those days, but I have forgotten completely, somehow, where and what I played on my last tour
through the cities of the Caucasus.

We received several telephone calls from old acquaintances, who
wanted only to make sure that we were leaving, and right away said
goodbye. A few colleagues of mine didn't dare to call. At the same
time, many others, sometimes not even close friends, were not afraid to
approach us in public places, at concerts or in the streets, to shake

hands, to cheer us up, and to wish us luck. Some did not conceal that under different circumstances, perhaps soon, they would venture to leave the country where their whole lives had been spent. Final leave-takings with many of my colleagues and the staff of the Ros- and Mos-concert were warm and moving.

The ad hoc committee of the ministry unexpectedly denied me permission to take my recently purchased piano out. I was not in a position to look for fairness; nonetheless, I had nothing to lose and so wrote a letter to the deputy minister, *Tovarishch* Popov, a man with a more humane reputation among the ministry staff, reminding him that Grotrian Steinwegs were not on the list of "taboo" pianos. Amazingly, permission was granted, with a line noting that my Grotrian would be the last allowed out of the country. Thanks.

On 23 February 1976 we received an exit visa, to be used within one month. We spent this time as if in a fog, bidding farewell to our dear ones, friends, Moscow. As is traditional, we had our photo taken at the Red Square. On 13 March, I played my last recital at the Gold-enweiser museum-apartment. All this will stay with us forever; but to the devil with our memories of the vile OVIR, a special KGB department in charge of emigration, along with the real den of thieves who checked our luggage and shook every book from our library onto the huge, cold cargo station's cement floor.

Our last night in Moscow was 18 March. A couple dozen of the people especially close to us gathered for a farewell party in our empty apartment—relatives, friends, a few neighbors, musicians and non-musicians, invited and uninvited. We all tried not to think about what lay ahead. At six in the morning we left for Sheremetyevo airport. My last two Soviet impressions were of an attractive young female customs officer, meticulously stony-faced, reading the several personal letters that I wanted to carry with me. Her male colleague revealed more traces of humanity, and even allowed me to return to the group who saw us off beyond the checkpoint to embrace my mother for the last time.

Everything is over. They announce the boarding. Half an hour later, the plane rose above the ground of Moscow. Ahead, a complete unknown. . . .

CHAPTER 5

America

S mall wonder that the tone of this book has changed with the passage of time—the years slipped by, taking with them naïve optimism and hopes. Hard everyday work, struggling for one's place in
life, strokes of good luck and disappointment, one after another, took
away too much energy, gradually leaving me with a more pessimistic,
passive attitude.

It is hard to avoid a painfully subjective account of our life after 19
March 1976. There is too much in this period that I would like to forget—much of it not exactly gloomy, but so alien that it is almost
unreal. Besides, and this is perhaps the main thing, my object in writing this book, mentioned in the Preface, is basically fulfilled. As far as
possible I have described the people and events with which my musical life was connected. I hope that it will add new, living features to the
images of those who are widely known and help preserve the memory
of many others, modest and deserving, whose lives were also dedicated
to music. This chapter is about several musicians with different des-
tinies, our meetings and conversations that brought back the unforgettable times of our youth. It tells about my life in America—by now
quite long and varied. It also includes a brief comparison of piano education in the U.S.S.R. and United States, as well as some of my professional observations, accumulated with time and my growing experience.

We found ourselves in a completely foreign situation from the very
first day of emigration. After the monotonous, passive flow of Moscow,
with several close people and our music, the twelve days in Vienna

passed swiftly—a cheerless hotel, official meetings, long walks through food markets and several museums of the beautiful but infinitely strange, frosty city. I went over to Die Hochschule für Musik. They appeared interested; at least my name was known there. I was invited to compete for a vacant teaching position, though naturally they had their own candidate, who in a few weeks became the new piano professor.

I had written a letter to Ashkenazy in Reykjavik, asking him to answer me at Rome, our next stop on the way to the Western hemisphere. It was a joyless time. My telephone conversations with my older friend and colleague Boris (Busya) Goldstein, then a violin professor in Hanover, were my only comfort. Goldstein had been one of the five most gifted teenagers of our prewar school (the Central School of Music), the winner of major international competitions, so rare in the 1930s. In fact, he won two fourth prizes—at the age of fourteen at the first Weniawsky Competition in Warsaw (1935), and two years later at the Ysaÿe Competition (later named after Queen Elisabeth) in Brussels. Almost fifty years after the Weniawsky, I met the old concert violinist Henri Temianka, who had been third after Ginette Neveu and Oistrakh; he told me that during a long life he had met few as generously gifted as Boris Goldstein. It is hard even to imagine the boy's popularity in the 1930s. He had even had his photograph taken with Stalin, after the presentation of the Badge of Honor.[1]

Like every child prodigy, Goldstein was not invulnerable to time, however, and after the war fortune seemed to part company with him. I can only say that his talent did not lose its luster; his playing was still artistic and elegant, his tone and phrasing enchanting. Possibly something else slowed his career after the war. Boris had always been an uncommonly kind and gentle person. When the next generation of bright and more aggressive performers emerged beside him on the big stage, he seemed to lose his poise for a while. What followed illustrated destiny's injustice toward its chosen ones.

In spite of a long series of bitter disappointments, Goldstein retained his kindness and distinctly charming smile. He performed in only two countries, Greece and Bulgaria, but with huge success. He still played once a year at the Grand Hall and made infrequent recordings—the situation did not allow him to hope for more. We'd last met in 1974, on an embankment of the Moscow River, and talked a little. He looked sad, hanging his head, with bitterness even in his smile. Shortly after, he left the country.

And now in March 1976, Busya tried persistently to persuade me to come to West Germany. His reasoning was that it might be the only country where good musicians were still in demand, that I would not regret it, and so on. Probably he was right, but I was with my family and did not dare to take this chance and deviate from the official process of emigration. I have not forgotten these conversations, as well as his sincere and warm letters to Chicago. No doubt sensing a touch of nostalgia in my letters, a couple of times Busya sent me Soviet postcards of the inevitable monument with the right arm stretched for direction. God knows how he had managed to preserve them.

Many years later, after my concerts in the Netherlands, my wife and I spent three wonderful days in the Goldsteins' house in Hanover. On the last evening, by coincidence, Slava Rostropovich played (and how!) three solo cello sonatas by Bach in the local church. When we ascended the stage after the concert, some force or presence united us for several minutes. Even the people around us seemed to feel it, seeing us embracing, laughing, sharing something known only to the three of us. It was our past, starting with the Central School of Music, half a century old by that time, which will stay with us forever no matter what.

It was heartbreaking to read Busya's letters after that meeting. It soon turned out that his illness was grave, and he knew it. His very last letter is, in essence, a tragic human document of enormous force. Many people around the world were deeply saddened by Boris Goldstein's death in November 1987.

Before we left Moscow, Elena Ivanovna Goldenweiser had given me the telephone number of the Ivanov family in Rome. The notable Russian symbolist poet and philosopher Viacheslav Ivanov (1866–1949) had emigrated to Italy in 1924 with his two children, Lidia and Dimitry. Who knows how our nine months in Rome would have turned out had we not met these unusual people. Their hospitality, kindness, and constant willingness to help were invaluable in our situation.

By amazing coincidence, Lidia had studied in the Moscow Conservatory with Alexander Borisovich almost sixty years earlier, and then taken composition with Ottorino Respighi at the Santa Cecilia Academy in Rome. After the liberation of Italy in 1944, she worked as organist and piano player at the American church on Via Napoli. Thirty years later, by another coincidence, the same church offered us its hospitality after I'd played my first recital there for the parishioners and music lovers. That is how we made our first American friends—Rev. Willbour Woodhams and his wife Margot, whose sincere and active participation in the Roman period of our lives we will not forget.

In Rome we had a warm reunion with Ashkenazy, whom we had not seen for many years. He played an all-Beethoven program, opening with the rarely performed Second Sonata in A; later that autumn Richter began his concert with the First Sonata in F minor. In December the State Department granted us permission to enter the United States. I had specifically requested that we not be sent to New York City; at forty-eight I did not want to start over again there. It is still difficult to say whether it was the right choice, but so the decision was made—Chicago.

We spent Christmas with the Ivanovs, New Year's Eve at the American church. On 13 January 1977 we took off from Rome and arrived in New York that same evening. The next day Chicago experienced a record cold.

Our first months in Chicago were marked by a sense of alienation and hopelessness, traces of which are felt to this day. It is hard to imagine what this country had meant for my generation in the U.S.S.R.; the more bitter, then, were the inevitable disappointments of our new life here. It seems humanity's faults and virtues are the same, regardless of the political system. In the Soviet Union, with its tragic destiny, and in the flourishing United States one encounters both people of high nobility and first-rate villains and crooks. So let us always remember: our America, despite all the turbulence of the last decades, remains the greatest country in the world, strong and fair, showing its hospitality to those who need it.

My first and strongest impression of the Chicago Symphony—a February 1977 performance of Bruckner's Symphony no. 7 with Claudio Abbado—will be hard to surpass. I found myself in the famous Orchestra Hall for the first time thanks to Arrand Parsons, then a professor at Northwestern University, who soon became our close friend. Another comforting recollection is our first meeting with an older, hospitable Russian couple, the Aleskovs. Having lived in the United States for more than fifty years by that time, Gregory and Zina kept their door open for all good people, primarily for musicians and music lovers. It was from them that I learned of an opening for a professor of piano at DePaul University, a Catholic institution. Earlier I had received the standard polite refusals from several American music schools, and not only because my name was unknown. There were no vacancies for years to come.

And then something happened that could have stripped away all that remained of any musician's optimism. As soon as I started to practice at the available places, I detected a problem with my left hand—the interaction of the second and third fingers in scalelike and broken passages inexplicably went wrong. If the same thing were to happen to my right hand, my performing career would be over. I had no choice but to adjust my quite wide repertoire to this new circumstance. In some cases, because of several passages that were no longer under my command, I had to part forever with pieces I had played for all my long concert career (Beethoven's Fifth Concerto, both sonatas of Chopin, much of Schumann, Liszt, Rachmaninov, Prokofiev). Pianists would not believe the kind of unnatural and "antipianistic" fingering I was forced to use in order to secure at least an appearance of velocity and evenness in my left hand. It was funny to think that there had been a time when my colleagues came over not only to listen but to watch me practice.[2]

A performance by Rozhdestvensky with the Chicago Symphony sometime in the spring of 1977 was a joy for us. A great talent in combination with genuine intelligence and an ability to stand up for himself (rare under Soviet conditions) had made Rozhdestvensky an uncommon figure in the Soviet arts. Although his worldwide popularity made him to some extent less vulnerable, from time to time he too bore hardships, like his forced resignation from the All-Union Radio and TV Symphony Orchestra in the early 1970s.

Gennady and I had studied together at the Central School of Music but had only a bowing acquaintance then. We were thrown together for the first time at a plenary session of the Composers' Union in the late autumn of 1966 in Leningrad. They called me up from the Philharmonie and invited me to substitute on one day's notice for the cellist Natalya Shahovskaya, who was taken ill. (Interestingly, seven years earlier, in 1959, I had appeared on the same legendary stage of the Column Hall of the Leningrad Philharmonic for the first time, replacing another cellist—Slava Rostropovich—and playing with Gennady's father, Nikolai Anosov, one of the most intelligent Soviet musicians. It

seems ages have passed since then.) I had just begun to "restore" Shostakovich's Second Concerto, after a yearlong break, for my English
tour, but agreed anyway.

Working with Rozhdestvensky was a pleasure—the rehearsals
were always effective, with constant funny comments. Onstage he was
a most reliable musical partner, and our first collaboration marked the
beginning of our friendly relations. By the way, the little adventure
that occurred at this concert was my own fault. As usual, I was more
concerned about the first movement, and when it and the marvelous,
lyrical second had passed with no problem, I allowed myself to relax
too much. A punishment followed immediately. In the very beginning of the finale, I repeated a bar that should not be played twice. I
rambled at the keyboard, trying to catch up with the orchestra, when
Gennady turned to me with his unmatchable smile and said with the
coming downbeat, "F-dur" ("European" for F major), but by that time
we were back together. All this lasted no more than a few seconds, but
it seemed as if time had stopped. After a few friendly curtain calls, we
returned to the famous light blue living room, where I asked my conductor to forgive this goof. "Don't even speak of it," Genya said. "You
didn't hear what [a popular violinist] 'arranged' yesterday in the Schnit-
tke Violin Concerto. That was real heat!" (Rozhdestvensky's professional slang, very distinct and imaginative, is inseparable from his
image.) My pals from the orchestra later told me that when the violinist was totally lost, Rozhdestvensky, whose sense of humor never fails,
turned to him and said, "Play on them all!" (meaning all four strings, no
matter what).

Rozhdestvensky is the only one of my Russian colleagues who has
visited all four of our Chicago residences. In 1978, he was very glad to
reencounter his Grotrian Steinweg, which I had bought from him only
a year and a half earlier, and both former and current owners were
photographed together at the piano. When he noticed his recording of
The Nutcracker in my phonograph collection, Gennady, in spite of
being "in his cups," wrote a funny, long inscription for our daughter,
Anya, on it, impromptu. His quips were spontaneous and witty, but
when he was serious, his integrity and convictions were palpable.

About eighty applicants were originally in the running for the position
at DePaul; eventually only two remained. My master class and a performance before the faculty were scheduled for 10 April 1977. Our

luggage, primarily the piano, library, and the family's memorabilia, which had followed us from Trieste by sea, arrived the same day. While helping movers to bring the piano up to the second floor, I scratched my hands slightly, but it did not affect my playing. My English was so inadequate that I conducted my master class with a translator.

In a few days the dean, Frederick Miller, invited me into his office, still in the old DePaul building downtown, and we spent a short time getting acquainted. I was about to leave when he asked, looking into my eyes, "Mr. Paperno, do you really want this position?" Apparently, he had already made his choice: at that time the names of Russian musicians were still impressive in this country. A month later I signed my first annual contract. In our circumstances, the rank of associate professor with an annual salary of $18,000 seemed to be the solution to all our problems.

Some notable Russian musicians preceded me as teachers at DePaul: Sergei Tarnovsky (Vladimir Horowitz's teacher in Kiev); the well-known composer and pianist Alexander Tcherepnin; the violinist Pavel Stassevich (he bore an amazing family resemblance to his cousin, popular Soviet conductor Abram Stassevich, who in spite of our long partnership and friendly relations, had never mentioned his relative in America). For different reasons they were not happy at DePaul. When I played my first faculty recital, the review from the Chicago *Sun Times* mentioned in this connection the fate of Tcherepnin, whom I had the chance to meet at the hospitable Aleskovs' apartment several months before his death in Paris in 1977.

The University of Chicago's Mandel Hall was the venue for my first American recital. In outward appearance, the concert went off very successfully, helping me to realize how important the choice of program, especially for the first half of the concert, had now become for me. This was proved again at my next recital, in Milwaukee's Vogel Hall.[3]

On 6 November 1977, I heard Vladimir Horowitz for the first time. Even before the concert, Orchestra Hall was electrified. It does not matter that some pieces in his program convinced me more than others (the works of Fauré and Rachmaninov's "Musical Moment" in E-flat minor). Simply to be in attendance at a concert by this great seventy-four-year-old pianist (my mother had heard his degree recital in the Kiev Conservatory fifty-five years earlier) was an event. Groups of

Moscow pianists used to gather in the evenings to listen as each of Horowitz's new recordings made its way to Moscow. We were enraptured with his diabolic technique and the spontaneity of his playing. I consider it impossible to express any critical remarks regarding this piano legend. Only such musicians as Rachmaninov, Neuhaus, Sofronitsky, who had known him and watched his gigantic gift develop, can do it, as his older contemporaries or fellow students. I can only be thankful to have had the opportunity to listen to this phenomenal pianist live three times.

Ironically, the next day I too appeared at Orchestra Hall, with an excellent chamber group of Chicago Symphony members. In different combinations, we played rarely performed works by Hummel, Schumann, and Ravel. Both leading Chicago newspapers included very generous reviews the next day. Unfortunately, the group dissolved after its leader left for another city.

My first encounters with my new students were disappointing—this was the level of the average pre-conservatory college back home. Even now, having taught here for five years, it still hurts to meet young people with an unprofessional approach to the business of their lives—to be specific, with an ignorance of music, harmony (sometimes, I must say, even of elementary theory), polyphony, and basic piano technique, apparent in stiff arms and wrists. Efforts to clear up this long-accumulated amateurishness are often hopeless—the process has included not only the inadequacy of a previous teacher but also the limited talent of the pupil, who has blindly followed him or her down the wrong road. The old saying, "A good teacher can do anything," is simply not applicable here. A good teacher can produce a good shoemaker, plumber, or foreman. When it comes to a businessman, doctor, or lawyer, I still consider it possible with some reservations. As for a successful scientist, artist, musician, or athlete, in my opinion, at least two conditions are musts—natural talent and inexhaustible curiosity (including a great capacity for work to satisfy it).[4]

When I refused to accept hopeless prospects into my studio, both the administration and the young people were not happy with me. Eventually, in order not to let my school down financially, I had to open my class door a little wider (after all, I am the only full-time piano professor whose salary does not depend on the number of his or her students); but this hardly corresponded to the dialectic concept that speaks of "a transition of quantity to quality." Besides, an important ethical dilemma is involved here. I am not speaking about the students who are minoring in piano, whose required piano course lasts for the first two years; some of them show at least some interest in the professional basics of piano and music in general. Problems occur when the student wants to go on as a piano performance major for the remaining two years, and the teacher has a hard time convincing the pupil that under no circumstances can he or she make a living as a piano performer. I simply cannot approve such an obviously wrong choice of career. It does not happen often; usually these students acknowledge reality, we part as friends after their sophomore year, and two years later, they come up to me during graduation and thank me for being their good and fair guide in music, which always makes me feel good. Some of them ask to stay in the studio for one or two years longer, without pursuing a piano degree. Needless to say, this group as a rule is welcome here, provided they prove their professional attitude during the first two years.

I am glad when my new students can at least communicate at a professional level. Then we can talk about the form of the piece and its creative problems, and so forth. They accumulate their repertoire faster and are more demanding of themselves. As for the others who bumble through selected simpler pieces with the same stumbles for months—God help us both. Luckily DePaul has decent alternatives for them to pursue, like a degree in liberal arts, or in the recording industry (that's a good one—nobody gets hurt).

My first years were not easy. I found myself working within a system of music education entirely different from the Soviet, a system based upon a commercial, or quantitative approach. That is, more students = more money = more degrees. In my opinion, only those well-established music institutions whose supply of students steadily exceeds the available openings can enjoy both financial well-being and a high professional reputation as well. For me, the categories are inseparable, because such schools can afford to eliminate up to seventy-five percent of the applicants, and are not forced to accept almost anyone who simply rises above mediocrity and can afford the tuition. I would prefer to be wrong, but it seems this is neither a fault nor a trouble of the system, it is just the way it is. It is rather *my* problem that my adjustment to it goes so slowly.

On 1 August 1978, I made a tape of the works of Scriabin for my first American record, commissioned by the Musical Heritage Society. My idea was to represent all three periods of Scriabin's creative work on each side. So I learned the two opuses I'd never played before—the Five Preludes, op. 16, and the poem "Vers la flamme," op. 72. Norman Pellegrini of radio station WFMT Chicago did an excellent job in only six hours, despite the less-than-professional conditions in the empty Mandel Hall (portable recording equipment, outside noise from flying planes and the sweeping of the university's yard, and so on). We became friends once and for all.

Those who have heard this recording (MHS 3998) would probably be interested to learn that three days after this session my late friend, orthopedic surgeon David Shapiro, opened my left palm in his hospital in Milwaukee in an attempt to discover the reasons for the deterioration, unfortunately with no result. David told me later how difficult it was for him, as both a surgeon and a friend, to undertake this operation.

When Pellegrini and I were editing the tape afterward, we could hear the faint noise of a plane in one bar of the A-flat Waltz, op. 38. Norman threw this three-foot-long piece of tape into the wastebasket. Then it turned out that in another take of this spot one note did not come out at all, which was even worse. So for an hour, he pulled pieces of tape out of the basket, listening to many wrong ones, swearing comically. Finally he found the right one and reattached it to the master tape. It's funny that four years later, when we were taping *The Seasons* by Tchaikovsky, again for the Musical Heritage Society, this time in a professional recording studio, the same thing happened with the last piece in the cycle—"December" (another waltz in the same key). After we spent a long time trying to find and use the first take, Norman said, "You know, for you I would do as many takes as needed, but please, no more Russian waltzes in A-flat."

Vladimir Ashkenazy comes to Chicago infrequently, but regularly. After every performance one remembers such stylistically different pieces as Schumann's Davidsbündler Tänze; Beethoven's Fourth Piano Concerto and his last two sonatas; Scriabin's Sonatas nos. 7 and 10; and more recently Ashkenazy's accomplishments as a conductor, like Schubert's Fifth Symphony, Rachmaninov's Second, and Shostakovich's Tenth. Once when he and his wife visited us on their free evening I started half-jokingly to list piano concertos at random; there were few that Vladimir would not ever play.

In his ethical credo, "To serve the music," Ashkenazy is a kind of opposite to Horowitz, who rather used his incredible gift to serve the audience. It is interesting, however, that it is Ashkenazy in practice who fully personifies a splendid definition of technique given long ago by Horowitz: "Technique means having an absolutely clear idea of what you want and possessing the full ability for a perfect realization of it."

The autumn of 1979 was joyful and memorable for us, since three pianists with whom my whole musical life had been connected played concerts in Chicago. Bella Davidovich, during her first visit here, stayed at our house, and we spent all the evenings till very late remembering old times, and playing piano four hands as we did then. From my school years on, I have played four-hand music with dozens of my colleagues. Bella, without a doubt, is among my most gifted partners in this kind of chamber music (the three others are Ashkenazy, the late Estonian pianist Bruno Lukk, and Isaak Katz, a close friend and fellow student of mine, long a professor in Gorky and currently in Jerusalem, at the Rubin Academy of Music). I do not mean here just excellent sight reading. Rare musical insight and an innate feeling for ensemble turn this music making into a genuinely creative process. (Some analogy could be traced here with highly gifted chess players, who sometimes create masterpieces playing quick "blitz" games.) I have always known that Bella Davidovich's talent is of the highest class. In the decades since her victory in Warsaw (1949) her playing has become more diverse and dynamic, gaining drama and inner strength. A special and highly important facet of her talent is the excellent steadiness of her nerves. It seems this petite, charismatic woman with the nature of a staunch fighter was born to be a concert pianist.

Lazar Berman arrived at the same time to play the Brahms First Concerto with the Chicago Symphony. On his very first evening he was our guest, and we had a good time together. This was his third American tour. The first time, he made a sensation with his phenomenal virtuosity and primarily Liszt program. The media gave him trenchant nicknames like "a devil at the piano," "the Soviet bomb," and so on. It seemed that his late mother's dream of seeing her son among the world's greatest pianists was about to come true.

Lyalik for a long time had been underestimated in our homeland, considered basically an outstanding virtuoso without a sufficiently expressed musical personality. It is enough to listen to his Liszt, his Brahms, to much of his Beethoven, to realize that this is not so. True, his career had not been easy, unlike, say, that of Davidovich with her early Chopin first prize. Perhaps in time his mother's constant participation had become a hindrance to his musical development. Besides, as I already mentioned, our teacher was so captivated by his phenomenal pianism that he seemed reluctant to interfere in this element of virtuosity. People like Neuhaus, even the reserved Sofronitsky, liked him; Lazar has always been kind, communicative, loved to make people laugh. So the years went by in expectation of success. His participation in two international competitions (Budapest and Brussels) did not bring him a first prize. Finally, in the beginning of the 1970s, he performed in Italy with great success. A dexterous American manager invited him to the United States, and recordings with the best world conductors, including Karajan and Giulini, followed, as well as a second American tour, this time without the element of surprise.

In 1973, I had gladly accepted a commission to write a review of one of Berman's Moscow recitals. In 1976, a few days before we left Moscow, he did not hesitate to sign his famous recording of Liszt's Transcendental Études for me. We met in Rome a couple of months later, and now, 1979, in Chicago. Lazar looked tired, nervous, and even dispirited. In private, he did not hide how hard he took the Soviet officials' refusal to let his wife join him this time. No wonder that his playing was slightly dimmed by all this. Nevertheless, Lyalik called me up after the recording session to say that he had played more brightly there (Erich Leinsdorf conducted).

So many years of friendly relations connect me with Berman—the Central School of Music, Alexander Borisovich's studio, the war evacuation, the Conservatory. We wish him the best of luck in Italy, where he moved with his family after the U.S.S.R. disintegrated.

Finally, in November 1979, one of the world's greatest pianists in recital—Emil Gilels. Knowing his complicated personality, I let Gilels know through mutual acquaintances in Moscow that I planned to see him after the Chicago recital, and got an encouraging answer: "Let him be sure to come see me." He appeared onstage in the huge, impersonal Auditorium Theater, grown old and reserved. Possibly the Third Chopin Sonata could have aroused objections, with its delayed tempos and the deliberately measured modeling of both the whole and the details. But in the first part one heard a great musician and a sovereign of the piano. His interpretation of the less-known Schumann cycle, *Klavier-stücke*, op. 32, and Schubert's "Musical Moments," op. 94, was a revelation of wisdom and simplicity, humanity and mastery. Only a genuine artist could capture an audience with this chamber—in the highest sense of the word—music. Gilels' piano penetrated every little nook and cranny of the quieted-down hall; no one missed a turn of his natural, speechlike phrasing. What a strong, memorable impression it was!

Our meeting turned out to be very natural and warm. My wife and I stood at the door of his dressing room, waiting until Gilels had signed programs for the last, most talkative fans. A couple of times he looked at us through his glasses, not recognizing us. (No wonder.) The next moment he raised the glasses to his forehead and exclaimed, "Mitya!" so sincerely that I thought to myself that I might not have warned him beforehand.

Even though he and his wife (a former student of Leah Levinson) were leaving early the next morning for New York, Gilels invited us to their suite in the Drake Hotel, where we spent about two hours skipping from one topic to another. After all, I had showed up in his home for the first time exactly twenty-five years earlier, and there was much to talk about. But we were not alone, it was already past midnight, and so we left, carrying away a marvelous memory and his photograph with a warm inscription. He hoped to come here again the next year to mark the twenty-fifth anniversary of his first American tour. "This time be sure to call me up before the concert, as soon as it is announced," he said. But the political situation soon changed again, and what followed I will describe in the Epilogue. A few months later he suffered a mild heart attack after his concert in Amsterdam. I was much obliged to Ashkenazy, who phoned me after talking with Gilels to let me know that Emil was getting better. This time, Gilels had luckily escaped the worst in the city where two other Russian musicians had died—Oistrach and later, the outstanding conductor Kirill Kondrashin.

I would like to talk a bit more about Kondrashin—a complex man and a very successful musician who eventually became another victim of a regime that he deeply despised yet had no choice but to serve, and thus to promote.

We had been well acquainted with Kondrashin since 1957, when we became neighbors in the same big housing co-op of the Bolshoi Theater and Mosconcert. And it was not music that brought us together. Kondrashin was an ardent player of the card game preference, and I admit I was close behind him. For quite a few years, at least twice a month, he gathered in his beautiful apartment three partners, people he felt comfortable with, and the game usually went on until very late at night. After the first long lap, about eleven o'clock, we had about an hour's break in the dining room, where attractively presented sandwiches and plentiful drinks were served. It was always the best way to relax completely, and these late suppers went off with candid and witty chat. Often, about two o'clock, when we rose from the card table almost yellow from exhaustion, Kondrashin (if he was the loser) would say, looking with his inquiring, slightly bulging eyes, "One last hand, guys?" And sure enough we all would sit down again in silence.

Kondrashin was very happy with all the success and fame that the first Tchaikovsky Competition of 1958 and the concerts with Cliburn had brought him. If I remember correctly, he was the first unofficial Soviet citizen to be invited to the White House by President Eisenhower; it was said that Cliburn had requested it. After returning from the United States, he showed us with childish pride his American record from the Great Performers series (I wonder, could I have seen the Rimsky-Korsakov "Spanish Capriccio" on it? It was so long ago). Two years later he became the music director of the Moscow Philharmonic. Before that, Kondrashin did not always get along with the authorities nor with some singers of the Bolshoi, where he had worked for many years. During his first years at the Bolshoi the authoritative musician Ari Pazovsky, then the leader of the theater, did not particularly spare his self-esteem; Isaak Zhuk, the concertmaster of the orchestra, told me that he witnessed situations humiliating for the young Kirill. Perhaps this left an imprint on Kondrashin's character.

The one thing that angered him was my view of conducting as a blessed profession: unlike other performers you do not depend on your imperfect anatomy with the trembling, cottony fingers; the orchestra plays by itself, the score is always in front of you, and if a gifted and strong-willed musician possesses a developed conducting technique as well, he can already be considered an advanced conductor. He does not spend hours every day of his life sitting and practicing at his damned instrument. Later I realized that it is not that simple (an unfortunate attempt to conduct by the great pianist Richter is one example of many). Moments of insecurity, a nervous overload, the "anticipation of danger," and so on can reveal themselves onstage anytime. As Rimsky-Korsakov said long ago, "Conducting is a dark business." (By the way, he was not good at it either.)

Kondrashin was not easy to live with, and could be arrogant and sarcastic. One could hardly call him a warm and open person—he was intelligent, ironic, and sometimes cynical. (This is not said reproach-fully—it was a trait of the Stalin era, with its fear, lies, hypocrisy.) Against this background, some of his actions seemed almost moving. I know two of his former students whose fledgling conducting careers he helped start; at the end of the 1970s, having already settled in the West, he virtually provided three immigrant violinists with jobs in Europe.

Incidentally, at the end of 1958, a few days after my first daughter Masha was born, the telephone rang and a male voice asked for Maria Dmitrievna. I must have been slow that day, for I said "Wrong num-ber" and was about to hang up when I heard, "Mitya, it's me, Kirill—my congratulations on the brand-new baby girl!" I was moved by such friendly attention. Yet I could never call him by his first name as he asked. Because of our fifteen-year age difference and my boyish awe-struck respect for one I'd seen conduct at the Grand Hall since 1943, he remained Kirill Petrovich to me.

Interestingly, despite our friendly relations, we performed together only once (Tchaikovsky's Piano Concerto no. 2, at Tchaikovsky Hall). His technique was very high, the gestures absolutely clear, maybe a little short, which could sometimes make his performance not "large" enough (as in his Rachmaninov Symphony no. 3, in the 1960s). He progressed over time and became more profound and emotional (for example, in Shostakovich's Symphony no. 4, whose premiere, delayed by twenty-five years, the composer entrusted to Kondrashin). I also believe Kondrashin was our best accompanist, and very good in Russian operas (I also remember his *Bartered Bride* by Smetana, in the 1940s) especially before the glorious emergence of Svetlanov and Rozhdestvensky.

By that time the situation in the Moscow Philharmonic was strained—several musicians did not return from tours abroad, and as always the person in charge was guilty. Some personal problems also contributed to Kondrashin's two heart attacks, and the 1968 invasion of Czechoslovakia was traumatic for him as well. The year we moved to the outskirts of Moscow, Kirill Petrovich and I, for different reasons, sharply reduced our "gambling activity," and after that time we saw each other sporadically.

We met again in the United States after crucial changes in our lives. At the end of the 1970s, Kondrashin made the very painful decisions to defect, which created a great sensation in the music world. In July 1980 he conducted the Chicago Symphony at Ravinia. Misha Dichter played the Grieg Concerto strongly but less spontaneously than we expected from him after Moscow. Then Kondrashin carried the whole audience with him in a magnificent Symphony no. 1 by Mahler—one of the most impressive performances in my memory. The ovation was long and sincere.

My wife and I went backstage to see him. When my turn came to shake hands, we embraced each other silently for several seconds. He introduced us to his wife, Nolda, a young and gentle Dutch lady, obviously devoted to him. I handed him our phone number and asked them to save the next evening for us. Next morning he called, and we arranged that I would pick them up at the Drake Hotel. Kondrashin was elegant, as always, even though he had grown stout and become somewhat slower in his speech and movements. At home when we were alone for a minute, I told him that I could imagine how hard it had been for him not to return home, considering all the aspects of his life. He just waved his hand bitterly. "Aah, Mitya, don't ask." He looked older, and tired; almost nothing remained of that jolly sarcasm, which used to spare no one. The eyes, once filled with authority, were now sad. In telling us about his concerts, he often turned to Nolda for help: "I do not remember who the soloist was," "When are we leaving?" and so forth. He became animated only when talk turned to the past, to our house in Karetny Ryad, and so on. Kirill Petrovich complained how much he missed those evenings around the card table, the old partners, the funny, risky late-night chatter. Like chess for Oistrakh, our preference games had been an important part of Kondrashin's life, a necessary release of nervous tension. One felt in him no hatred for his former colleagues, who had spoiled his last years in Moscow. He praised Rozhdestvensky's ability to communicate with the Soviet officials in a manner at once intelligent and stiff.

This warm and nostalgic evening turned out to be our last. That December we exchanged Christmas cards, and on 20 February 1981, Kirill Petrovich Kondrashin died suddenly in Amsterdam, having con-

ducted the same Mahler First Symphony the day before. He was one
day short of his sixty-seventh birthday.

With my modest concert ambitions, I could not complain of my concert schedule in the United States between 1977 and 1985, which
included solo recitals and concertos with many orchestras, for both
regular city audiences and colleges. Often I conducted master classes,
from Grand Forks, North Dakota, to the Oberlin Conservatory in
Ohio, to the Manhattan School in New York City (twice). In 1982–
83, I made my second recording for the Musical Heritage Society
(Tchaikovsky's *The Seasons*) and played with one of the "big" American orchestras, the Rochester Philharmonic, in the 3,000-seat East-
man Theater.

I confess that I turned down two opportunities to play in New
York City. First, the Chopin Concerto in the summer of 1978 or '79,
when I was invited to substitute for one of the big guys, who canceled
on short notice; and then a couple of years later when my uncle generously offered to sponsor a recital in an important New York concert
hall. The reasons? Frankly, not only was it caution about my left hand
but perhaps even more my overall insecurity.

My schedule, of course, is hardly comparable to the stormy activity of my former Russian colleagues in New York, but it was about
what I had in mind for myself. Besides, having played more than fifteen
hundred concerts since 1955 as a full-time artist in Moscow and all
around that huge country, in Europe, Cuba, and now in the United
States, often under extreme nervous pressure, I did not regret a reduced
number of performances. For a musician it goes without saying: our
profession is not only beautiful, it is uncompromisingly demanding,
logical and at the same time irrational. To a music lover, perhaps this
book has revealed some aspects that we as musicians prefer not to talk
about. Basically, the struggle is connected with one's personal qualities—insecurity, nervousness, the nonstop effort to conquer yourself
(remember, "we have to make efforts"?), and then to start all over
again next time. As I discussed in the beginning of Chapter 3, the concert stage is only the tip of the iceberg, hidden from the uninitiated.

According to popular wisdom, an early death is the ultimate price for
being among the elect. The somber martyrology of the exceptionally
gifted, of whom only a handful made it to their forties, includes Pur-

cell, Pergolesi, Mozart, Schubert, Schumann, Mendelssohn, Chopin, Bizet, Mussorgsky, Scriabin; from the great performers, add Karl Thausig, Emanuel Feuermann, Rosa Tamarkina, Dinu Lipatti, Mario Lanza, Julian Sitkovetsky, Ginette Neveu, William Kapell (the latter two died in plane crashes, but that counts here) as well as Pushkin, Lermontov, and many others who suffered a violent death. Certainly quite a few of the great ones crossed the threshold of their sixties, and rarer, the seventies, but whose life is more typical for the musician with the divine gift: Papa Haydn or his pupil Mozart, Liszt or Chopin, Pablo Casals or Rosa Tamarkina?

Still, it is only a half-baked theory, put into practice in 1982: within three December days, the music world lost both Arthur Rubinstein, a man of great vitality, at the age of ninety-five and Leonid Kogan, at fifty-eight (like Poliakin, Kogan died suddenly on the train, on his way to play a concert in Yaroslavl). Two months earlier, at age fifty, the "insane genius" Glenn Gould had gone. Those in Moscow and Leningrad lucky enough to have heard Bach's *Goldberg Variations* from this young Canadian in 1957 will never forget the impression. The magic of a kind of shortened tone, and a corresponding, less connected articulation was something much more than a masterful stylization of the old clavier music. It seemed as if Bach himself spoke to you as your living contemporary—in person, wisely, trustingly. In his interpretations of other composers (Beethoven, Brahms) and in his general views of music performance, Gould was paradoxical, sometimes unacceptable, but always deeply principled, which he proved with all his creative work.

Many Russian musicians had concertized, taught, and in some cases lived for a time in Chicago. Here I met people who remembered not only Rachmaninov but the concerts of Yosif Levin and Nikolai Medtner in the 1920s (I have copies of their programs at Orchestra Hall—11 January 1920 and 21 and 22 November 1924, when Medtner played his C minor Concerto, op. 33, his first, with the Chicago Symphony). Prokofiev visited Chicago more than once. The Lyric Opera premiered his *The Love for Three Oranges* on 30 December 1921. With his independent and ambitious character, Prokofiev was generally much more comfortable here than Scriabin or Medtner.[5]

During Medtner's second American tour (1929–30) he became the victim of a rogue manager who had paid him a lump sum with a bad check. Only the noble intervention of Rachmaninov saved the Medtners from a painful financial blow: secretly, he "bought" the bounced check from Medtner's wife, intending to press charges against the crook. It turned out that by that time the bad guy had already spent not only Medtner's but Glazunov's and Horowitz's money as well, and attempted suicide. Many years later Anna Mikhailovna Medtner told the editor of Medtner's *Collected Letters*, "After all, Rachmaninov stopped this civil suit, telling me that for him this money was, in essence, a trifle. He never betrayed me to Nikolai Karlovich." (*Soviet Composer*, 1973).

Scriabin, who performed here in 1906–07, also felt estranged in America. It is interesting, though, to compare passages from three of his letters to his wife and friends. In the very beginning of the tour: "Concerning art, they talk nonsense, of course, and limit themselves in the main to exclamations." Soon after returning to Paris: "I really do not know whether anybody needed me with my music, but I was greeted everywhere with triumph. America loves noise and publicity." A year later: "I was pleasantly impressed with America. It seems to me that the common judgments of it by the Europeans often are very immature and one-sided. The Americans are far from being so dry and giftless in the arts as is commonly thought."

Rachmaninov settled in the United States in 1917, when he was already in his forties and famous worldwide. With his stern, reserved disposition he opened himself only to a few close, primarily Russian friends, like Medtner and Chaliapin. Thoughts of Russia never left him, and the nostalgia revealed itself with a particular bitterness in his last big works—the Symphony no. 3, op. 44 (1936) and especially in the tragic "Symphonic Dances," op. 45 (1940). His last performance with orchestra took place at Orchestra Hall in Chicago on 11 February 1943 (Beethoven's First Concerto and his own Paganini Rhapsody, Hans Lange conducting). On 17 February, already in a lot of pain, he played his last recital in Knoxville, Tennessee. A rapidly developing lung cancer sent him to his grave on 28 March, three days before his seventieth birthday. The next day, in remote Penza, I cut from *Pravda* a few short lines about his death, which shook us all then, the teachers and students of the Central School of Music. This clipping, turned yellow, is still with me.

It is quite natural that performers like Jascha Heifetz and Vladimir Horowitz, who came to America as young men, found their second motherland, in the full sense of this word, here. Perhaps the same could be said about the younger generation from the Soviet Union. I hope that a majority of them will preserve forever their Russian roots and will know, love, play, and spread the music created by our great countrymen—from Glinka and Tchaikovsky to Prokofiev and Shostakovich.

As it was during our last years in Moscow, my favorite time here comes late at night when it is quiet, and everyday problems and fuss are left behind. I open a Russian book and move for a couple of hours into another world, which will remain mine forever.

I thought long ago that the remarkable motto of the World Chess Federation—*Gens una sumus* (We are one family)—would be very appropriate for musicians. That was one more of my illusions, which gradually turned into the bitter disappointment of the last few decades of my musical life. And yet I do not want this book to end on a sadly subjective note, like other memoirs of Russian musicians. If for our outstanding writer Ivan Turgenev the Russian language was the "only support and foothold in the days of doubts and distress," then we musicians have also the most beautiful of the arts—Music.

> Thank you, my motherland,
> Thank you for such a bitter distance.
> Filled with you but not recognized by you
> I talk to myself.
> And in the nightly conversations
> Even the soul itself would not come to know
> Whether it's my insanity mumbling
> Or your music growing stronger.
>   Vladimir Nabokov

Epilogue

The years from 1983 to 1985 were a turning point for me at De-Paul. After this time, the number of new students who applied to my studio, not randomly but by specifying their choice of teacher, began to grow. (This did not mean, of course, that there were no more of the "basic minors" in my class; with some of them, our first-year lessons continued to be as much elementary theory as piano playing per se.) Into DePaul's interesting and progressive technical syllabus, I brought some more creative items from my Russian background. So now the piano seniors' final exam in technique lasts about twenty minutes and consists of a comprehensive demonstration of scales and arpeggios with inversions, double notes, and chords from the same key. Not only does it help to develop and consolidate a sense of harmony, but it constantly involves the student's mind in the performing process, since it discourages playing "with the fingers only."

From that time on, at least one third of my new students, both undergraduate and graduate, have been better prepared professionally and more intelligent; their aspirations for learning and improvement have made their years with me mutually encouraging and satisfying. Practically all received some kind of recognition sooner or later, like successfully participating in a competition, entering prestigious doctoral programs, or becoming good teachers around the country or abroad. One of my best students is Pedro Burmester, who in the mid 1980s came to me for two- to three-month sessions on the recommendation of Ashkenazy. I continue to receive reports of his quite successful concert career, both in Europe and here, and his growing reputation as a teacher in his native Porto.

In 1980, after three years, I was granted tenure, and I began the 1985 academic year as a full professor, a change that was initially opposed by the school's ad hoc committee of three faculty members, mainly because of my insufficient teaching load. I suppose this decision might have been motivated by somewhat irrelevant reasons as well—after all, many of my fellow teachers would wait more than seven or eight years for this highest promotion. Frederick Miller, the dean of the school, with whom our relations had been candid and respectful though not always smooth, decided to dispute the committee's decision. The case was turned over to the University Council. After my presentation (I had nothing to lose and my English at that time was cooperative), and a two-day hearing, including my recordings, reviews, and student evaluations, my promotion was confirmed. I mention it here since it was highly unusual in university practice to overthrow a school committee's decision.

In 1988, I received an unexpected offer from one of the country's strongest schools of music, Indiana University at Bloomington, to serve as a visiting professor for a semester. It seemed to me that DePaul was both pleased and kind of jealous, but the OK was given, and I am glad to have gone through this challenging and interesting experience. Now I can say openly that toward the end of my term I had a conversation with the person in charge at Bloomington about the possibility of staying on in a tenure-track appointment. Certainly I was flattered by this offer, but I hope I found the right words for my polite refusal. My reasoning had little to do with students or salary; by that time, having survived thirteen years of agonizing adjustments of all kinds, we had settled in Chicago, and I realized that DePaul University and the School of Music had become an important part of my life, professionally and personally alike. The sincere friendship of Rev. John Richardson, then the university president; of Deans Frederick Miller, and later, Donald Casey; and a few faculty and staff people, as well as my first dear saviors in Chicago, Arrand Parsons and Norman Pellegrini, helped us enormously. I can hardly imagine my life since 1977 without these people.

In some cases, emigration à la Soviet, with no return ever, even to one's mother's funeral, and yet with a constant and sharp nostalgia, was quite devastating. One of the best poets of the so-called third Russian emigration, Naum Korzhavin, expressed it in two spare lines, as only a poet could do:

> I died there
> And will not rise here.

But I thank God again for saving enough of my sense of humor to let me appreciate the following American humor as well:
"Are you homesick?"
"No, I'm here sick."

Beginning in 1985 I played in Europe again, in Palma de Majorca, Paris, then the Netherlands, Portugal, Belgium, and elsewhere. With the exceptions of Palma, Lisbon, and Diligentsia Hall in the Hague, these were neither big nor popular concert halls, accommodating a range of between 150 to 500 people. Inevitably for me, I did not feel good about some concerts (one in Leiden, one in Lisbon, another in a small town near Munich). What I found interesting and in a way encouraging was that these unfortunate recitals were sometimes followed the very next day (in Paris, Arnhem, Porto, and Antwerp) by ones that were possibly the best in the last period of my concert career, and practically impeccable pianistically as well.

I had included several new pieces in my repertoire, such as Schubert's Fantasy from the G major Sonata, D. 894; Brahms' Seven Fantasies, op. 116; Liadov's Variations on a Polish Theme, op. 51; and Medtner's A minor Sonata Reminiscenza, op. 38 (the latter was especially noted by a Parisian reviewer). As always, as soon as I felt myself master of the situation I started to communicate spontaneously what I could lately do better—a sense of timing and phrasing. With no false modesty, I felt very satisfied when several critics noticed and appreciated these qualities.

The year 1985 had its dark side too—we lost several people close and dear to us. In January, my uncle Mark Millard died in New York City, an uncommon man in many respects. An intelligent businessman with an artistic nature, he spoke six languages and was modest to the point of shyness. Soon after the 1917 revolution, his parents had taken the nine-year-old boy abroad to Hungary, Germany, France, and finally to the United States, where his career developed rapidly. My mother, his older cousin, always remembered him warmly and with a kind of peculiar pride, as the one successful member of the Paperno clan.

It was hard to believe, looking at this modestly dressed, reserved man who quoted Tolstoy or spoke knowledgeably about his Piranesi collection, how successful his business career was. Any kind of publicity was alien to him; he did not encourage the mention of his name in the original *Notes*, nor even the expression of our gratitude for his generosity. Only once did he allow his emotions to show slightly, after reading my book, when he sensed again the family ties lost long ago. Mark died three months after our last meeting in New York, just collapsed in his office one morning. I decided not to tell my mother about his death.

From a letter of Lidia Ivanova (1896–1985):

4 March 1982. Rome.
In the memoirs of my father, I tried to speak of myself as little as possible. Therefore, there is not much about our teacher [Goldenweiser], who was so closely associated with my musical life. Here are two short sketches from the chaotic period soon after the revolution:

"Alexander Borisovich possessed an amazing self-restraint. A young Conservatory student came into our class once. He startled me by talking with Alexander Borisovich for several minutes in an impudent, almost insulting tone. I was shocked and expected a strong reaction from Alexander Borisovich. He covered his face with both hands, and kept quiet while the student talked, then calmly but dryly and politely said goodbye.[1] He obviously kept control of himself, and I am sure that it was Lev Nikolayevich Tolstoy who had helped him.

"In 1918–19, Goldenweiser invited me to illustrate on piano the patterns of sacred music for a public lecture by V. G. Chertkov [1854–1936, a close friend and follower of Tolstoy]. At first, I was happy and flattered that he entrusted it to me, but later started to look at it differently—what would Chertkov talk about? Would he come out against the church at this terrible period of our life? Having overcome my extreme bashfulness I called him up. 'I am the one Goldenweiser wants to play for your lecture, but first I want to know whether you are going to talk against the church.' He was surprised and then said with Tolstoy's straightforwardness, 'Of course I am.' I told him that I declined to play. When I informed Goldenweiser, he got very angry. 'Are you out of your mind? What did you tell Chertkov? Why did you call?' I explained, 'To make sure about the lecture.' 'You have nothing to do with this. You were just to play the religious music.' 'No, Alexander Borisovich, it would be participating.' And that was that. Yet I felt that Alexander Borisovich appreciated my being firm in my principles."

Even in her elderly years, Lidia Ivanova kept composing, and also got involved in literary work. In 1981 she and her brother Dimitry came to the United States to take part in Yale University's symposium on their famous father's literary legacy and were our guests in Chicago. In late June 1985, my wife and I were among the last friends who saw the dying Lidia in Rome. Two weeks later, Dimitry called us up with news of her death. We will always keep in our memory this amazing family, who embodied the high spirituality of the genuine Russian intelligentsia.

Yet I have more reasons to remember Lidia than my wife does: she was a gifted and refined musician, and the one who taught me to appreciate a good scotch and soda. But seriously—thank you, Lidia, for everything.

From a letter of Xenia Leontieva (1901–1985):

27 June 1983. Gulfport, Florida
I read [your book] through for a day and a half, and then could not sleep, it stirred up so much in my memory. The photograph of the dying Heinrich Gustavovich Neuhaus with Arthur Rubinstein, both of whom I had known well, made me cry bitterly. . . .

In 1917 I studied with Heinrich Gustavovich in Tbilisi, where my family moved from the Bolsheviks. Only then did a new world in music open for me. I still remember how he explained the Chopin pieces. . . .

In 1935 I met Neuhaus in Warsaw, where he and Abram Ilyich Yampolsky brought David Oistrakh and the fourteen-year-old Busya Goldstein to the Weniawsky Competition. . . . They both had Stradivariuses, which was a subject of long talks in Warsaw. Oistrakh should have had the first prize, not the second. At his final recital he came onstage, very skinny, in shabby dress, with a long tie like a cord. Those in elegant Warsaw who were used to seeing the soloist in tails were shocked.

The next day, Neuhaus gave a lecture on music education in the Soviet Union. They did not allow anyone to see him backstage and talk (exactly as it was many years later here, with Gilels

and Richter). During his lecture, Heinrich Gustavovich noticed
me and stopped for a second. Later I learned that he told his
friend, the conductor Fitelberg, that to live in Poland would be
his dream but his family in Moscow would be held there.

You wrote that before lighting a cigarette, Heinrich Gustavovich scented it with perfume. My God, I remembered that he
did it with my first cigarette in 1918! He was very depressed then,
felt the revolution keenly, and all the cruelty and murders. He
lamented that his small hands did not allow him to be in complete
command over the piano, but it was news to me that he tried to
commit suicide after Rubinstein's concert. You see, I remember
Rubinstein before he was forty, when he used to miss and
"choked" a lot, sometimes even seemed not to care about his
playing. I remember a soiree at my guardian's home in Warsaw
when Rubinstein, while playing Chopin's Fourth Ballade for a
crowded gathering, switched suddenly in the middle to a popular tango and finished again with the Ballade. Could such a wild
thing occur to Neuhaus? After that, I was disappointed in him
until he became a "real Rubinstein." It was the conductor Mly-
narski who exerted a strong positive influence upon him, when
Rubinstein married his daughter—mature behavior was said to be
a condition of the marriage.

The old Russian lady who wrote this warm and spontaneous letter—one of the first responses to the *Notes*—had lived a long and difficult life. Xenia Leontieva lost her parents at an early age, moved to
Warsaw in 1922, where she graduated from the Conservatory, and
then lived in Paris for thirty years. She taught both French and Russian
at several universities in the United States before retiring to Florida. A
Russian to the core, Xenia found her second motherland in France.
She met and communicated with a long list of outstanding musicians—
Stravinsky, Liszt's famous pupil Emil Sauer, and "our genius Chalia-
pin," with whom she worked for three months as an extra at the Grand
Opéra in Paris.

Her first years in the United States were very hard; she missed Paris
and her French and Russian friends. But it was fifteen years before she
could afford to return there, and she looked forward to spending three
months in the familiar atmosphere of her past. A bitter disappointment
awaited her—this atmosphere no longer existed: the country and its
people had changed, many of her friends had died, those still alive
turned out to be different. Apparently she made the same impression

on them. In two months she was ready to leave. When a customs officer at the New York airport told her "Welcome home, ma'am," she
could hardly keep her composure and thought, "He is right, it really is
my only home now."

We met with Madame Leontieva only once, when I played my
concert in St. Petersburg in 1984, and we spoke to our heart's content.
After this meeting, through letters and long telephone conversations I
could imagine her as clearly as though our acquaintance had lasted not
two but many years. In May 1985 I opened the Russian-American
newspaper and a familiar name framed in black struck my eyes.

In mid October 1985, Norman Pellegrini called us up from WFMT.
"Mitya, sad news. Gilels died in Moscow of a heart attack. Knowing
what he meant to you, I decided to tell you before it goes on the air."

After his recital in Chicago and our meeting at the Drake Hotel in
1979, our relations with Gilels had grown richer in trust and confidence, despite our never seeing one another. In the spring of 1983,
Gilels was the only one of the Soviet artists, in those years of broken
Soviet-American cultural contacts, to give a concert in New York
City, unexpectedly even for him. I learned of it from a student of mine
who was leaving the next day for New York. Unfortunately, instead of
making immediate reservations for concert and plane tickets, all I did
was to draft him in haste a very candid letter, in which there was more
than just token admiration. Without even making a fair copy, I handed
it to the student along with the just-published *Notes*, which book was
to be given to my old Russian friend and colleague, Nina Svetlanova,
who had taught in New York for years. But in the backstage confusion,
both the letter and the book came into Gilels' hands.

This was by no means part of my plans, and I was apprehensive that
Gilels, with his complex nature, might take offense at several lines in
the book describing his long-lasting rivalry with Richter. In my situation, I could not risk losing his goodwill, as had happened many times
with people closer to him than I. In short, when the telephone rang the
next morning my first thought was that it could be him, and the next,
that I wouldn't be ready if the conversation took an undesirable turn.
I was so unprepared that when he said "Good morning," I could only
ask, instead of greeting him, "So, are you mad?"

And here a long, rambling, candid conversation began, which
revealed Gilels, for me, as I think not many people had known him—

kind, natural, and frank. For the first minutes he talked about the book nonstop, as he had read it off the night before at one sitting—how many accurate observations and portrayals there were, and how much the Soviet readers, especially in Moscow, needed it, and so forth. I do not want to appear boastful, but one can understand what I felt, receiving such appreciation from the idol of my youth and the oldest friend of the last twenty-five years. It was a conversation that one remembers forever. Only one phrase of his cut me sharply and made me fall silent, when he said with an unusual intonation, "You know, Mitya, I was sure that I would see you this time in New York."

We called each other up a couple more times, talked again for half an hour, moving from his concerts to my current situation, from pre-war Moscow to Stalin's role in his life. (Incidentally, Gilels, unlike me, assumed that Stalin might have listened on the last day of his life to the Mozart D minor Piano Concerto, as the Shostakovich-Volkov *Testimony* has it.) Everything was like a continuation of the first talk, which had really drawn us together, cordial and trustful. We had been awaiting Gilels' next trip to the United States for more than two years. Finally, the tour was announced, including Chicago—1 December 1985.

I first heard him live in the autumn of 1943, from the gallery of the Grand Hall, and he was only twenty-seven then. Since then this image has stayed in my memory, of a stocky, unsmiling, robust fellow; this wonder of a projected yet velvety *piano* and a powerful *forte*, without knocking, which he could create with his hands—very handsome ones, by the way, strong and flexible. More than half a century has passed since then, and what years these were! Already we anticipated hearing his recital at the other end of the world and then having him as our guest. And instead—he is gone, and it is still difficult to accept.

A telegram concerning my mother from Elena Ivanovna Goldenweiser, received 20 November 1985: "Ida passed away peacefully on the 18th. Letter follows." From the letter:

> She died simply from weakness, as they say—went out like a candle. Till the last day she was the same, wishing everyone well, satisfied and thankful for everything, as always—complained of nothing. On the 18th at 1:10 p.m. she stopped breathing. She lived in this world with dignity and left it in the same way. Let the memory of the woman who was more than a mother to you pre-

serve you on all your roads. I know from my own experience that our dearests sometimes help us more from there than they could do when they were near us. I have never stopped feeling, with absolute reality, the presence in my life of Alexander Borisovich and my wonderful parents alike. Love is a genuine, real miracle, you know.

In August 1988, after a summer festival in Finland, I finally found myself back in Moscow. Those few days were filled with mixed and hard-to-describe emotions. I shall never forget being at my mother's grave, especially the first time. It was also hard to believe it was happening when I entered Alexander Borisovich's classroom, studio 42, in the Conservatory. Elena Ivanovna and I walked upstairs to the fourth floor of my alma mater, almost deserted in summer. She had the keys to the classroom and both pianos. We spent about half an hour there, almost in silence, took a few pictures. I circled the studio, sat down and played on his piano (Beethoven, Andante Favori) and at the students' one (Scriabin, the first movement from the Second Sonata). Of course, several times I met my other beloved old lady—Leah Levinson, who was then eighty-three, and spent a couple of hours in the Goldenweiser museum-apartment, where I had given my last Moscow performance twelve years earlier.

During this visit, I copied a short correspondence between my dear teacher and Neuhaus, two great but very different men. The letters were given to me by Elena Ivanovna. When the opportunity to publish my book in English first emerged, I gave the idea of making them public a lot of thought, and consulted with E. I., who approved and gave her permission for publication. Here in their entirety are these two deeply personal and moving documents, which have sat for almost forty years in Goldenweiser's archive:

10 January 1958
Dear Alexander Borisovich! Forgive me my behavior last Wednesday. About 16–17 years ago something went astray inside me (personal adversities, the incurable illness and death of my son). I struggle against the tireless desire for putting an end to my life, even though I love life, but not myself in it. I have an almost pathological striving to be offensive to people. But I have never done vile things to people personally even though I was capable of outraging them, including you.

Somehow I am not suited to this life. A melancholy and suffering, from which one often wants to howl, will not leave me alone. The only two months I was happy I spent last summer in Tsihisjavari, where I worked a lot and did not drink wine at all. I am dreaming of retirement, and then . . . Forgive me this incoherent letter. Maybe you will feel that I deserve compassion rather than anger.

Your old and ill-fated colleague, H. N.

Dear Heinrich Gustavovich, your letter affected me deeply enough to make me cry. Thank you for the moral trust, without which you would not write me this way. I love you and appreciate highly your beautiful talent and exceptional culture.

I have always tried not to blame people, and I always suffer and feel deeply sorry for you. What you are doing is the very "blasphemy against the Holy Spirit" about which Christ spoke so sharply. I embrace you as my friend, and wish wholeheartedly you may free yourself from the heavy burden that poisons your life physically and morally.

Your *very* old friend, A. Goldenweiser

January 10, 1958

And one more general impression, present every minute in Moscow—"language shock." Receiving and understanding every word said at the noisy emotional parties each evening, in the crowded streets, metro and buses, cemetery, stores and food markets—everywhere— was a long-forgotten feeling.

In the middle of my first night back in Chicago, I was awakened by an airline employee, returning my lost suitcase. Lucya and Anya still recall with laughter my state of exhaustion and confused sense of time and place, when I shook his hand, and kept saying "*Spasibo*," thinking to myself, "Since when are the delivery guys in Moscow so polite— and black?"

Before turning sixty I became, almost by accident, keen on stamp collecting. After an initial disorderly period I narrowed my philatelic interests down to one country (Russia) and two topics (music and chess). This hobby not only gives me hours of sheer enjoyment but happens to be quite educational—I started bringing my book of musical stamps and covers to my piano literature students, and we would spend one lesson observing and discussing the role of music in history in this new and interesting light. For instance, thanks to the first-day cover of the beautiful Czechoslovak Chopin stamp of 1949, I finally got factual confirmation of e-natural (for C major) in the third bar of the short C minor Prelude, op. 28, no. 20, instead of the e-flat that appears in many editions, including the Paderewski, and which has always sounded wrong to me: Chopin's manuscript on the left side of the envelope, the so-called *cachet*, clearly shows no restored e-flat on the fourth beat.

In the beginning of 1989, a few days before my sixtieth birthday, Slava Rostropovich and I played a cello-piano recital in Pasadena, California. First I flew to Washington, D.C., where he had been for many years music director of the National Symphony. Three years earlier he had invited me to attend one of the premiere performances of Rimsky-Korsakov's *The Tsar's Bride* under his baton and directed by his wife, soprano Galina Vishnevskaya, at the Kennedy Center. It was a very impressive and moving production, truly Russian, without all those sham accessories, costumes and make-up *à la Russe*, which often reveal the producer's and director's lack of education or taste. Slava then very nicely handed me the afterword he had written for my second, shorter book *Postscriptum* (published by AMGA the next year), part of which concludes this book.

That is when I witnessed for the first time his enormously over-loaded work schedule—rehearsing both operatic and symphonic repertoire, studying the score alone, and so on. Yet what I experienced in 1989—when I flew to Washington a couple of days before our concert in Pasadena and became a part of Slava's insane pace—was not something an ordinary professional like myself could survive. Just to give an idea of these days—two of our three rehearsals started after his concerts, at midnight, from scratch. You can imagine our last night in the capital, and yet we took off for Los Angeles at nine o'clock in the morning, tried the big concert hall in Pasadena for an hour or so, had a late lunch, a lousy sleepless rest, a cup of coffee, and left for the concert. No wonder I did not feel well; my hands were shaking slightly and felt like cotton, which Slava did not even worry about. In the exposition of the last Beethoven Cello Sonata, op. 102, no. 2, I had to push my way through, which fortunately worked out that time, and before the repeat I managed to catch my breath. We really did it well, especially the powerful final fugue. There was another big work in the

second half, Nikolai Miaskovsky's A minor Sonata, no. 2, op. 81 (dedicated to the young Slava in 1948), which the large audience received
very warmly. The only concession I asked of Slava was not to play the
Weber piece for an encore, the score of which he had given me only
the evening before.

The concert was met with a big, enthusiastic reception. Both
newspapers gave me brief but appreciative reviews. "Technical assur-
ance, interpretive eloquence, and accommodating dynamics—even
for Rostropovich's most feathery playing—characterized the accom-
paniments of Dmitry Paperno" (Los Angeles *Times*, 14 February 1989);
"Dmitry Paperno was the evening's more-than-adequate piano partner." (Los Angeles *Herald Examiner*). The day after the concert, we
departed in different directions, cordially as always.

Back in 1988 I had received a telephone call from James Ginsburg, a
young man who said he had played for me once several years before.
He made me some sort of business offer, regarding a "commercial
recording." Either my English was not at its best that day, or I simply
did not take it seriously. But he obviously did, since after two recording sessions in the summer of 1989 Cedille Records issued a compact
disc—*Dmitry Paperno Plays Russian Piano Music* (CDR 90000 001)–the
first for both of us. This marked the beginning of a friendly and fruitful business relationship. All the reviews were favorable, and the next
summer our second disc followed (*German Program*, CDR 90000 002).

On 19 March 1990 during a recital in Columbus, Ohio, I noticed
for the first time a very slight discomfort in a few descending technical
patterns, similar to what I'd experienced in 1977, but this time in my
right hand. I got the message right away and shared it plainly with my
wife and our friend Dora Levenstein as we left the concert hall, pleasantly excited at a successful recital: "That's it."

My feelings were mixed. I realized that since whatever it was had
now touched my right hand, it was only a matter of time. (Nobody
even knew what the impairment was, because there had been no firm
diagnosis thirteen years earlier.) Maybe some of my readers have noticed my response to what happened in 1977, when, after the initial
period of frustration (and maybe, more than that), I took full advantage
of my chance to survive as a concert pianist. At forty-eight, in the very
beginning of my American career, it was simply a must for me. True,
I couldn't have done much to help myself if it had happened to my

right hand, and the fact that it started in the left gave me my fifty-fifty chance.

Since then there have been other quite serious "tests" of different kinds, and I would prefer to unite them all in one pattern—of survival. When I try to figure out what the few sinister happenings in our life here might have in common, I come up with an unexpectedly positive result: they all could have ended up worse, much worse. . . .

It is natural that age draws us toward meditation and religious thoughts. Even those who have spent most of their lives in atheistic surroundings discover the comforting sense of some higher power that does not abandon you, or at least watches over you in hard times. And I want to believe that my right hand's being effected was another interference in my life of this power whose intentions we cannot always comprehend right away.

In 1990 I was already over sixty; I had a long and interesting concert career behind me and at least one more year onstage ahead, a steady teaching position, and a second compact disc in preparation. There were actually no problems with making the German disc: the "it" had been taking its time, unwinding very gradually. My third finger was getting weaker, but the coordination of the three middle fingers was disturbed only slightly. I kept playing both recitals and performances with orchestra; some of them were quite successful (the second one in Lisbon, and in Antwerp, where my friend of recent years, the late Denise DeVries-Tolkowsky, simply did not believe my story).

At the end of 1991 I decided to accept an invitation for another concert in Columbus, and scheduled it for 19 March 1992. It was the date of our departure from Moscow in 1976, my first American recital in Chicago the next year, of my memorable concert on the very stage two years earlier. To feel freer in conveying my musical message on this particular evening, I addressed the hundreds of people who packed the hall, emphasizing the very special meaning of this last full-size recital in my career. For the same reason, I also decided to play with an open score in front of me, most of the time without looking at it. To crown it all, I played on Horowitz's beautiful piano, which was touring the country for some promotional purpose and was placed for a couple of days at this particular concert hall in Columbus. It is hard, is it not, to imagine a better way to end one's long career?

Meanwhile, Cedille, in spite of knowing the whole story, sug-

gested making one more CD. It was a wild plan, but Jim Ginsburg
eventually convinced me to give it a try, whatever might come of it,
even a complete waste of time. I picked sixteen short pieces for this
disc, including several piano transcriptions, embracing almost two hundred years of music history (from Bach to Shchedrin), as well as great
stylistic and pianistic diversity. God knows how I made it. I can only
say that decades of mastery and handicraft served me well. Taking
into account the unusual circumstances of these two seven-hour
recording sessions in July 1992, and the hours of editing, this disc might
well be considered "highly uncommon." (*Uncommon Encores*, CDR
90000 007).

In 1991–92, two outstanding Russian musicians visited us for the first
time after their concerts in Chicago. We had become more closely
acquainted with the very talented composer Rodion Shchedrin in the
1960s, when I added several of his pieces to my repertoire and could
not find the score of his most popular Basso Ostinato. I came over to
his apartment to pick it up and stayed awhile to talk and play some
Chopin at his request. We were on informal terms with him, no more
than that. I have always found him a great musician, a man of impeccable uprightness and intelligence. In October 1990, Rodion and his
wife, the legendary ballerina Maya Plisetskaya, came to Chicago for
the premiere of his *Russian Circus Music* commissioned by the Chicago
Symphony, a witty and brightly orchestrated piece as always. The next
day I picked them up from the Drake Hotel, and we had one of those
unforgettable evenings at our place.

Miss Plisetskaya, one of the greatest ballerinas ever, does not need
any introduction for those who have even once seen her dancing.
Maybe not everybody knows, though, that Shchedrin, besides being
one of the most notable composers, is also an advanced pianist, a pupil
of Yakov Flier, who had greatly influenced his musical growth. Without Flier, the list of Shchedrin's works for piano (Twenty-four Preludes
and Fugues, sonatas, concertos, solo pieces) would not be as impressive.

Another of our guests was especially close to me, even though we
might not have seen each other in Moscow for several years at a time.
One crucial fact always brought us together with Tatiana Nikolayeva,
no matter what—we belonged to the prewar Goldenweiser Old
Guard. I have mentioned already that we both came to Moscow to
his class in the Central School of Music in 1937 and were even assigned

to the same assistants—first to Nadezhda Andreevna Svetozarova, and two years later to Kliachko. We had many shared memories from those bygone years—lessons with our Old Man, numerous students' concerts, both public and before the jury, even a couple of children's parties at the end of the 1930s. Early on, my mother had noticed this typical Russian girl, with her two braids, always serious, friendly, and neat. I am sure that even then the grown-ups sensed under the teenage appearance some solid substance commanding their respect.

After the war, along with her amazing accumulation of piano repertoire, Tanya became very successful in composition as well. In 1950 she won—triumphantly—the Bach Competition in Leipzig with Shostakovich first on the jury panel and later in the closing concert as one of her two partners in Bach's Triple Clavier Concerto. Instantly, she began a long and brilliant career—including the historic premiere of Shostakovich's Twenty-four Preludes and Fugues, written expressly for her, and the highest Stalin award for her piano concerto.[2] Soon after, she started to teach at the Conservatory, performed often in the big Soviet cities and also abroad. She seemed never even to notice the inevitable jealous and unfair whispers behind her back, which as usual came from colleagues on a less sophisticated intellectual level. With all her dignity, Tatiana had never been arrogant with anyone, maybe just less smiling with some. I can hardly imagine her complaining or being outraged—angry sometimes, but always self-controlled. And such was her playing, full of wisdom, dignity, always conveying a strong message. Her steady success and worldwide popularity as a performer and teacher had made her life happy and satisfying in spite of the loss of her two husbands and many inevitable complications. She was born to be a major artist.

One of the most striking qualities of this profound musical personality is her phenomenal memory. Balzac once said that talent is first of all a matter of quantity. In Nikolayeva's case there was much more to it than that, yet her ability to keep an incredible amount of music in her memory and recall it quickly could be an unsurpassed world record. Nowadays more and more pianists play the whole of Bach's *Well-Tempered Clavier*, or all Beethoven's sonatas, or Chopin's preludes; not many do the complete set of Shostakovich's Preludes, op. 34, and almost nobody the ingenious Twenty-four Preludes and Fugues, op. 87. But all this, combined with literally hundreds of hours of piano works of many stylistic periods, genres, and durations, played by a female performer, a wife, mother, and grandmother, a successful composer and teacher herself—does it not deserve our utmost amazement and admiration? In my course on piano literature I usually give a few short Bach pieces (like the inventions) played by Glenn Gould and Tatiana Nikolayeva for a comparative evaluation. Drastically contrasting presentations, but each highly convincing. In no way would Tanya lose this anonymous competition.

So in October 1992, Tatiana played Shostakovich's Twenty-four Preludes and Fugues at Orchestra Hall in Chicago. I could not make it to the first performance, but on the second afternoon I took a seat not far from the stage. I felt a kind of warm sadness when she came out, an old Russian woman, quite heavy and walking slowly. Only the familiar kindly interest in her eyes, her readiness for another session of the labor of her life—to communicate music to people—and her spontaneous facial expression while playing (like raised eyebrows when something new was coming) carried me back to our common past. What a wise and humane performance it was! For encores she played only Bach this time—a fragment from *The Art of the Fugue*, and the Preamble from the Fifth Partita in G, which simply could not be played better.

Our meeting backstage, after almost twenty years, was very warm, in spite of Tatiana's reported disagreement with some aspects of my *Notes*, which had been circulated at the Moscow Conservatory even before the period of *glasnost*. Her visit to our apartment next day was so friendly that we simply could not stop talking. Tanya's memory amazed me again. She remembered some things about me that I did not—a few details from my tenth birthday party and how I played Bach's three-part A major Invention for Alexander Borisovich at about the same time. We had a little vodka, and she did two short impersonations, of "Shostakovich after a few drinks" and of our Old Man, covering his face and saying in his high-pitched voice, "I don't understand . . ." when he was not happy with our playing. It was so good, full of artistry.

One year later, soon after starting the same Shostakovich cycle in San Francisco, Tanya suffered a mild stroke and left the stage,[3] but a second blow, this time a deadly one, followed, and she died a couple of days later in the hospital without regaining consciousness. Another tragic loss, Tatiana Nikolayeva, 1993, at age sixty-nine.

Music lives by thought.

—Scriabin

One plays piano with one's head and ears first of all, and only then with the hands.

—Neuhaus

Having recalled my fifty years' experience as a student, concert pianist, and teacher, it might make sense to state briefly a few of the practical observations I try to implement (and not always unsuccessfully) in my studio. To begin, let us acknowledge, in a very simplified form, two special features that make piano performance truly unique. For one thing, having the whole structure of a piece of music under his or her two hands, a pianist is the single representative of the composer to the listener. Secondly, piano playing is probably the only case when the performer, after producing a musical tone, cannot prolong or amplify it in the way a bow, breathing, or vocal chords can. So it is up to us (providing that we are at least moderately gifted, clever, and caring) to compensate for the piano's shortcoming, or even turn it to our advantage.

Let me remind you of von Bülow's declaration: "In the beginning there was rhythm." In Chapter 3, if you remember, I mentioned a kind of voluntary self-limitation ("frames of rhythm"), which some initial monophonic set of tones imposes upon itself. After that, any rhythmically organized musical line could be considered a melody. Chaos becomes music.

Recently I have given several lectures on the role of harmony in piano performance. My constant care as a teacher was to implant in students a sense of harmony as our best ally and guide.[4] Since it appeared "the day after melody and rhythm," harmony has been an integral part of music, and for us, the pianists, a real blessing. In fact, I'd say that the main difference between a skilled amateur (a category I deeply respect) and a mediocre professional hack is a knowledge of harmony, even though the amateur *senses* only its mysterious beauty, and the mediocre hack *knows* only its theoretical side. But what will happen in music education if a person with a degree in his pocket does not know harmony, but only elementary theory at best? How many and what kind of students can this kind of teacher cripple and launch into a highly competitive professional life? And how about the generation of these students' students? Will I ever forget my first freshman's question during our lesson, "Excuse me, Mr. P, but what's a subdominant?" I can hardly call it depressing; it's disastrous.

But enough of these pessimistic digressions. Let's think positively—good professional piano playing is in progress. All its components function smoothly in full accord with each other, bound together into long lines. Thanks to a projected tone, lively rhythm, natural dynamics, and so on, you begin to feel that the music speaks to you, communicating its images and messages. The miracle of musical communication cannot be expressed in words, and so I won't even attempt to decorate this simplified picture. I only want to approach, logically, the cornerstone of musical performance: "To speak."

When in 1969 I worked on my essay about phrasing in piano performance, I was encouraged to observe how much attention our great predecessors paid to the subject. I'll mention just one brief example, from Marguerite Long's *Le Piano*: "Our fingers should pronounce the notes as our lips pronounce the syllables. Well-articulated playing, without dryness, is as precious an advantage for a pianist as good articulation is for an actor." Since human and musical speech are so closely associated, let us take the analogy a step further and talk about one of the most characteristic qualities of speech—pace, or tempo.

Nikolai Gogol, one of the greatest Russian writers, said that you would never prevail in an argument by getting into a temper and proving points hastily. In other words, one can hardly convince someone else by speaking too fast. I have in mind here an inner sense of timing that tends to make our spoken intonations more credible. Without falling into vulgarization, one can apply it to musical speech as well. Every performer loses some technical precision and reliability with age, but achieved experience and human maturity help him to convey a musical idea in his and only his way—distinctly, without choking over words (musical intonations) and syllables (short motives, notes). For me, a direct connection between the manner of speaking and playing is obvious in many cases. As a rule, the "quick talkers" play in the same accelerated fashion, often as if swallowing the points of meaning. The only difference is that in the first case the thought is outstripped by the tongue, while in the second, by the fingers. It takes a person with a real artistic nature to transform himself in his art, including his manner of speech. (In his book, *My System*, Stanislavsky even cites a few examples of stuttering actors who once onstage, in character—"within the image"—stopped stuttering.)

Think how much playing a piano and driving a car have in common, where speed is taken for granted, but haste translates to danger; they both require fast reactions and plasticity of performance, an ability to differentiate "in motion" the more important from the less important, and a proper "average pace," as Igumnov put it. And don't we all know how many aggressive yet slow-thinking drivers there are on our roads!

Just listen to old recordings and you'll see how much faster, in general, the tempos were before 1930. The concept of virtuoso playing corresponded fully then to its root meaning, *virtus* (valor). We in the Conservatory had fast, reliable fingers ourselves, and everybody was flattered to have a reputation as a virtuoso. Then, with maturity—and thanks to Sofronitsky, Ginsburg, Gilels, and later Richter, Michelangeli, and others—something new started to emerge in our own playing—very gradually, though. Probably it was a desire for a more distinct, colloquial way of expression. In 1958 Van Cliburn contributed much to this development of "drawling," time-stretching playing. Now, several decades later, a performer cannot surprise us with fast tempos (or maybe only as a great technical trick)—it goes without saying that pianists with insufficient technique do not make it to the concert stage. The priority of intellect; a natural, speechlike phrasing; clarity of intent; and very few but powerful culminations—these, in my opinion, define contemporary performance style.

The great musicians of the past lived so much ahead of their time that some of the following statements on this topic still sound fresh and vital. In a letter to his father, Mozart wrote, "It is much easier to play the piece faster than slower. You can skip several notes or make changes in both hands and nobody will notice it. But what's the good of it?" Or (attention, my young fellow pianists!): "They all get surprised when I always keep an exact time. They cannot imagine a tempo rubato when the left hand knows nothing about it; in their playing it is always subordinate to the right."

Compare this with Chopin's instructions to his students: "Let your left hand be your conductor." Chopin wrote to Liszt, "You always have something to hit your audience over the head with, a gift I do not have." This is not about Liszt's technical superiority, or faster tempos, as it may seem at first, but rather the different aesthetic principles of their magnificent arts. Now we can better appreciate the wise observation of Grigory Kogan: "If Mozart had lived in the nineteenth century he would be composing the music of Chopin." (Maybe it is not an accident that Mozart and Chopin are the best embodiments of the Midas touch in music.) Liszt, in his turn, put it this way: "If you cannot play a piece in a slow tempo, it is not ready yet." And finally, from George Enescu, possibly the most versatile musician of our century, a statement which so strongly appealed to Oistrakh that he quoted it in his *Recollections*, 1966: "Declare war on speed in order to phrase naturally—it is a must. When you are playing, make your musical speech absolutely clear." I cannot help expressing my admiration for these golden words.

Returning to the latest achievements in the performing arts, I would say without hesitation that the contemporary performance style is rooted in historic and social developments as well. Indeed, it is necessary for people living in this mad, mad world—full of cruelty, cynicism, tension, and haste—to escape from time to time into a completely different realm. Music speaks to us on equal ground, with both dignity and trust, without pushing or trying to convince us of anything. A sense of being part of something eternal, strong, and kind elevates us above the surrounding fuss (not to say vileness) and saves our self-esteem.

I want to believe that at least some readers might accept this postwar phenomenon as a natural evolution of the public's preference in music. But since both the musicians and the public are parts of the same society with its changing cultural needs, new modes of expression are inherent in the tastes and aspirations of each. In other words, a slower, more dignified manner of communication is becoming common for musicians not simply to satisfy public demand, but because it is now the most natural expression for them.

> The service of the Muses does not tolerate a fuss.
> The beautiful should be stately.
> —Pushkin, 1825

Recent years have brought another generation of my graduates, summer festivals in the Czech Republic, and several more master classes, in Israel, in Portugal, and most significantly, at the Moscow Conservatory.

A poster on the first floor announced my master class, conducted on 5 December 1996 in studio 42. I addressed Sergei Dorensky (the dean), Gleb Axelrod, Naum Starkman, and the several dozen other people who had gathered, trying to emphasize the special meaning the event had for me: for the first time I was sitting at Alexander Borisovich's second piano, in his chair, as a teacher. It took several minutes for me to pull myself together, despite the many familiar faces and friendly atmosphere. Running behind even more than usual in the three-hour class, I did not have a chance to hear the fourth student, a girl who had prepared to play Debussy, to our mutual regret. But the performances of the other three students (which included a Chopin polonaise and several numbers from Schumann's *Kreisleriana*, op. 16, and *Klavierstucke*, op. 32) were decent overall, with communication, reactions, and receptivity on the level of my best students, which did not surprise me.

During the course of my ten-day stay in Moscow I met once again with Elena Ivanovna Goldenweiser, Leah Levinson, and many other dear people who had been a part of my Soviet life. Twice I visited with Nikolai Vedernikov, a classmate of mine since pre-war days and through my Conservatory years, and now a leading Russian Orthodox clergyman; he has been a confessor to quite a few Russian musicians, including Tatiana Nikolayeva. Our first reencounter, at St. John the Warrior, his beautiful small church, was particularly emotional, as his parishioners could attest. Even as we spoke and laughed casually over our shared recollections of some sixty years past, a calm and wise force radiated from him. Russia's hope for resurrection depends on people like Father Nikolai.

It looks like we have finally made it through almost six decades of places and characters. In 1995 my granddaughter, Alexandra (Sasha), was born; the next year brought my grandson, Sam. No one can tell what destiny life has in store for us. I am old enough to take every day with my family, friends, and students—as well as with my music, books, and the world around—as a bonus.

I thank my good Lord again for letting me fulfill in my life what I have.

And I thank you, my patient reader, as well.

Afterword

Here we are, meeting at the end of Dmitry Paperno's book. I am glad that, between Vladimir Ashkenazy's Foreword and this Afterword we have been able to frame the testimony of our friend.

One reads this book so easily that it sometimes seems as though you are having a conversation with a highly intelligent person—certainly a stroke of good fortune nowadays.

My friend, Mitya Paperno, was one grade below me at the Central School of Music in Moscow. Apart from his musical talent and clean-cut look, he distinguished himself among us Moscow urchins of the 1930s and '40s by his intellectual skepticism. Now, a half-century later, this quality has grown noticeably stronger and developed into a nostalgia for our past. And I, who do not share this attitude, can hardly claim that this seems a shortcoming in him as an author (or, I would add, as a person). Dmitry Paperno has scrupulously retained in his soul and memory the golden period of our studies in the Central School and Conservatory: the period when we first started to fall in love with music, girls, and our Teachers (exactly so—with a capital letter). . . . He is a kind of curator of the honey of our youth, and like a queen bee who gives away a little sweetness to each of her workers, so our Mitya gave to us, his lucky school fellows, this excellent *book* about the unforgettable years of our youth and our Teachers.

Mstislav Rostropovich
From Postscriptum *(AMGA Editions, Paris, 1987)*

Notes

CHAPTER 1

1. Mikhail Afanassievich Bulgakov (1891–1940), an outstanding Russian-Soviet writer and dramatist. His most significant work, the novel *The Master and Margarita*, was banned until 1966. Bulgakov escaped arrest and persecution because Stalin was fascinated with his best play, *Days of the Turbins*. In both the play and the novel version (*The White Guard*), Kiev, where Bulgakov was born and where the action takes place during the civil war of 1918–20, is never mentioned by name but only as City (*Gorod*).
2. Black Hundred was the most aggressive and militant of the antisemitic groups of Czarist Russia.
3. In justice, it should be noted that my first really good student in Chicago was an American girl who came to my class at DePaul University from another city. She not only possessed an interesting and receptive personality but also was curious and well-prepared professionally. Elizabeth Parker, who received a Ph.D. from Juilliard, was the first of my students to be a winner or finalist in a fairly prestigious nationwide competition. I promise to offer more encouraging observations on my American teaching experience later in this book.
4. An excerpt from a 1982 letter from Elena Ivanovna Goldenweiser, my teacher's widow: "Poliakin's son-in-law . . . gave me a few details about his death. His accompanist Vladimir Yampolsky and Shostakovich were on the same train, but in another car. Poliakin had asked a woman who was in the same compartment with him to wake him up. When she returned from the restroom in the morning, she found him dead. Their stories contain some (not very significant) inaccuracies, which just proves how difficult it is to rely upon verbal and later written testimony, especially secondhand."

5. In the time since the first publication of these *Notes* I received a call from a cellist who had studied at the music college in Dushanbe when Yakovlev taught there. She told me that the students appreciated him highly for his genuine talent, but the authorities had transferred him to a remote region as a troublemaker. This humiliation, in her words, had been fatal to his health, heavily undermined by the years of his disorderly life.

6. Let us remember that this was written in 1982, at which time it meant "closed forever," so I could hardly sympathize with those three charming characters. By the way, the proper pronunciation of the playwright's name is che' hov.

7. Even into his eighties, Richter (d. 1997) found himself in the first ranks of the musicians of our century.

8. This Moscow Philharmonie building, with its numerous offices and rehearsal studios, has nothing to do with the Tchaikovsky Conservatory.

9. I cannot guarantee that this story is one hundred percent authentic, but so many people have enjoyed it that I couldn't resist sharing it.

10. In the Russian edition of this book I listed several of our general education teachers. I was deeply satisfied to learn how many of their students, now scattered around the world, appreciated seeing these names in print many decades later. I want to mention here only that they remain in our memory, not only as excellent professionals in their fields but also as special people, loyal to the very idea of the school, with a good understanding of the psychology of their not-quite-common students. We thank them all.

CHAPTER 2

1. In the beginning of the war, Lev Mazel, for some reason, found himself with our Central School of Music in Penza, before rejoining the Conservatory in Saratov. Then deeply pessimistic and depressed, he nonetheless entertained us older boys with ribald jokes meant "not for the girls' ears." At the end of 1941, we were both taken ill simultaneously and spent several days in the one-room isolation ward. For the first time (I was twelve then) Mazel astonished me with his splendid analysis of the popular Chopin E-flat Nocturne, op. 9, no. 2. I realized then what a harmonious design lies behind this beautiful music, so simple in essence.

2. Apropos, Neuhaus loved to recall what he witnessed in Petrograd during the spring of 1915. Prokofiev was sitting and leafing through magazines at a party when a youthful officer approached him. Saying,

innocently, that he had attended Prokofiev's concert a few days back, he confessed, as it were, that he hadn't understood a thing. To which, without lifting his head, Prokofiev replied, "There's no telling to whom they'll sell tickets."

3. Andrei Alexandrovich Zhdanov, Stalin's favorite ideological hench-man; he died later the same year.

4. In the Russian edition I cited a few of his puns. It's a pity that they are untranslatable, but take my word for it—they were quick and sharp.

5. Let us not forget that arrest in the period of terror meant, if not an inevitable death, at least ten years of Siberian camps, so the word *purges* is hardly adequate here—we are talking of *tens of millions of ruined lives*. Think of it.

6. A terrifying manifestation of the criminal, anti-human nature of Stalin as a person and leader, the Doctor's Plot was an organized campaign, based on slanderous denunciations, against the country's medical elite. A large group of the best, most revered physicians, mostly Jews, were arrested and charged with attempts to kill several party and state lead-ers through improper medical treatments. Amazingly, a few of the accused did not "confess" despite long nightly interrogations with merciless beatings. All were doomed to receive death sentences (pos-sibly by public hanging!) following a mass trial, which didn't take place only because Stalin died first. The survivors were freed imme-diately. The ultimate goal of the provocation was to ignite a "spon-taneous," open outburst of general antisemitism to justify further actions.

7. I read somewhere shortly before writing this book that in the 1930s a gang of hooligans had terrorized one of the workers' suburbs near Moscow. The chieftain, nicknamed Karzuby, during the following years of terror made an incredible Comsomol career under his real name, Mikhailov. The same? The devil knows. In any event, in War-saw he made the impression of a complete nonentity. And why wouldn't he? Weren't we used to it by then?

8. In 1995 Cedille Records, under whose label I have made several compact discs since 1989, managed to obtain the rights to use a part of my second round, the F minor Concerto, and gala performance on my Chopin-live disc (*Paperno Plays Chopin*, CDR 9000 026). The difference between my youth and current performing periods is too striking for me to enjoy some of this very fast, though technically very well-equipped playing. My further thoughts about this meta-morphosis of performance style, typical for the second half of this century, are offered in the Epilogue.

CHAPTER 3

1. Here are two lines from the early 1950s concerning my restrained performing style as a student. From Goldenweiser: "If one could combine Paperno and Bashkirov [another of his students, known for his excitable playing] and then halve them, we would have two not-bad pianists." And my favorite, from Neuhaus: "Paperno skillfully hides his emotionality."

2. Perhaps the story has been slightly enhanced; during our telephone conversation in 1983, when Gilels played his one recital in New York, he did not deny it.

3. Speaking of Cliburn, if I remember correctly, it was Konstantin Ivanov who introduced us. We talked awhile in a friendly way, in particular about Medtner's music. I took his picture, which remained in my archive for about thirty-five years, when I took a convenient opportunity to pass it to him through my Portuguese student Pedro Burmester, a participant in the Cliburn Competition in Fort Worth. I've never heard from Mr. Cliburn, which is perfectly all right with me; my short letter simply may not have made its way to his hands. I remember him gratefully.

4. Lev's father Kirill, a handsome, charismatic man, combined the genuine heritage of the Russian gentry with the unique outlook of the typical orchestra violinist, having spent many years in the pit of the Bolshoi Theater. After losing his wife, who was many years his senior, he married our outstanding pianist Tatiana Nikolayeva, who was much younger than he. I was lucky to be close to this remarkable Russian family from the gloomy 1940s on.

5. Goldenweiser was Russian Orthodox. His father, descended from an intelligent Jewish family, had converted to Christianity to marry the Russian gentlewoman Varvara Petrovna Shchekotikhina, with whom he fell passionately in love.

6. Unfortunately, many examples of Argamakov's biting jokes, including a verse epigram on Neuhaus based on complicated homonymic rhymes, are untranslatable. I'll take the liberty of quoting one of his impromptu remarks from the 1920s, which can be appreciated in English. At a meeting of the piano department, Igumnov proposed Anna Pavlovna Ostrovskaya as a candidate for the dean and addressed her from the podium, "Anna Pavlovna, be our leader!" At which Argamakov immediately and loudly commented from his corner, "It would be *Lieder Ohne Worte!*" meaning by this pun (on Mendelssohn's *Songs Without Words*) that Ostrovskaya could be only a wordless leader, that is, no leader at all.

7. Some time after the Russian-language edition of *Notes* was published,
   either my editor or I received an unexpectedly angry letter from
   Khokhauser's lawyers, claiming that I was allegedly blaming him for
   breaking some agreement between the Western managements not to
   invite Soviet performers in order to protest Soviet actions in Hungary
   in 1956, and he had done it only to make more money. Needless to
   say, nothing of the kind was in my mind when I wrote these few
   lines. Either the gentlemen did not pay attention to the quotation
   marks around the word *boycott* (which, along with the fact that the
   word *another* is clearly ironic in this context, specifically indicates that
   there never was any existing agreement or boycott to break), or they
   were simply given a careless translation.

   Putting aside the tone of the letter, which recalls that of Dickens'
   Wackford Squeers, it was so obviously groundless that it still is not
   easy to figure out its original intent. Maybe they in London realized
   that too, because this unpleasant tempest in a teapot ended as suddenly as it began.
8. Punchinello is the blabbing character from Italian *commedia dell'arte*,
   similar to the English Punch and the Russian Petroushka.

CHAPTER 4

1. Ekaterina Alexeevna Furtseva, the U.S.S.R. minister of culture.
2. By the way, Vedernikov and Richter had introduced Prokofiev's
   Seventh Symphony (his last) to the special commission of the Soviet
   Composers' Union, on two pianos, shortly before Prokofiev's death
   in 1953.
3. A later note (1995): Nikolai Petrov, now a successful and truly athletic
   pianist, called me up several times when he was playing in the United
   States. He confirmed that there really had been problems with his
   hand, despite the rumors inevitable in such cases.
4. A later note (1995): For the sake of fairness, I will add that the truth
   eventually prevailed. I have heard some very favorable references to
   Sokolov's playing lately—a broad and diverse repertoire offered in
   very convincing, bright, and logical interpretations. I was truly glad to
   hear this.
5. A later note (1995): I am happy to mention the amazing Evgeny
   Kissin, who luckily has had nothing to do with any competition.
6. Neuhaus loved to quote Anton Rubinstein's half-joke: "The one
   who always plays right notes is a suspicious person."
7. The ominous groups of three henchmen (a typical manifestation of

the Stalin era's mockery of law) who determined a person's fate, even sometimes immediate execution, within minutes.

8. A later note (1995): Jeffrey Swan's concert career deserved broader development and acknowledgment in this country, but as we know, fairness is not always on the menu in our profession.

CHAPTER 5

1. Busya played for Jascha Heifetz during the latter's concerts in Moscow in 1935, and Heifetz did not forget the impression he made. The great violinist, known for his toughness in dealing with people (especially in his last years), recommended Boris Goldstein for a teaching position in the United States forty years later.

2. After the Russian publication I received many friendly and sympathetic words related to this not-too-encouraging start in the United States. Some of my colleagues expressed their reservations about making such a delicate professional confession public. I've never regretted it. Somehow further deterioration had slowed down. In fact, the very next year I made my first American recording and played quite a few solo recitals and with the Orchestra. Starting in 1985, I regularly performed in Europe. And all this having suffered this mysterious impairment. But wait, and keep reading.

3. I will allow myself to give two short fragments from the review: "Wednesday night, before a packed house, Paperno was competing again—against a high-powered advance billing. He pressed through almost half the recital before he could forget the strain and get down to the music at hand. . . . Here suddenly flowered insight, agility, shape, balance, grace, brilliance, and poetry" (*Milwaukee Sentinel*, 30 June 1977).

4. "There are as few utterly giftless people as there are musical geniuses." This is one of the very few of my teacher's assertions that I do not share; for me it sounds too paradoxical to be taken seriously. But even if it were so, what is the criterion for complete lack of talent, musically speaking—the level of really bad students, or of cavemen? Another of Neuhaus' favorite quotes was Tchaikovsky's comment about Brahms, which sounds so wild that I found it hard to believe—until I discovered these lines in *The Book of Failures* (Stephen Pine, 1979), taken from Tchaikovsky's diary, 9 October 1886: "I played over the music of that scoundrel Brahms. What a giftless bastard! It annoys me that this self-inflated mediocrity is hailed as a genius." Wow!

5. "When the young shopgirl in Chicago handed me the two music sketchbooks with impolite indifference, I thought to myself, 'If you

only knew, silly little thing, how much good music will be written down in these lines.'" Mirra Mendelssohn-Prokofieva, quoting Prokofiev in her short memoirs (Gosmusizdat, 1956).

EPILOGUE

1. This pose was typical of Goldenweiser when he was sitting or listening to music. Here is one more sketch from another letter by a former Soviet musician:

> In 1948, Alexander Borisovich was the chairman of the state jury in Baku. One student of Prof. G. G. Sharoyev, whom he later married, got badly lost in some sonata, sat back and grabbed the left side of her chest. The tender-hearted professor got anxious. "Uh-oh, something is wrong with her heart!" Upon which Alexander Borisovich, sitting in his favorite pose, having covered his face with both palms, reacted right off. "And I think something is wrong with her head."

Remember the earlier comment about "playing with the fingers only"? I am sure this was the case here.
2. Alexander Borisovich allegedly said in that dark time of Stalin's last years, "It hurts me deeply to realize that if Tanya's surname were not Nikolayeva, even this great talent would not win recognition." Goldenweiser meant "if she were a Jewish girl"—Nikolayev(a) is as typically Russian a family name as Johnson or Smith are American.
3. A few concert artists have actually died onstage during their performances, among them two Russian conductors, Vladimir Dranishnikov, 1939, and Abram Stassevich, 1971; three American singers—Leonard Warren, 1960, Nelson Eddy, 1967, Richard Versaille, 1995; and a pianist of phenomenal virtuosity, Simon Barere, 1951.
4. I was greatly satisfied to read, a few years ago, an interview with Misha Dichter in one of the popular music magazines; the similarity of our thoughts on harmony in piano playing was obvious and encouraging. Even more satisfying was to hear my students' impressions of John Browning's master class at Northwestern University in 1996; his observations on subordinate voices, the dynamic and textural "waves" leading to the next culmination, sounded very familiar to them.

Discography

C D s

Dmitry Paperno Plays Russian Piano Music (CDR 90000 001)
German Program (CDR 90000 002)
Uncommon Encores (CDR 90000 007)
Paperno Plays Chopin (CDR 9000 026)

L P s

Alexander Scriabin: Selected Works for Piano (MHS 3998)
Tchaikovsky: The Seasons, op. 37a (MHS 4626)

Around the time of this book's publication, Cedille plans to release a CD of performances broadcast live or recorded for broadcast by Chicago radio station WFMT and is also looking into the possibility of releasing performances archived on tape in the Moscow Recording House and elsewhere, and/or re-releasing recordings previously issued on LP by Melodiya.

Index